THE BROOKINGS INSTITUTION, 1916–1952

THE BROOKINGS INSTITUTION, 1916–1952

EXPERTISE AND THE PUBLIC INTEREST IN A DEMOCRATIC SOCIETY

DONALD T. CRITCHLOW

NORTHERN ILLINOIS UNIVERSITY PRESS · DeKalb, ILLINOIS

Library of Congress Cataloging in Publication Data

Critchlow, Donald T., 1948–
    The Brookings Institution, 1916–1952: expertise and the
public interest in a democratic society.

    Bibliography: p.
    Includes index.
    I. Brookings Institution—History.   I. Title.
H67.W338C75   1985   001.4'06'0753   84–20699

ISBN 0–87580–103–x

Frontispiece: Robert S. Brookings.
            (Courtesy of Brookings Institution Archives)

To William J. Marchinton and Anne Marchinton, Who Taught Me the Meaning of Love and Devotion

Contents

ILLUSTRATIONS

PREFACE

ALTHOUGH based on extensive records found in the Brookings Institution's office files, which were opened to me by special arrangement, this study is not an institutional history per se. Charles B. Saunders's official history, *The Brookings Institution: A Fifty Year History* (1966), provides a terse chronicle of the first years of the institution. With Saunders's work to build on, I have been able to place the history of the institution into a larger context of politics and public policy. I portray the institution as playing both a negative and a positive role in public policy. On the positive side, the Brookings Institution contributed to the establishment of a modern budget system in the United States, the reorganization of the Bureau of Indian Affairs in the 1920s, the drafting of the National Industrial Recovery Act, and the founding of the United Nations at the end of World War II. Such contributions stand on their own and testify to the influence of the institution. Yet the Brookings took a stand against certain other programs—the National Recovery Administration, Keynesian economics, and Truman's proposals for national health insurance and for the extension of Social Security benefit payments. Its economic analysis of the depression of the 1930s and inflation in the postwar period were often superficial. In showing such aspects of the institution's history, I have endeavored not to debunk Saunders's work, but rather to show that the history of the Brookings Institution has not been one-dimensional.

This study presents the history of the Brookings Institution in a broad interpretive framework that emphasizes the relationship of elite groups to the American political environment and economic order. If our view of the world is to be comprehensive, we must study the history of elite groups and their role and power in a capitalist society, as well as studying the history of the masses from the bottom up. I hope that my work will encourage other public policy historians and political scientists to undertake studies from a similar perspective. If this study contributes in a small way to the development of a comprehensive view of our past and present society, then I will have achieved a major objective.

ACKNOWLEDGMENTS

M ANY people contributed to the completion of this book. Dr. Barbara Moulton made possible my access to the Brookings files, then closed to the general public. During my subsequent stay at the institution as a guest scholar, Edna Birkel and James Farrell, director of public information, ensured that I was given complete freedom to pursue my work.

At the University of California, Berkeley, this manuscript was critically read by Samuel Haber, President Emeritus Clark Kerr, and my close friend Charles Sellers. During my three-year stay at North Central College, Naperville, Illinois, Barbara Sciacchitano, chair of the Department of History, encouraged and supported work on this book. Further assistance came during my two years at the University of Dayton from Leroy Eid, chair of the history department, and Dean Francis Lazarus, who provided funds for the typing of the manuscript. Other colleagues in the history department created an atmosphere that spurred the ambitions of a young scholar. The manuscript was completed at the University of Notre Dame, where Phillip Gleason brought to the study his wide-ranging knowledge of American history and his fine sense of style. My colleagues Thomas Kselman and Gary Hamburg offered sound advice concerning the publication of this work.

Many others shared in the writing of this book. Without their help this book would have been far different. I especially want to thank those scholars who graciously commented on the manuscript, including Richard Abrams, University of California; William H. Becker, George Washington University; John Braeman, University of Nebraska; Jerome Clubb, University of Michigan; Joanna Cowden, Chico State University; Ellis Hawley, University of Iowa; Stephen McNamee, University of Dayton; Sidney Ratner, Rutgers University; Jordan Schwarz, Northern Illinois University; and William C. Widenor, University of Illinois. My friends Gail Bates, Walter Feeser, Anita Graham, John Hansen, Joel Meisenheimer, and Joseph W. Phillips helped this project from the start to its conclusion. Lu Cooper and Cheryl Reed typed the manuscript with patience and without complaint. I want to thank especially Ann Bates of the Northern Illinois University Press for her help in preparing the manuscript for publication.

I acknowledge with thanks the financial assistance provided by the Rockefeller Foundation Archives, and by the University of California at Berkeley during my tenure there as a Eugene Irving McCormic Fellow.

I owe a special debt of gratitude to three individuals in particular: to Paul Kleppner, a friend and a scholar, who after reading the manuscript urged me to submit it for publication; to Elizabeth Johnson, a student of Russian history, who read and reread many versions of this book; and finally to Patricia Powers Critchlow, who lived with this book through six years and four institutions, and throughout it all continued to provide encouragement, understanding, and a sense of humor.

Notre Dame, Indiana
February 1, 1984

THE BROOKINGS INSTITUTION, 1916–1952

1 · THE "THINK TANK" AND PUBLIC POLICY

I F THE significant decline of voter participation in the last decade is indicative, there is a growing feeling in the United States that political control of the government by the people has been lost and cannot be regained through the present electoral process. This conclusion has been reinforced by a substantial scholarly literature proclaiming the failure of democratic governance. Popular political campaigns, coming from both the left and the right, have promised to overturn bureaucratic government and to restore control to the people, but the failure to fulfill these promises has heightened a cynical disillusionment with the system. A consensus has been reached, it seems, that our political system is chaotic and our economy unmanageable. Many feel that any public policy that may be devised will prove to be so complex as to be fruitless. Special interests exert a disproportionate influence on government. And government organization itself seems to operate on principles impervious to the influence of the electorate. Furthermore, since the end of World War II Americans have seen the growth of "think tanks"—organizations such as the Brookings Institution, the Rand Corporation, and the American Enterprise Institute—which play an ambiguous role in public policy. These think tanks not only are commissioned to evaluate and to formulate governmental policies, but also provide a substantial number of high government officials. Such institutes form what some have called a shadow government; yet their exact role in the political process is not altogether clear.

Following a tour of the prestigious Brookings Institution, a high-ranking Soviet official asked an obvious question, "If in a democracy, such as you have in America, the people are ultimately responsible for political decisions, why is there a need for the Brookings Institution?" This question suggests other, closely related ones. What role does a policy-oriented organization like the Brookings Institution play in a democratic society? What influence does the Brookings Institution exert on public policy? What is the meaning of "nonpartisan" in the political process? If conventional political science wisdom is correct in assuming that political parties, party leadership, and political institutions in America respond to and articulate the will of the people, then why is there a necessity for a nonpartisan research institute? Moreover, what role does the Brookings Institution play as a mediator between public interests and the state? This study seeks to provide a historical basis for answering such questions.

On the surface, these questions could be answered simply. The Brookings Institution is a nonpartisan, independent organization, free from government supervision, but a primary participant in government policy making. The main purpose of the institution is to stand above specific economic, political, or class interests and to speak for the general welfare of society. The Brookings Institution is a kind of university without students, where learned men of high reputation contribute expertise to current discussions on public policy. The Brookings Institution, like other research organizations, does not decide public policy. This job remains the task of Congress and the President. Instead, the Brookings Institution formulates, recommends, and evaluates public policy.

Today the Brookings Institution stands just off DuPont Circle at 1775 Massachusetts Avenue in Washington, D.C., in a large, rather austere, imposing stone building. The complex also includes an annex and a conference center. Founded in 1927 following a merger between the Institute for Government Research, established in 1916, and the Institute for Economics, organized in 1922, the institution remains the nation's oldest research institute. Its reputation has been built on its service to government. During the first fifty years of its existence, its staff participated in the creation of the modern budget system, the settlement of war debts during the 1920s, the reorganization of the Bureau of Indian Affairs in the Hoover administration, the drafting of the National Industrial Recovery Act during the early New Deal, and the organizing of an administrative structure for the Marshall Plan. In recent years the institution's work has been equally significant. The Brookings Presidential Transition Plan submitted to the incoming Kennedy administration led Theodore Sorenson, who participated in the transition between administrations, to write that the Brookings "deserves a large share of the credit for history's smoothest transfer of power between opposing parties."[1] During the Kennedy-Johnson years, Brookings men, and men who would later become associated with the institution, played key roles in the Democratic administrations. Kermit Gordon, later appointed president of the Brookings Institution, served as Johnson's budget director, and Arthur Okun, who followed Gordon to the Brookings, served as chairman of Johnson's Council of Economic Advisors. This involvement with government led President Johnson to declare at the celebration of the Brookings's fiftieth anniversary in 1966, "You are a national institution, so important to, at least, the Executive branch—and I think the Congress and the country—that if you did not exist we would have to ask someone to create you."[2]

The institution continues to exert a subtle, but evident, influence in Washington public policy circles. Composed of a resident staff of 160 people, with an additional group of 85 scholars located in the nation's leading universities, the Brookings Institution is organized around three areas, Economic Studies, Government Studies, and Foreign Policy Studies; the last includes a strong defense-analysis group. With an operating budget of over $9 million, mostly from grants from private foundations and government contracts, the institution conducts approximately 100 research projects a year on topics ranging from the crisis in the Middle East to the politics of deregulation; publishes an average of ten books a year, including the influential annual *Setting National Priorities*; provides technical assistance to various governmental agencies, commissions, and congressional staffs; and serves as a conference center that attracts the nation's leaders in business, government, and academia. Furthermore, the Brookings Institution acts as a stopping point for those entering or leaving government. Alice Rivlin, former Brookings senior fellow, held the influential post of director of the Congressional Budget Office, while Stephen Kaplan, a Brookings specialist in defense, joined the Pentagon to work in a high-level capacity. Above all, observes Leonard Silk, economic affairs columnist of the *New York Times*, "Brookings is part of the Washington System."[3] Although the current president, Bruce M. MacLaury, has consciously moved the institution in a more conservative direction to compensate for the liberal reputation it gained in the 1960s and to attract more corporate financial support, the Brookings Institution maintains a reputation for objectivity that remains unchallenged by the proliferation of newer research organizations.

This brief description of the Brookings Institution does not, of course, give a sufficient answer to the question of why this institution (or others of its kind) exists. The ideal of a nonpartisan public policy research organization, operating outside the university and free from government supervision and from domination by special interests, is unique to the United States. In fact, the concept of nonpartisanship has captivated Americans since the late nineteenth century—no doubt because of the considerable suspicion of party politics that is so common among Americans, in contrast to both Eastern and Western Europeans, who have found more virtue in the political party.

Some social scientists have explained the existence of nonprofit research institutes such as the Brookings Institution in terms of "corporatism" or "corporate liberalism"—though in this context, as elsewhere, the term "liberalism" means different things to different people. Basic to the corporatist interpretation is a belief that the public interest has been subverted by private corporate interests that have sought increased state intervention in order to rationalize the market and to maintain their monopolistic positions. Liberal reform, declares James Weinstein, a proponent of the corporatist view, should be seen as a movement for "state intervention to supervise corporate activity, rather than a movement for the removal of state control over private enterprise." Therefore, the corporatist interpretation posits a "conscious and successful effort to guide and control the economic and social policies of federal, state, and municipal governments by various groupings in their own long range interest as they perceive it."[4] Although some historians of the corporatist persuasion stress the voluntaristic aspects, as opposed to the imposition of compulsory state control, the corporatist interpretation sees business elites in America as having a consciousness that welcomes state intervention in the economy. R. Jeffrey Lustig maintains that, although historians use the term "corporate liberalism" in a number of ways, they consistently apply it to a point of view that is "pro-business" and "pro-state," dedicated to private profit and to the regulatory state. Lustig holds, therefore, that corporate liberalism is a way of maintaining social control, a political program of the most farsighted capitalists, and that it sets "a climate for conscious class thought."[5]

In the corporate liberal model, organizations like the Brookings Institution act as mediators between the state and these enlightened corporate interests. G. William Domhoff argues, for example, that the "power elite" in America shapes social legislation through private research institutes "initiated, directed, and/or financed by members of the upper class." Domhoff specifically cites the Brookings Institution as one of the key organizations of the power elite.[6]

Not all New Leftists construct, as Domhoff does, such a tight relationship among the state, corporate business, and private research institutes. For instance, Nicos Poulantzas, a neo-Marxist, views the state as an autonomous "structure," able to act on its own as it sees fit to protect and maintain social and economic stability in the capitalist order.[7] Thus, the state acts to legitimize existing class relations by offering reforms, which members of the capitalist class, ironically, may oppose because of their own shortsightedness. The managers of the state, on the other hand, because of their positions within government may see more clearly what needs to be done in order to preserve the system.

Although structural Marxists have not specifically addressed the role of private research institutes in the capitalist system, their argument can be easily extended to include such organizations. Organizations such as the Brookings, the Committee for Economic Development, and the Council on Foreign Relations, the structuralists would argue, act independently, in most cases, from corporate interests, but their primary purpose is to devise social and economic policies that provide stability to the capitalist system. At times, particularly during social crisis, these research institutions offer programmatic reforms to state managers anxiously concerned with preventing a complete rupture in the body politic.

Recently Fred Block and Theda Skocpol, by elaborating on the causal mechanisms leading to reform, have offered sophisticated explanations as to the role of the state and its managers in times of social crisis.[8] Block observes that reforms most frequently come when the state is threatened from below by an agitated working class. Thus class struggle pushes the development of capitalism along reformist lines. In turn, Skocpol, although somewhat critical of Block's emphasis on class, argues that Marxists should see the state and political parties as "organizations with their own structures, their own histories, and their own pattern of conflict and impact upon class relations and economic development."[9] In order to meet constituent needs, Skocpol contends, political parties act as purveyors of reform during periods of crisis.

While New Left studies have enriched our understanding of the relationship between corporate elites and government, the history of the Brookings Institution suggests that relations between public policy groups and the state are far more complex than suggested by the corporatist or structuralist interpretations. Common to both these interpretations is the belief that enlightened capitalists or their representatives will demand state intervention to enact reforms designed to mislead and to mollify working-class elements that threaten the existing system. Contrary to what the neo-Marxist model predicts, the history of the Brookings Institution reveals little concern with social upheaval. Furthermore, although the institution has participated in reform efforts, including the movement to establish an executive budget system and Indian reform in the 1920s, it vehemently opposed the liberal program presented by Franklin Roosevelt and Harry Truman in their respective administrations.

This opposition to New Deal and Fair Deal liberalism reflected a strong antistatist bias on the part of the Brookings Institution, as well as a belief in the ability of the marketplace to correct economic and social maladjustments. The institution's antistatism should not be mistaken for laissez-faire liberalism of the nineteenth-century variety; on the contrary, the economists at the Brookings were managerial institutionalists, rather than neoclassical economists. They called for managerial expertise in business and government in order to rationalize an economy dominated by large corporate organizations. Nevertheless, they called for minimal state intervention in the economy.

Moreover, the hostile response to the liberal program suggests that the Brookings Institution had developed a unique character of its own that enabled its staff to respond in a myriad of ways at different times to public issues. If Theda Skocpol is correct in assuming that political parties have their own structures, histories, and patterns of conflict, is it not reasonable to assume that an institution such as the Brookings, set within a general social and economic context, will also gain a certain autonomy of its own? Indeed, this study, although sympathetic to certain aspects of class analysis, finds that the history of the Brookings Institution was shaped by its elitist origins, its continuing belief in nonpartisan expertise, and its faith that public policy could be depoliticized by separating administration from politics.

This study argues that nonpartisanship in politics and in research emerged during the Progressive Era, at a time when industrial

America was undergoing an organizational revolution that demanded technical expertise in corporate business and in state and federal government. Clearly the collection, evaluation, and dissemination of information vital to public policy formulation was seen as necessary to a government and a society that had become increasingly more complex. Nevertheless, other industrialized nations did not turn to independent, nonpartisan research institutes to meet this need for technical expertise. The nonpartisan research institute was a peculiarly American response to what was perceived as a breakdown in the political order.

Nonpartisan expertise gained its power and its form in America as a response to the very strength and potency of partisan politics in America in the late nineteenth century. That is, nonpartisanship was developed into a political strategy by an elite group of social scientists, mostly economists, and businessmen who sought to undermine the existing control of government by political parties. Political parties were seen by these elite reformers as spokesmen for special interests that corrupted and distorted the general interests of society. Thus the founding of the Institute for Government Research in 1916, and subsequently the founding of the Brookings Institution in 1927, were part of a grand political strategy to limit partisan influence in government by depoliticizing public policy.

In short, this study proposes that the origins of the Brookings Institution are found in a movement by a self-designated "better element" who persistently disclaimed democracy and party spirit. This element, under the guise of progressive reform and efficient government, consciously sought to weaken partisan interests in public policy and to shift decision making as much as possible from elected officials to appointed bodies. The IGR was organized to bring efficiency to government and to the budgetary system, but beneath the rhetoric of "efficiency and economy" lay a deep distrust toward popular democracy.

This study follows an interpretive framework which views American history as a conflict between the popular forces of democracy and those elitist forces that distrusted the ability of the masses to rule themselves. By seeing themselves as standing above partisan politics, by operating outside the political arena, yet formulating and passing judgment on public issues, the staff of the Brookings Institution perceived themselves as a professional elite, the guardians of the Republic.

Throughout the nation's history various groups, because of their natural abilities and moral virtues, have felt that they were best suited to represent the general interests of all members of society. Even Thomas Jefferson spoke occasionally of the benefits of rule by a natural aristocracy. During the Jacksonian era, however, with the formation of the second party system and the spoils system, partisan politics became equated with democracy. The Jacksonians saw the realization of democratic government through the political party. As the nineteenth century drew to a close, though, partisan politics, and thereby popular democracy, came under attack by reformers who wanted to restore representative government by lessening the strength of political parties and by placing experts into government. In this situation, the idea of representative government took on new meaning for reformers. Representative government came to mean the establishment of a bureaucratic state effectively administered by professionals. The ideal of a natural aristocracy was replaced by the ideal of the nonpartisan expert.

Writing in 1901, Woodrow Wilson conveyed this change in political attitudes. "It is no longer possible to mistake the reaction against democracy," he told the readers of the *Atlantic Monthly*. "The nineteenth century was above all others a century of democracy; and yet the world is no more convinced of the benefits of democracy as a form of government at its end than it was at the beginning." Wilson was not discouraged by this reaction, however. For if democracy had failed, representative government would succeed by placing the "best men," the educated professionals, into government administration. Representative government now meant government by nonpartisan expertise. "Representative government," Wilson observed, "has its long life and excellent development, not in order that the common opinion, the opinion of the street, might prevail, but in order that the best opinion, the opinion generated by the best possible methods of general counsel, might rule in public affairs." For Wilson, the "best opinion" meant professional opinion; and the "best possible methods of general counsel" meant efficient government administration. "Nonprofessionalism is nonefficiency," Wilson concluded, while warning that America must develop professional leadership and "expert organization, if our government [is] to be preserved."[10] It was not mere coincidence, therefore, that Wilson had proposed the establishment of an independent research institute as early as 1897. The founding of the Institute for Government Research two decades later fulfilled Wilson's hope that government would be supplied with professional opinion that spoke for the public interest.

This history of the formative years of the Brookings Institution is in many ways a history of this ideal of nonpartisan expertise in America, of its development in the twentieth century. This study is also an account of a small group of economists and political scientists, led by the institution's first president, Harold Moulton, who dominated the institution for twenty-five years. Like earlier social scientists, the small staff at the early Brookings Institution, never numbering more than twenty, saw themselves as nonpartisan social scientists working in behalf of the objective interests of society. Just as the staff of the Institute for Government Research sought to bring efficiency to government, so would the Brookings staff seek efficiency in economic affairs. Nevertheless, contrary to their perceptions of themselves, by the time Harold Moulton retired in 1952, the institution had gained a reputation, especially among liberals, as a spokesman for "big business." The staff under Moulton had not consciously assumed this role. Still, their critical studies of the New Deal and Fair Deal programs found a receptive audience among the most conservative elements in the country.

At the same time, the complaints of the Brookings Institution in respect to the Democratic Party program were not totally without foundation. Brookings studies voiced legitimate concerns about Roosevelt's political manipulation of the economy. They accused Roosevelt of spending money with an eye to gaining political benefit for himself and his party. Recent quantitative studies indicate that Roosevelt's spending program in fact did target constituencies most likely to vote Democratic. Moreover, Brookings studies warned of the inflationary consequences of increased deficit spending. Once programs were established, they observed, Congress would find it difficult to retrench government spending in periods of economic prosperity.

When Moulton retired from the Brookings in 1952, however, he and his staff were replaced by a group of younger economists generally sympathetic to Keynesian fiscal policy. Moulton's retirement therefore marks a new chapter in the history of the Brookings Institution. The differences between Moulton's prescription for the state and its relation to the economy, and the views of those who succeeded him at the institution, present for the historian subtle distinctions. Staff economists who followed Moulton at the Brookings maintained a belief in a capitalist society, but they rejected past notions of a self-adjusting economy. Not to accept fiscal planning, they claimed, was to deny the advance of economics as a science. The trustees of the institution deliberately sought to reintegrate the institution into the mainstream of current economic thought. The reestablishment of the institution's reputation as an economic research institution is another story, one that deserves telling. But because that story is so involved, and because the primary material for the more recent period is not yet available to the researcher, this study ends in 1952. The study is primarily concerned with tracing the problems inherent in the concept of nonpartisan economic expertise and the meaning of the general welfare in a capitalist society. The issues confronting Moulton during the years under consideration nevertheless provide a warning to the plethora of research institutions that have sprung up since the end of World War II.

Three general themes emerge from this history of the Brookings Institution. First, the Brookings Institution's relationship to corporate capitalism, which emerged in this period of American history, proved to be multidimensional and varied. A second theme follows from the first: Just as men shape their own history, so do men shape the history of their institutions. Society and its social structures are formed by people making choices, with unforeseen consequences, as to the direction and form of their society. Finally, contrary to the interpretation of those historians who have placed the political consciousness of business and social science elites within a corporate liberal framework, the history of the Brookings Institution reveals that a strong antistatist bias prevailed throughout its early development.

Concerning the relationship of the Brookings to corporate capitalism, there seems to be no necessary reason to envision the institution as some sort of corporate-class conspiracy. On the contrary, there has been little need for conspiracy. Those businessmen and social scientists who were involved in the "good government" cause quite frankly expressed their disgust with "party spirit," while readily linking the ills of universal suffrage to "corruption in government." Most of these reformers genuinely felt that if people knew the facts, if research for government was conducted on a nonpartisan basis, society would be bettered. And middle-class taxpayers, who were tired of government inefficiency, sickened by machine politics, and doubtful of the future of democratic society, willingly received the messages sent by the "good government" reformers.

The Brookings Institution was financed primarily by capitalists such as Robert Brookings and by the Carnegie Corporation and the Rockefeller Foundation. It would be easy to conclude after looking at the financial records of the institution and at the policies pursued that those who paid the piper selected the tune. But such was not the case. Staff members of the Brookings Institution who had been trained at the nation's leading universities would have resented any such imputation concerning their objectivity. Furthermore, the founders of the Brookings realized from the outset that the institution's prestige rested on its objectivity and absence of party spirit. To ensure the good reputation of their institution, therefore, they wrote into the bylaws that "the primary function of the trustees is not to express their views on scientific investigations conducted by the institute, but only to make it possible for such scientific work to be done under the most favorable auspices." This bylaw has been strictly enforced throughout the institution's history.

This study considers the history of the Brookings Institution in the larger social and political context of the times. Because of its inquiry into the nature of nonpartisan research in the twentieth century, it offers more than an institutional history of a specific research organization. Nevertheless, the Brookings Institution must be seen in terms of its own unique nature. The institution, from its very founding, developed an identity and character distinct from the larger social and political forces operating outside it. Thus a major theme of this study is that the Brookings Institution functioned with a logic of its own, largely the creation of its early staff.

In this respect, the work addresses a crucial problem within the social sciences: To what extent is an individual able to act independently in an environment shaped by powerful social forces? Early social scientists expressed an ambivalence in deciding between a voluntaristic approach, which stresses individual action, and a deterministic model, which considers social forces in history and society as causative. Both approaches within the discourse of sociological thought, as Jeffrey C. Alexander shows in his fine study *The Antinomies of Classical Thought: Marx and Durkheim*, have contributed equally to our understanding of society.[11] Yet both traditions, Alexander observes, hold obvious drawbacks for the social scientist. The voluntaristic approach has significantly increased our understanding of individual interaction within collective bodies, but it frequently ignores the larger context, often less apparent, within which the individual operates. In turn, the deterministic approach often assumes that individuals act on motives that are always calculating, efficient, and ultimately predictable.

If classical sociological theory, for all of its insights into voluntaristic and deterministic behavior in society, remains undecided in addressing the individual's role in a larger context, recent organizational theory, which would at first seem useful for understanding the development of the Brookings Institution, only further obscures central issues for the historian. Organizational theory suggests that organizations can be framed in ecological terms.[12] Thus organizations act as competing organisms, existing within their own life cycles, vying with one another for survival. The most adaptable (the strongest) survives. This neo-Darwinian approach to organizational behavior only reifies the problem of understanding the role and actions of individuals within organizations, because the model downplays the significance of the individual.

This study of the Brookings Institution does not purport to resolve major tensions within the sociological tradition. Nonetheless it suggests that recent American historians have overemphasized the deterministic aspects of the relationship between the state and corporate business, and similarly between corporate business and policy-oriented organizations such as the Brookings Institution. Even the best scholars of recent American history have been too easily persuaded that America is best seen in rigid bureaucratic terms. For instance, James Gilbert, in his astute study *Designing the Industrial State: The Intellectual Pursuit of Collectivism in America, 1880–1940*, downplays the ability of individuals to act independently within a bureaucratic society. Gilbert argues that at some time in the early 1960s, "It became more difficult to claim that man could make his way to success or fulfillment without bargaining away his liberty to some institution."[13] Gilbert maintains that even in the early twentieth century some intellectuals had come to view the individual as insignificant in history. America, for these intellectuals, was becoming a "mass society—a collectivity, not a chaos of competing egos and regions."[14] Other historians, many of them less sophisticated than Gilbert in their approach to history, have joined him in viewing America in the late nineteenth century, after the decline of laissez-faire capitalism, as a "collective," "corporate," or "bureaucratic" society which, it seems, many social thinkers, at the turn of the century, embraced.[15]

Finally, this book does not deny that certain social thinkers, and a few businessmen, envisioned a collectivist or corporate society. The history of the Brookings Institution, however, shows that many social scientists, especially those who sought efficiency and economy in government, resisted collectivist solutions to America's problems. In fact, many social scientists, and most businessmen, remained peculiarly distrustful of collectivist and statist approaches to economic problems. Although social scientists and businessmen accepted, by the late nineteenth century, a limited role for government intervention in the economy, and although they viewed the economy in institutional terms, they remained deeply ambivalent toward the state. Their primary faith remained in the marketplace (even though they realized that the traditional marketplace had radically changed with the emergence of the large corporation). Thus social scientists and businessmen often rejected proposals for business to enter into a partnership with government to form a new associative state.

Contrary to those who have posited a widespread desire among businessmen and social scientists for the formation of a corporate liberal state, this study argues that an underlying suspicion and a profound mistrust of this concept of the state has pervaded the consciousness of both groups in the twentieth century.[16] This mistrust of the state distinguishes American businessmen from every other bourgeoisie in advanced industrial societies. The American economic order, instead of being brought under the management of a centralized bureaucracy, has proved to be one of the least interventionist in the advanced industrial world. In turn, many social scientists have expressed a profound hostility toward the state, which has frequently been seen as a body particularly vulnerable to the machinations of partisan interests intent on manipulating the economy for their own political benefit.

The economists at the early Brookings Institution expressed a consistent belief in the market's capacity to correct economic and social maladjustments. In particular, the institution was an adamant defender of the market economy in the late 1930s, when that economy was perceived to be under attack from liberal economists who advocated deficit spending as a remedy for the Depression. The Brookings Institution led the attack on Keynesian economics through its criticism of the National Resources Planning Board (disbanded by Congress in 1943), the full-employment bill of 1945, national health insurance, and state intervention in the economy, and thus played a crucial role in shaping postwar history. Because the efforts of the government to establish state planning on a federal level were largely unsuccessful, it turned of necessity to private research organizations for advice, consultation, and specialized studies. In turn, political groupings and special interests, in order to ensure themselves a voice in the policy process, if not to exert complete dominance over the process, established their own think tanks to rival the Brookings. Thus the postwar period saw a proliferation of research institutes: the American Enterprise Institute, the Hudson Institute, the Heritage Foundation, and far too many others to enumerate. In this way the Brookings Institution, with its historical distrust of the electoral influence on public policy and its fear of the "excesses" of democracy, helped to ensure that a plurality of opinions, expressed through a myriad of institutes and organizations, would be heard in Washington. The cacophony that ensued sounded an alarm to a nation unable to set a national agenda and created an anxiety that democracy was in disorder.

2·DEMOCRACY, EFFICIENCY, AND THE FOUNDING OF THE IGR

A T THE turn of the century, social scientists were convinced that the nation was threatened by a dangerous mass electorate consistently manipulated by machine politicians who showed unscrupulous and flagrant disregard for any notion of public morality. The social scientists therefore joined forces with reform-minded businessmen in an effort to take partisan politics out of government administration. These "scientific" reformers, as social scientists and businessmen saw themselves, hoped to restore political order and representative government to American society. All of the measures proposed by the reformers—the elimination of party labels in municipal elections, the shortening of the ballot, the reduction of the number of elected officials, the weakening of the legislative branch of government, the enacting of an executive budget system, and the shifting of decision making as far as possible from elected bodies— were intended to accomplish a single goal: *the depoliticization of the political process.* In response to machine politics and other perceived excesses, reformers sought to take power away from the partisan politicians who dominated government in the post–Civil War period and to place government administration in the hands of nonpartisan experts.[1]

Beneath the catch words "efficiency and economy," the rallying cry of the reformers, lay strong antimajoritarian values fused with antiparty perspectives. Under the guise of progressive reform and efficient government, social science reformers deliberately sought to create a nonpartisan administrative state. This goal entailed the

destruction of machine politics and the subjugation of a mass electorate, particularly the uneducated mass of urban voters who supported the corrupt city machines, in favor of a governance system
seen as more appropriate to a modern capitalist order. It was from
this movement for nonpartisan reform that the precursor to today's
Brookings Institution, the Institute for Government Research
(IGR), emerged in 1916. Founded specifically to bring "science" to
government, the IGR became the chief advocate of a national executive budget system.[2] From these roots in the budget reform movement, the Brookings Institution would grow and expand into other
areas of public policy.

The demand for an executive budget expressed a particular distrust of popular democracy. This movement, which began on the
municipal level, soon became a national crusade that was eventually
supported by both the Republican and the Democratic Parties.
Budget reform was a technical solution to the problems of democratic government, and technical issues by their very nature usually
do not arouse the passions of the general populace. The proposal
itself was simple: The chief executive, with the help of experts in a
budget bureau, would review all departmental estimates of expenditure before submitting a proposed budget, complete with detailed estimates for appropriations for the upcoming year, to the
legislative branch of government. Following the enactment of this
proposed budget by the legislature, a comptroller general, again
aided by nonpartisan experts, would oversee the proper administration and expenditure of funds.

Perhaps no man better epitomized this social-science reform impulse than did Henry Bruere, who began his career as a social worker
after studying economics at the University of Chicago (under
Thorstein Veblen), law at Harvard University, and political science
at Columbia University.[3] Though more highly educated than most,
Bruere represented the new social-work professional who appeared
at the turn of the century, the specialist whose concerns were often
little more than an expression of dissatisfaction with inefficiency in
an industrial society. Bruere's first professional success came in 1903
when he organized the McCormick Work Men's Club, an inhouse
YMCA established by McCormick Harvester, following the strikes
of the 1890s. The turmoil of the nineties encouraged companies
such as McCormick Harvester to recognize that personnel managers and lawyers like Bruere could serve to disarm grievances and
outflank disruptive organizing drives by militant unions.

Two years after establishing the McCormick social program, Bruere moved to New York City to begin working for the Association for Improving the Condition of the Poor (AICP) and the Citizens Union, a "good government" group. The AICP, one of the oldest relief associations in New York, had been established in 1843 by wealthy merchants to elevate the moral and physical condition of indigents, but it had recently undergone a radical shift in its philosophy. Shortly before Bruere's arrival, the AICP staff under a new general manager, William H. Allen, a young Ph.D. from the University of Pennsylvania, had decided to "substitute result for motive, efficiency for goodness, as a test of their own efficiency."[4] This change meant that the association's work now became more centralized. Association files were centralized; all AICP recipients received vouchers for relief funds; periodic checks on recipients were instituted; and a budget system was established to keep a close watch on the allocation of funds. At the same time, Allen brought in a staff of accountants, lawyers, and professionally trained social workers who would "apply the process of research, and the disinterestedness of research, and the techniques of business management to public and civic problems."[5] Those older social workers who protested that this change had "exalted the expert and the professional at the expense of the volunteer" were now dismissed as old-fashioned sentimentalists.[6] To such sentimentalists the new efficiency expert would reply, quoting Andrew Carnegie, "One of the most serious obstacles to the improvement of our race is indiscriminate charity."

When he joined the staff of the AICP, Bruere became part of the reform establishment in New York City. This small group of men, mostly social scientists and businessmen, saw themselves as the scientific guardians of the public welfare and community interest in a modern age. Bruere was invited to become a member of the prestigious University Club, the Players Club, and the Century Club. His social acquaintances now included men like R. Fulton Cutting, who was a scion of an old-line banking family and a former president of the AICP, and had been a leading supporter of "good government" in the city since his days as a mugwump. Through his new contacts, Bruere arranged for his older brother Robert Bruere, a specialist in industrial relations trained in Berlin, to become an associate editor of the influential progressive magazine *Survey*. Together these men—Allen, Cutting, and the Bruere brothers—along with those few who gathered around them, became central figures in municipal reform in New York City. These men would galvanize New York politics, as one reformer later observed, by initiating the call for an executive budget system in the city. This call in New York soon spread to other cities, then to the state level, and finally took on national prominence during the Taft administration.

Budget reformers, although disdaining the emotionalism of early reformers, became zealots in their crusade to bring "science" to government. Whatever inadequacies these men might have felt about their status as members of a new profession in a changing society they overcame by their complete confidence in American business culture. They believed in progress and evolution. In this respect they reflected the influence that Darwinism had had on American thought in the nearly forty years since its introduction into this country. Translating Darwinian ideas into a language of American business, the reformers would equate progress with the emergence of the corporation and "businesslike" methods, design with management, and natural selection with cost accounting. In the process, social scientists such as Bruere provided an ideological rationale, based on technical knowledge and scientific objectivity, for reforming government along the lines of business.

In the latter half of the nineteenth century, social science had been radically transformed from a discipline of deductive reasoning based on natural law to one of inductive procedure founded on historical analysis and empirical research.[7] During this intellectual transition, social scientists became professionalized, career-oriented, and established in academia and, to a lesser degree, in government. The new ideology and methodology allowed social scientists to mask any preoccupation with political matters in the terminology of scholarly objectivity and empirical research.[8] Men like Allen and Bruere seldom acknowledged their political and partisan concerns. Nonetheless, the transformation of political impulses into administrative solutions reflected the aspirations of a new professional class anxious to gain influence in a highly industrialized society through its expertise. Members of this class were not, however, disingenuous in their concerns with social issues. They saw the proposed administrative solutions to social problems as an avenue to addressing such larger questions as industrial relations, distribution of wealth, and stability in the political order. Most social scientists in the late nineteenth century sincerely believed that their expertise could correct the flaws they perceived in the political and social structure.[9] They sought success by placing the "best men" in public office. In this way, social scientists at the turn of the century shared much in common with the mugwumps who had tried to reform American politics in the 1880s. The mugwumps were a group of reformers who gathered around Edwin L. Godkin and the *Nation* in their disgust with the presidency of Grant. They promulgated a program based on civil service reform, an executive budget, hard money, and free trade, but they exerted little practical influence on the politics of their day, especially after they deserted the Republican Party in 1884 in order to support the Democratic nominee, Grover Cleveland. They were elitists whose remedies for the excesses of democracy boiled down to getting men like themselves into government on the basis of merit. Such a political goal was hardly the sort around which to rally the masses or on which to build a base of support within the party.

Historians have generally, and quite correctly, characterized the politics of these mugwumps as an upper-class reaction to political corruption during the Gilded Age.[10] Nevertheless, the ideological continuity between the mugwumps and the new scientific reformers has been obscured by historians who have tended to see two distinct movements bearing little relation to one another. Much of this confusion has occurred because initially the mugwumps, acting on the advice of Godkin, bitterly assailed scientific reformers such as Richard T. Ely and other young economists who had recently returned from graduate studies in Germany. This group, with the impulsiveness that youth affords, quite consciously rejected past liberal principles, specifically the laissez-faire doctrines that had been the cornerstone of liberalism in the nineteenth century.

While studying in Germany, Ely and his associates had been greatly influenced by scholarship showing that the expansion of a strong government was necessary for reform and that the emergence of a more centralized state was completely in accord with the evolutionary tendencies of society. Edmund Janes James, a close friend of Ely's, declared that "the state, so far from being the source of innumerable evils, has always been not only the absolutely essential condition of human progress, but also one of the most important, if not, indeed, the most important factor in the economic evolution of society itself."[11] To these young economists, state intervention in behalf of social progress was essential and inevitable. Moreover, their view of the state as an active protector of social rights offered a new ideological basis from which reform could oc-

cur and which at the same time was compatible with the compla-
cent view that certain people were best suited to design and administer this new activist state.

Any suggestion of intervention by the state beyond its rightful
powers, interpreted in a narrow sense, proved to be anathema to
Godkin and his crowd. Godkin lashed out at the young upstarts
who threatened to undermine the very principles upon which the
reform tradition had operated since the time of Adam Smith and
John Stuart Mill—particularly Mill. Godkin assured his readers
that, contrary to Ely, when human legislation tries to transcend the
natural laws of political economy, no matter how worthy the motive may be, "it works the more injury as it strives to attain an ideal
good."[12] Despite Godkin, Ely continued to make converts through
a prodigious list of publications including *An Introduction to Political
Economy* (1894), which in its various editions became the largest-
selling economics textbook of its time. The same year Ely published his textbook, Godkin bluntly warned President Daniel Coit
Gilman of Johns Hopkins University, where Ely was making a
name for himself as an up-and-coming political economist, that
"Professors of Political Economy preaching their own philanthropic
gospel of 'science' are among the most dangerous characters of our
land, and Ely [is] one of them."[13] Two years later Godkin attempted
to drive Ely from his new post as chairman of the economics department at the University of Wisconsin. The attack opened when
Godkin published a letter written by the Wisconsin superintendent
of public schools charging Ely, who was described as an "anarchist
and socialist," with having incited printers in Madison to strike as a
means of unionizing. Forced to defend himself against these serious
charges, Ely appeared in a public trial before the regents of the university.[14] In the end, after much hullabaloo, the charges against Ely
were quietly dismissed because the school superintendent refused
to testify at the trial.

These attacks by Godkin obscured the elitist assumptions underlying both the older mugwump tradition and the new scientific reform outlook represented by Ely. Long before his trial, Ely had
been quick to point out that he was not a radical but an elitist whose
writings were, as he put it, "designed for men of wealth and culture, for those called the upper classes and by them chiefly my
books have been read." Following his trial he reiterated this point:
"I am a conservative rather than a radical . . . an aristocrat rather
than a democrat." By aristocrat he specifically meant a member of a

"natural" aristocracy based on natural ability and special training. "I have in mind, of course," Ely elaborated, "not a legal aristocracy, but a natural aristocracy . . . an aristocracy which lives in fulfillment of a special service."[15] What Ely offered, as most older mugwumps would come to see, was a new conception of the state that promised to expand the social basis of the "best men" to include the new professionals—accountants, social scientists, professors, engineers, and college-trained civil servants. By modifying German statist economics to fit the conditions unique to America, economists such as Ely proposed a greater role for these new professionals as guardians of an emerging administrative state. Clearly implicit in Ely's plan was the older mugwump assumption that the state should be depoliticized through management by nonpartisan experts. The mugwump tradition, however, had been tied to laissez-faire economics and thus was not amenable to the idea that activist administrators should pursue positive state action. In his polemic against the older liberals, *The Past and the Present of Political Economy* (1884), Ely struck on exactly this point when he claimed that laissez-faire economists deliberately cut themselves off from policy making because they viewed economics as a "pure" science. The laissez-faire economist not only saw man as fallible, but saw state policy as "a changeable, fluctuating factor which introduced a disheartening element in what was otherwise immutable."[16]

Moreover, with the rise of professionalism in the social sciences, scholarly research now determined what was nonpartisan and disinterested. Of course, social scientists were involved in interpretation as well as presentation of the "scientific" facts, but whether their final conclusions were biased or objective was a matter to be decided by a self-contained professional community through book reviews and tenure committees.[17] Such a professional procedure for judging political disinterest protected, as Ely proved at his trial, the new academic mugwump from open class attacks. Politicians and the electorate might not always accept the conclusions for reform derived from "scientific" research, but the professionals' claim to disinterestedness gave their views more credibility than those of genteel reformers. The emergence of the social science profession paved the way for Bruere and other staff members of the AICP to join forces with older mugwumps such as Cutting to bring about "scientific" reform in government.

Yet this movement to modernize government by placing administrative authority in the hands of a professional aristocracy would have been doomed without the political breakdown of party organization in the late nineteenth century. After this time the American masses acquiesced in their loss of political control, as evidenced by the general decline in voter turnout following the election of 1896. A comparison between the elections of 1896 and 1916 shows that of the 34 non-Southern states only 8 experienced increased voter participation. The majority of the industrial states lost 15 percent to 20 percent in voter turnout.[18] This decline marked a radical shift in the social basis of political culture from local, predominately rural communities to diversified, economically integrated urban centers with organized group interests. Institutional reforms enacted during this time—the Australian ballot, antifusion laws, and personal registration laws—only hastened the decline of partisan identification and voter turnout. The result was the demobilization of the armies of partisan voters who had marched to the polls throughout the nineteenth century.

With the decline of party feeling, nonpartisan independence found new vitality. The professional class discovered that it could appeal to the majority in its campaign for nonpartisan government. The emergence of the demand for a depoliticized administrative state perfectly suited the objective political conditions characterized by an apathetic lower class and a middle class fed up with partisan politics-as-usual.

Thus when the reformers announced a crusade against machine politics in New York, they met with a favorable response where the older mugwumps had failed. "Efficiency and economy" in government now became a popular demand, a revolutionary slogan raised to oust the Democratic machine, Tammany Hall, from city government. The crusade to bring "efficiency and economy" to New York City began only after independent, anti-Tammany reformers had failed in the electoral arena. In 1902 the Citizens Union, a good-government organization that had been formed in 1896 to educate in a "properly superior manner" the ordinary citizen, had successfully backed the candidacy of Seth Low for mayor. Low came into office with the highest of patrician credentials, having formerly been the Independent Republican mayor of Brooklyn and president of Columbia University. Two years later Low's administration had proved disastrous. He had failed to reduce the cost of government, as he had promised, and moreover he had insisted on enforcing prohibition laws that divided his German constituency.[18] In the 1904 election New Yorkers, completely disillusioned with the "pompous righteousness" of Low, returned a Tammany Hall man, George B. McClellan, to office.[19] The lessons of the Low debacle seemed obvious. Henry Bruere, who had come to New York shortly after Low's defeat, spoke for many when he concluded that poor administration, not the lack of good men, had thwarted independent reform. "There was a search for a great administrator," Bruere wrote. "He wasn't found because he doesn't exist. A great administrator needs tools and techniques of sound administration."[20] William H. Allen, Bruere's associate at the AICP, had reached a similar conclusion. It was Allen who suggested to R. Fulton Cutting the establishment of a research bureau to "study the underlying administration of government." "Almost without exception," Allen told Cutting, "so-called reform governments have emphasized goodness rather than efficiency." What was now needed was an independent research agency "dependent neither upon politics nor *average* public intelligence. . . . The Supreme [sic] need is for an Intelligence center that will substitute facts for calamity or scandal."[21] Such an agency could effect reform through government administration, and this kind of reform, Allen suggested, was beyond the vagaries of popular whim. Allen's proposal struck just the right chord with Cutting. An elitist by nature (he insisted on wearing formal evening dress to political rallies), Cutting agreed to have the Citizens Union sponsor a new research agency, the Bureau of City Betterment, later to be expanded and renamed the Bureau of Municipal Research (BMR).[22] Financial support for the new agency came from Cutting and his close associates, John D. Rockefeller and Andrew Carnegie.

The sponsors of the bureau selected Henry Bruere and William H. Allen to direct its efforts. These two men were soon joined by Frederick Cleveland, a finance professor at New York University. Allen, Bruere, and Cleveland formed a trio soon known among New York reformers as "the ABC." Just as Allen and Bruere typified the new social science professional, Cleveland exemplified the new accountant. In 1905 accounting was still a young profession.[23] The Wharton School of Finance at the University of Pennsylvania had just begun the first undergraduate degree program in accounting when Cleveland enrolled as a student in 1897. After completing his accounting degree at Wharton, he went on to receive a doctorate in economics under Allen's mentor, Simon Patten. He later took an LL.B. at Bruere's alma mater, New York University.[24]

Cleveland's educational background bore a striking resemblance to that of Allen and Bruere. So did his world outlook. A friend of Frederick Taylor, the father of the "efficiency and economy" movement in America, Cleveland also proved to be a fanatic about the need for efficiency and economy in government.[25] Furthermore, he shared Bruere's and Allen's disgust with the "inefficiency" of boss-ridden politics. He described elections as little more than "marionette shows" staged by political bosses for their own selfish gains. Like Bruere, Allen, and other social scientists of the age, including Woodrow Wilson, Cleveland saw himself as a "practical" man who rejected the visionary world of the sentimentalist in favor of tough-mindedness. He was an economist and accountant who remained, above all else, a realist concerned with the practical. This realism reflected itself in his view of economics. "It has long been recognized that the old time treatises on political economy," he declared, "have little in common with the experiences of businessmen." Past treatises on political economy, he continued, had been little more than partisan pleadings directed toward legal and social reform. Now, however, "science has turned to the field of business for its data. It has developed treatises on commerce, transportation, banking practices, insurance, and other specific employments. . . ."[26] And in turn, Cleveland maintained, economics had emerged as a field dominated by "business specialists actively engaged in and in close touch with business affairs."[27]

The BMR soon bustled with activity under the ABC. The bureau's first investigation targeted the notoriously corrupt boss of the Manhattan borough, John F. Ahearn. Aided by a staff of young accountants and efficiency experts, the ABC submitted a detailed report to Low's successor, George B. McClellan, showing Ahearn's fraudulent and flagrant misuse of public funds. A subsequent investigation headed by special counselor John Purroy Mitchel, who later would become mayor of New York, substantiated Bruere's charges. Eventually the governor would personally remove Ahearn from office.[28] The reformers' first campaign ended in victory. Other successes were to follow.

The bureau found a further avenue of political influence through the office of the city comptroller, Herman A. Metz, who had been elected in 1905 on the slogan "A Business Man for a Business Office."[29] Metz asked the bureau to study the problem of the misuse of public funds by politically appointed city officials. By 1907 Bruere was ready to present a detailed proposal to the Board of Estimate and Appointment for enacting a new budget system, which would include a centralized accounting system and standardized forms to be used by all departments in preparing estimates for future expenditures.[30] To rally public support for such a centralized budget system, the BMR organized a persuasive "budget exhibit," which attracted nearly 50,000 people to its presentation demonstrating how a city budget could bring efficiency to government and prevent political appointees from grafting public money. Impressed with the bureau's campaign, J. P. Morgan contributed $10,000 to the cause of good budgeting in New York.[31]

Of course the ABC denied that any political intentions were behind their proposal for an executive budget. Nevertheless Tammany was not so easily fooled. Party followers accused the BMR of being a front for independent Republicans and termed it the "Bureau of Besmirch." Clearly the BMR relied heavily on those classes who would be most opposed to Tammany. Cleveland reported that nearly half his time was spent in meetings with "professional and business men" to ensure their support for the bureau's activities.[32] Contrary to the claims of the bureau, its "objectivity" proved fragile. For instance, during the 1909 election for the Board of Estimate and Appointment, Cutting phoned Bruere to tell him that unless his friend, John Purroy Mitchel, accepted the Fusion Party's nomination for board membership, Cutting would end all support of the BMR.[33] Bruere subsequently spoke with Mitchel, who, after some hesitation, finally accepted the nomination.

Four years later, on November 4, 1913, Mitchel won the mayoral election on the Fusion ticket. Mitchel quickly enlisted the aid of the BMR in conducting the city's affairs. Bruere was appointed to the post of city chamberlain, while a young bureau expert on civil service, Robert Moses, began his career in New York City politics as a technical assistant to the Municipal Civil Service Commission. The bureau was intent that only university men and "gentlemen who had inherited breeding and culture" should fill city posts.[34] Nevertheless, the partisan nature of independent reform was manifested in the line of political appointees who stepped into clerkships and judgeships, after being approved by Fusion ward leaders. The bureau did little to promote nonpartisanship in government. In fact, Cleveland announced, "When its friends are in power, a citizens' agency should not publish unfavorable information."[35] Only a few liberals seemed to worry about what the *New Republic* saw as a "tendency to make the municipal research work largely a matter of agreement between the bureau and the public official." The *New Republic* specifically pointed to Henry Bruere, a man holding "mechanical views of government," as an example of this tendency. The magazine warned that "this private agreement [between the bureau and the Fusionists] about public matters is the rock upon which the municipal research ship may founder."[36] The ship did not founder, but instead became a model for reformers in other cities.[37] Businessmen in Philadelphia invited Bruere to their city in 1908 to establish a bureau that promoted business methods in city government. Two years later the City Club of Chicago raised money to establish a Bureau of Efficiency whose purpose was to establish proper accounting principles for Chicago government. Capitalists were not the only sponsors of municipal research bureaus, however. When the Social Democratic Party captured the city government in Milwaukee, one of its first acts was to organize a Bureau of Efficiency and Economy to be headed by John Commons of the University of Wisconsin. By 1916 research agencies had been established in Rochester, Detroit, Cleveland, Akron, Toledo, and San Francisco, the forerunners of numerous quasi-governmental institutions that would become involved in city government. Not directly accountable to the electorate, these shadow institutions exerted a new and subtle force on urban government, and in the process became as much a part of the governmental process as the traditional branches of government. The stage was now set for the emergence of a research bureau concerned with national government. The efficiency and economy movement was now prepared to address national issues, specifically the national budget system.

The issue of a national executive budget was now a matter of urgency. Reformers warned that if America was to progress and if representative government was to survive, an executive budget system, nonpartisan in nature, must be created. They quickly pointed out that the current budget system, dominated by a myriad of congressional committees, was abhorrently archaic. Throughout the latter half of the nineteenth century, the congressional budget system had become increasingly politicized and diffused in a labyrinth of appropriation committees, each dominated by a chairman who ran his committee as a feudal lord would his own fiefdom. Such a system encouraged Congress to squander public money on waterway and harbor improvements, pensions, and a long list of other pork-barrel projects to ensure support in the home districts of individual congressmen.

This congressional budget system was in fact a fairly recent development. It had been established in 1885 when the speaker of the House, John G. Carlisle of Kentucky, turned over that session's appropriation bills to the jurisdiction of six committees instead of to the single Committee on Appropriations, chaired by Carlisle's rival, the powerful Samuel J. Randall. Carlisle's action, deliberately designed to weaken Randall's authority in Congress, only opened the door for further political manipulation of the budget by Congress. By the end of the next decade, twenty-nine separate committees in the House and the Senate were involved in appropriating money.

When President Taft called for the establishment of a commission to study government administration in 1910, he gave budget reform national attention. The budget-reform movement now shifted from New York City to the nation's capital, Washington, D.C. In calling for such a commission, Taft pursued a progressive impulse that had been evident in his support for the first federal corporate tax, an income tax amendment, a postal savings plan for low-income wage earners, and the initiation of antitrust suits against corporate interests.[38] Taft hoped that his call for reform in government administration would add to his credentials as a serious, although not rash, reformer. To the dismay of many, the federal budget stood at over a billion dollars when Taft assumed office, and the federal debt had reached disturbing proportions, largely as an aftermath of the Panic of 1907.[39] Under mounting public pressure to make the federal government more economical, Taft was able to secure from Congress an appropriation of $100,000 for his proposed commission to conduct an investigation of government costs. Taft then instructed his private secretary, Charles Norton, to find a director for the study. Taft and Norton tacitly agreed that any inquiry should ultimately be directed toward designing an entirely new budget system, one that would be more centralized and that would be under the jurisdiction of the president. So even before a director had been selected, Taft and Norton had in effect enlarged the charge of the inquiry, and as a consequence budget reformers now were given a key role to play in reforming the federal government.

Although Norton solicited nominations from all of the prominent accounting firms in the nation, Frederick Cleveland's name kept coming to the surface. Norton particularly liked Cleveland's reputation as a "realist" sympathetic to corporations and business methods. In contrast, in a secret memorandum to Taft, Norton summarily dismissed Cleveland's only rival for the job as a "visionary."[40] Once chosen to head the project, Cleveland assembled an impressive staff of less than a dozen men to constitute what became known as the Taft Commission. Among these men were two who would eventually play leading roles in the early history of the Institute for Government Research (IGR), the precursor to the Brookings Institution: a professor of administrative law at Columbia University, Frank Goodnow, and a statistician with the Labor Department, William F. Willoughby. Goodnow later became the first chairman of the board of the IGR and Willoughby its first director.[41]

The Taft Commission, after two years of painstaking work, presented to Congress on June 17, 1912, *The Need for a National Budget*. The report called emphatically for efficiency in government, a demand that would be carried into the conservative decade of the 1920s. Government expenditures must be cut, services retrenched, and taxpayers' money saved. The report marked a subtle shift in emphasis for the budget-reform movement. In the past, budget reformers had maintained that with the enactment of an executive budget, additional funds could be reallocated for social welfare from the money saved by reducing waste and corruption. Cleveland's final report gave little emphasis to the benefit social programs might receive as a result of good budgeting.

Of particular interest in this regard is a memorandum submitted by Henry Bruere to the Taft Commission during its preliminary investigations into government waste. The memorandum, "Suggestions for . . . a Social Welfare Program for the National Government," proposed that the commission examine the possibility of establishing programs for the "regulation of hours and conditions of labor, the encouragement of means for old age insurance, and the elimination, so far as possible, of the causes of poverty."[42] In expressing such concerns Bruere showed himself to be more than a mechanic of government administration, as he had been described earlier by the *New Republic*. Nevertheless, the commission chose to ignore his memorandum. Instead, the commission in its final report to Congress stressed the great savings that would ensue with budget reform and left it at that. Savings had become an end in itself.

The Need for a National Budget called for the institution of an executive budget in which the president, after reviewing all departmental estimates with the help of a Bureau of the Budget, would propose and introduce to Congress a budget to serve as a "guide" for congressional appropriations. The proposal also suggested that a single committee be solely responsible for appropriating funds. Such a system, Cleveland declared, was the "only effective means whereby the Executive may be made responsible for getting before the country a definite, well-considered, comprehensive program with respect to which *the legislature* must also assume responsibility either for action or inaction."[43] By phrasing the proposal in these terms, Cleveland deliberately sought to disarm the opponents of a new budget system by insisting that he was not seeking to subvert traditional relations between the executive and the legislature. He was particularly concerned that congressional foes of budget reform not accuse the commission of trying to impose a highly centralized, "English" budget system on Congress.[44] Nonetheless, it was obvious to many that the president would gain at the expense of Congress under the new system. Government bureaus, it appeared, would be held accountable to the president and the Bureau of the Budget. In turn, congressional committees that were once able to appropriate money directly to these bureaus would have their powers placed in the hands of a single congressional committee.

By framing the budget issue in terms of cutting government costs, budget reformers sought to persuade a recalcitrant Congress, while rallying an apathetic public, to support an executive budget system. Most congressmen realized, though, that the slogan "economy in government" served as a subterfuge for reformers who sought to strengthen the executive branch at the expense of Congress. Furthermore by 1912, an election year, it had become obvious that Taft was using the "economy" issue as a political device to bolster his sagging public support. The president publicly declared that he had reduced the fiscal budget in 1911 by $42.8 million. Members of his cabinet cited his support of the executive budget as proof that he was in fact a scientific reformer and a true progressive.[45] Taft supporters were particularly anxious to make such claims in order to counter Theodore Roosevelt's growing support in the liberal wing of the Republican Party. Budget reform had once again been turned into a political issue, a phenomenon that would recur in succeeding decades.

Taft, fully aware that Congress for a variety of reasons would be slow to act on the report, directed his department heads to prepare two budgets, "one in accordance with the present practice, and one following the proposal of the Taft Commission."[46] Under the existing system, department heads, acting independently of the president as well as one another, submitted budget estimates directly to Congress. Usually their estimates for future expenditures were inflated, by as much as 20 percent, in the expectation of congressional cutbacks. Taft now proposed a new system in which the executive office directed all budgetary estimates for the upcoming fiscal year. Jealous of its prerogatives, Congress responded to Taft's two proposed budgets by insisting that regular annual estimates be prepared and submitted "only in the form and at the time now required by law." Undaunted, Taft ignored congressional strictures and submitted his two budgets anyway. An affronted Congress, led by a number of chairmen from key appropriation committees, immediately canceled further appropriations for the Taft Commission.[47] Two years of work by the commission had seemingly come to naught.

The demise of the Taft Commission did not dismay reformers, however. Instead the movement gained increased momentum as reformers took their cause to the academic and business communities. Frank Goodnow, who had become president of Johns Hopkins University, organized a special session on the national budget at the 1912 annual convention of the American Political Science Association.[48] Shortly afterwards, the Chamber of Commerce conducted a national referendum—the first in its history—which revealed overwhelming support from businessmen for a national budget system. Frank Goodnow and W. F. Willoughby were subsequently asked to direct the efforts of the Chamber's Commission on Efficiency and Economy to lobby in Washington for an executive budget system.[49] More importantly, talk was now heard in reform circles of the need to establish a new research organization to play the role of the New York Bureau of Municipal Research, but on the national level. Frederick Cleveland picked up this idea and soon brought it to the attention of Jerome D. Greene, secretary of the newly endowed Rockefeller Foundation. Cleveland's suggestion immediately precipitated a discussion among New York businessmen. These discussions came to a head when Greene and Charles Norton, who had left the Taft administration to become vice president of the National Bank of New York, agreed to push the proposal. Greene wrote a confidential letter to a select group of nine leading figures from business, calling for the establishment of a research organization to "study the problems of administration and to interest the public in the solution of these problems."[50] This original committee of nine formed the basis for the board of trustees of the new institute.

By 1915 the newly formed board had been expanded to include a well-balanced group of liberals and conservatives who were "to vouch before the public for the integrity of the enterprise and its freedom from the slightest political bias." The organizers were particularly pleased to recruit President Charles Van Hise of the University of Wisconsin and Felix Frankfurter, men whose affiliation was considered likely, as Jerome Greene later recalled, "to win the confidence and disarm any hostility on the part of liberals."[51] Greene worried that Midwestern and Western progressives would openly attack the institute because of its ties with Rockefeller. Such worries, in fact, were realized when Senator Henry F. Ashurst of Arizona charged that the new institute was a front for Rockefeller. Even the press continued to call the institute the "Rockefeller Inquiry." In spite of such criticism, Greene attempted to show that the institution was "nonpartisan" by balancing the committee's liberals with conservatives such as Arthur Hadley, president of Yale, and corporate leaders such as Cleveland H. Dodge, vice president of Phelps Dodge. Also asked to join the board was a St. Louis businessman and philanthropist, Robert Brookings, who in the post–World War I years would ensure the survival of the institute. Brookings's interest in budget reform stemmed from his participation as a consultant to the Taft Commission.

The newly formed board of trustees chose Frank Goodnow as its chairman. By the spring of 1916, Goodnow decided that the full board should be convened in order to select a director of research for the new institute, which was to be called the Institute for Government Research (IGR). To the surprise of some, W. F. Willoughby, instead of Frederick Cleveland, was chosen to direct the institute's activities in Washington. Before the meeting it had been arranged that R. Fulton Cutting would place Cleveland's name in nomination. But when Frank Goodnow, seconded by Jerome Greene, nominated his former associate on the Taft Commission, W. F. Willoughby, any discussion of Cleveland as director of the new institute ended. Greene's support for Willoughby must have carried extra weight; after all, Rockefeller was providing $10,000 of the seed money for the institute.[52] The Rockefeller crowd had come to know Willoughby when he had served on the Rockefeller Foundation's Special Committee on Scientific Research. Moreover, Greene felt, and most trustees concurred, that Cleveland lacked the "capacity for concise and lucid expression so necessary in obtaining congressional and public support for a national budget."[53]

With the establishment of the Institute for Government Research, the Rockefeller Foundation shifted its funding away from the New York Bureau of Municipal Research to the IGR. Finally in 1918 Cleveland, seeing that his influence was on the wane, submitted his resignation from the BMR. He would be replaced by a young historian, Charles Beard, who had recently resigned his post at Columbia University in protest over what he considered the suppression of academic freedom at the university.[54] Frederick Cleveland's role as a national figure in the "efficiency and economy" movement had come to an end. After leaving the BMR, he retreated into academia, taking a position at the University of Pennsylvania. Similarly, William H. Allen drifted into various municipal crusades supported by the Republican Party in New York. In turn he became increasingly more conservative. His last book would be *Teachable Facts about Bolshevism*. Henry Bruere remained an influential figure among the city's elite, eventually becoming a vice president of Metropolitan Life Insurance Company, and later president of a New York bank.

Willoughby's selection as head of the Institute for Government Research reflected the ascendant role political scientists would play in the efficiency and economy movement. The status of accountants was clearly on the decline in the social sciences. Of the half-dozen men who initially staffed the new institute, only Lewis Meriam, a Harvard-trained political scientist, and Henry Seidemann, an accountant with extensive government experience, would come over from the BMR.[55] Political scientists such as Willoughby brought to the IGR a wider theoretical knowledge, a greater clarity in argument, and more respect for the IGR on the part of academics, foundations, and government—the three major constituencies the IGR desired to serve.[56]

Willoughby also had extensive government experience. Following graduation from Johns Hopkins in 1884, he had joined the Labor Department as a statistician. In this post he advocated voluntary arbitration, child labor laws, and collective bargaining rights for unions.[57] His reputation as a progressive was further enhanced when Theodore Roosevelt appointed Willoughby to fill simultaneously the key posts of treasurer of Puerto Rico and president of the principal governing body of the island, the Executive Council.[58] As treasurer Willoughby completely reorganized Puerto Rico's colonial financial system and drafted a lax corporation law, modeled on New Jersey's, to "stimulate the influx of foreign capital" into the country.[59] Following this service in Puerto Rico he joined the

Census Bureau and the Taft Commission, before becoming a professor of political science at Princeton University under Woodrow Wilson.[60]

A prolific writer, Willoughby showed no hesitancy in expressing his beliefs concerning democracy. Democracy by majority rule, he had written in 1901, often was "little better than mob rule." Willoughby counterposed democracy with representative government, which was based "on the principle that, though sovereign authority resides in the people, the latter are incompetent to exercise it, except in the most general way." Under modern conditions, "decisions in respect to matters of legislation and administration, if they are to be wise, must rest upon . . . a relatively small body of officers specializing in this work." More specifically, he declared, "the conduct of government affairs is a special work requiring special abilities, training, and knowledge and therefore one to be performed by a special body having these special qualifications." Partisan politics, he proclaimed, were irrational and selfish. "Selfishness is the controlling power in politics. Expectations of material gain and pecuniary rewards, not altruistic feeling, are the motives that . . . supply the incentives for political pursuit."[61] Willoughby expressed the views of the social science mugwump.

Willoughby expressly welcomed the decline in voter interest and the coinciding growth of government commissions staffed by experts. He observed that "the states have entered new fields of usefulness . . . through the establishment of special boards and commissions, as railroad commissions, bank and insurance commissions, boards of health, etc." The advantage of government commissions lay particularly in their ability to take over from legislative bodies the duty of drafting new laws. "Many abuses can be more effectively remedied by permanent officers than by legislation. . . . The custom of originating bills in bureaus of government is increasing, and has been followed by the best results."[62] Willoughby believed his role at the IGR was to help further such means of efficient administration.

Willoughby expressed the sentiments of the mugwump tradition, but in many ways he was even more of an elitist. He wanted a government of specialists; and he did not include in this group every "educated" man. Indeed, Willoughby criticized the "American view" that "in education is to be found the cure of all social evils." Facts showed that the "proper conduct of public affairs had not come into existence as a result of the wider diffusion of education. Bad governments exist in our highly educated as well as in our less progressive municipalities." In Puerto Rico, Willoughby had observed that the educated classes, *particularly* the educated classes, were corrupt and showed "little if any desire to subordinate selfish ends to public consideration." He concluded that virtue could not be attained from education alone. "Political education is primarily and essentially one of training rather than one of education, of character building rather than scholastic instruction." The best way to build character, to develop political education, was through "efficient, disinterested and impartial administration."[63] Willoughby came to the IGR suspicious of the ability of even the "best men" to run government properly, so he had narrowed the old mugwump base to include only specialists. Social science ideology, at least as expressed by Willoughby, had become increasingly more elitist in sentiment in comparison with that articulated by Ely's generation. A major step toward the creation of an efficient administrative state, managed by "a relatively small body of officers specializing in this work," would be the establishment of an executive budget system.

"The establishment of a genuine national budget," Jerome Greene later recalled, "was clearly the first objective of the Institute for Government Research."[64] In January, 1917, shortly after his election to a second term, Woodrow Wilson met with a committee from the IGR composed of Willoughby, Goodnow, and Felix Frankfurter to discuss the establishment of an executive budget. Wilson was naturally sympathetic to the work of the IGR. As a graduate student at Johns Hopkins, Wilson had discussed with Richard Ely the possibility of establishing a research institution in Washington. At his meeting with the IGR representatives, Wilson, who claimed a longtime interest in government reorganization, expressed his desire to abolish or consolidate the many administrative agencies in government. He spoke with particular approval of the centralized budget system in Great Britain. Nonetheless, Wilson was "very pessimistic" about "the possibility of a new budgetary system under our current political system."[65] Still, at the end of the meeting, Wilson asked Willoughby to submit a memorandum summarizing the IGR's views on the budget.

The outbreak of World War I and America's entry into the European conflict proved Wilson's pessimism to be unwarranted, however. Support for an executive budget system now became fiscally prudent. Government expenses soared at an alarming rate during the war. For instance, in order to meet government expenses be-

tween April 5, 1918, and March 23, 1919, the secretary of the treasury transmitted to Congress a total of 232 supplementary requests
for appropriations. On the political front both the Democrats and
the Republicans had already pledged their support for a national
budget system at their party conventions in 1916. Popular sentiment for a national budget could only have been further reinforced
by the Victory Loan injunction, "Make a Budget and Save." Frederick Cleveland reported that "we can scarcely pick up a magazine
without seeing something about . . . the national budget."[66]
Congress now seemed ready to act. James N. Good, chairman of
the House Committee on Appropriations, and later secretary of
war under Herbert Hoover, deserves much of the credit for pushing
a budget bill through Congress. To assist him in drafting the bill,
Good called on Willoughby, whose recently published book *The
Problem of a National Budget* had elicited considerable support on
Capitol Hill. At the suggestion of Willoughby, Good held congressional hearings on the budget in 1919. Over 700 pages of testimony were collected. Willoughby himself provided key testimony,
along with other notable reformers including Goodnow, Henry
Stimson, Charles Beard, and the young Assistant Secretary of the
Navy, Franklin Roosevelt, who declared unabashedly that his department alone would save 20 percent under a budget system.[67]
   At the end of the hearings, Willoughby drafted what was to be
called the Good Bill for a national budget system.[68] The bill provided that the president, and only he, should transmit a budget to
Congress on the first day of each regular session. In addition, provisions were made for a Bureau of the Budget acting under the
president, along with a comptroller general who would audit expenditures. The Good Bill formed the basis for the Budget and Accounting Act of 1919, which overwhelmingly passed both houses
by a large majority. Congress agreed, as New Jersey Senator Walter
Edge so aptly put it, that the new act "is not a panacea for all evils
of extravagance," but that "it will have a wonderful moral effect on
the present state of mind of the American people."[69] Feelings were
running high among the budget reformers in 1919. Then, unexpectedly, Wilson vetoed the budget act.
   At issue was the constitutionality of Section 303 of the act, which
provided for the presidential appointment of a comptroller-general
and his possible removal from office for neglect of duty, by means
of concurrent resolution by the houses of Congress. Wilson argued
that, under Section 2, Article II of the Constitution, the power to

appoint entailed the power to remove from office. Therefore, Congress could not remove a comptroller-general who was appointed by the president. Wilson's argument had a long history in constitutional law, but also expressed his desire to ensure absolute presidential control over the budget process.[70] Congress had been willing to give the president increased powers over the budget; nevertheless, Wilson wanted more. Congress's failure to override the veto brought to a close the budget issue in Wilson's administration. Ironically, the benefactor of Wilson's insistence that presidential powers be extended would be his successor, a notably weak president, Warren G. Harding.

Willoughby continued to lobby for a new budget law. In early February, 1920, acting on a suggestion from Good, Willoughby met with President-elect Harding at his retreat in St. Augustine, Florida, to discuss the matter of budget reform. Following their meeting, Willoughby jubilantly wrote to the trustees that Harding had given the go-ahead on a new budget bill.[71]

In the meantime, Good had drafted a new bill. To meet any objections from the new president it was agreed that the comptroller-general would be limited to one fifteen-year term and could be removed from office only by a *joint* resolution, which would need the president's signature. Not taking any chances on the passage of the bill, Willoughby hired a professional public relations man to place editorials and news items in favor of an executive budget system in the nation's leading newspapers.[72] Willoughby's actions went beyond what one might normally expect from a "nonpartisan" expert. A thin line divided partisan from nonpartisan, and nonpolitical from political activity. At this point in the IGR's history, these lines would be frequently blurred, contrary to institute rhetoric.

Willoughby's efforts proved successful. On June 10, 1921, President Harding signed the Budget and Accounting Act and declared that the bill marked the "beginning of the greatest reformation in government practices since the beginning of the Republic."[73] Harding appointed the highly political Charles Dawes to become the first director of the Bureau of the Budget. Dawes initially attempted to follow the goal of keeping the bureau out of politics, which he equated with policy. "We have nothing to do with policy . . . ," he assured Congress. "If Congress were to pass a law that garbage should be put on the White House steps, it would be our regrettable duty . . . to advise the Executive and Congress as to how the amount of garbage" could be placed in "the most expeditious and

economical manner."[74] This subtle, if not confusing, distinction between administration and policy proved impossible to maintain for
very long.

Within a year after assuming his post, Dawes ordered his investigators to expand their activities from questions of "efficiency and
economy" to what he regarded as the policies behind the government programs under investigation. He instructed his small staff to
provide information in their reports as to "whether limitations
should be put upon existing policy and what, if any, new policies
should be recommended."[75] In this way, experts within the Bureau
of the Budget began to extend their interests from administration,
defined narrowly, to larger issues involving policy. Nevertheless,
during the Dawes years the bureau remained primarily concerned
with trimming the federal budget. Yet its concern for efficiency and
economy in government did little to hinder the growth of government, but instead restricted its own activity. Dawes took great
pride in reporting at the end of his tenure in office that the bureau
had spent only $123,313.54 of its $225,000.00 budget. In fact, the
bureau was operating with roughly forty-five employees who were
provided with only one adding machine, one calculating machine,
and one bookkeeping manual.

Yet the staff at the IGR continued to maintain a sharp distinction
between administration and policy. By confining their role to that
of nonpartisan technicians, they limited their interests to questions
of administration. For instance, Henry Seidemann, who was assigned to work at the Bureau of the Budget, prepared the analytical
tables for the national budget. Similarly, Lewis Meriam, another
staff member at the IGR who had come from the BMR, provided
technical assistance to the Joint Committee on the Reclassification
of Salaries while it was drafting the Classification Act of 1923.[76]
When Willoughby published his influential *Reorganization of the Administrative Branch of the National Government* (1923), which called
for a Department of Public Health and a Department of Education
and Science, he framed his arguments in terms of functional efficiency, not in terms of policy outcomes. By 1924 Congress had ta-
bled Willoughby's reorganization plan, thereby marking the end of
the early budget-reform movement.

By the 1920s most people had lost interest in administrative reform. Even budget reformers like Charles Beard, Henry Stimson,
and most of the board at the IGR had turned to larger social questions. Nevertheless, Willoughby continued to insist that the IGR

was a research institution concerned with administration, not policy. Fear of being seen as a "political" institution led Willoughby and his small staff to evaluate the "efficiency" of government through a series of incredibly dull monographs that described in minute detail how each agency within government was organized. As to questions of why these agencies existed or if these agencies were accomplishing their missions, the IGR refused to comment. The IGR had fulfilled its early promise to enact an executive budget system, but it now seemed unable to go beyond that one accomplishment. To many the IGR was an organization without purpose and without vision. Only one member of the board of trustees saw new possibilities for the institute. If the IGR had sought efficiency in government administration in the past, this member queried, why should not it broaden its mandate and bring expertise to economic policy? World War I had shown the importance of economic questions and the dire need for economic expertise. The man who raised this issue had not been particularly active in the IGR, but he would now revitalize the IGR. In the process he established a new institution bearing his name, which was Brookings.

3 · ROBERT S. BROOKINGS AND HIS VISION OF A BETTER SOCIETY

HISTORIANS, IN writing about the founding of the Brookings Institution, have too often mistaken corporate involvement in the institution as further evidence of the subversion of democratic government by "big business."[1] In a certain sense these critics are correct. Corporate interests, through the Carnegie Corporation and the Rockefeller Foundation, sponsored the Institute of Economics and the Robert S. Brookings Graduate School, which merged in 1927 to form the Brookings Institution. Nevertheless, it appears that this desire to influence governmental policy through the establishment of an independent research agency based in Washington, D.C., stemmed less from a conscious attempt to undermine the public interest in favor of business per se than from an effort to bring order to the public policy process.

The First World War revealed all too readily the sheer ignorance with which public officials were operating in making major economic decisions that affected an entire nation at war. It soon became apparent that administrators lacked basic information concerning the nation's net financial reserves, aggregate industrial output, transportation, and employment potential. This situation, which one reporter writing at the time described as "everything going wrong," particularly shocked those American businessmen who came to Washington to serve their nation in time of war.[2] Businessmen, having experienced the corporate revolution in the late nineteenth century, knew all too well the importance of reliable information in making managerial decisions. These men, realizing that government operated in a manner that would not be tolerated in private business, sought to introduce modern business methods and management to government. Professionally trained economists and statisticians were subsequently mobilized and appointed to the War Industries Board, the War Labor Practices Board, the United States Railway Commission, and a myriad of other wartime agencies.[3] Robert S. Brookings, from his wartime experience as one of these new appointees on the War Industries Board, saw with more clarity than most the new role demanded of economists in the postwar period. The government and the public needed economists to collect, analyze, and disseminate economic information if the country was to operate efficiently. Yet Brookings's distrust of partisan politics precluded his thinking in terms of lobbying for a governmental agency along the lines of a latter-day Council of Economic Advisors. Because of his own prewar involvement in the Institute for Government Research and its campaign for an executive budget system, Brookings turned to the establishment of a nonpartisan economic research institute and an allied graduate school to fulfill his purpose. He envisioned this Institute of Economics (IE) and the Graduate School as serving as sister organizations to the IGR. The purpose of the two new organizations would be to collect objective economic data, to investigate economic problems, to evaluate current economic policy, and to develop a cadre of scientifically trained men to enter into government administration.

The establishment of an independent research institution, the Brookings Institution, through the merger of the IE and the Graduate School, served to "rationalize" the public policy process within the capitalist system. Brookings's outlook can be described as "corporatist" in the sense that he sought to bring order to postwar capitalist America. This development, he felt, would benefit both American business and the nation as a whole.

Yet to discuss the founding of the Brookings Institution only in terms of economic interests or corporate ideology misses the essential character of Robert S. Brookings and his motive in establishing the new institution. Moreover, such emphasis on corporate support confuses the role of the financial sponsors of the institution and the role of those professional social scientists who staffed, managed, and shaped the institution once it was established. In the end, the social science experts translated and narrowed Robert S. Brookings's vision in ways the financial founder neither foresaw nor intended. Both Brookings and the social scientists, of course, accepted the claim that the collection and analysis of economic data would allow for more efficiency in government administration and in public policy. Nevertheless, Brookings's own intuition suggested that more than efficiency in government was needed in order to address the social ills of a society marred by great inequalities of wealth. Thus Brookings in his later years grew increasingly more critical of the existing system, while the social scientists at the Brookings Institution became increasingly moderate in their social thinking.

Those who knew Robert S. Brookings described him as a somewhat eccentric, and talkative, entrepreneur. Above all else, though, Brookings was a builder. A nearly compulsive desire to build, to organize, to leave to posterity monuments of his work was the outstanding characteristic of this St. Louis businessman who became the chancellor of Washington University, the cochairman of the War Industries Board, and the founder of the Brookings Institution.

Brookings shared this creative impulse with other capitalists and philanthropists of his day, including his close friend Andrew Carnegie. Such men prided themselves on being architects of a new age. They maintained bolder dreams for American society than did the new professionals, the managers of business and the social scientists.[4] The founding of a nonpartisan economic institute marked the culmination of Brookings's efforts to bring harmony to the world. The institution also manifested an activist faith, accepted by many businessmen of the day, that the world could be reordered according to man's desires. Yet if these capitalists, the Carnegies, the Rockefellers, the Brookingses, reflected the optimism of an age, they also were men, shaped by their own backgrounds and by their idiosyncrasies of character, who stood as unique individuals within the broad sweep of history. Surely, Brookings's own peculiar rise to success set him apart from the other capitalists of his day. Brookings, for all of his desire to "belong" in established social and business circles, always remained a bit of an outsider.

Later, students at the Graduate School would joke that Brookings's fortune was built on clothespins, and they were close to being right. Raised in Baltimore by a Quaker stepfather and a Presbyterian mother, Robert Brookings inherited the Protestant values of hard work, moral stewardship, and civic responsibility.[5] His mother, who had been left a widow with three children when Brookings was two years old, showed a strength of character that carried the family through the next few years until she married her cousin, Henry Reynolds. A sensitive child, Brookings developed a particularly strong attachment to his mother, who provided the protection and support he needed. She encouraged Robert to take up the violin and to pursue his musical interests. His stepfather, an enterprising carpenter known in the community as "the quiet Quaker," inculcated in Brookings a belief that man's highest duty was not to himself but to others.

In the winter of 1866, at the age of seventeen, Brookings left home to travel to St. Louis, where his older brother Harry had settled. His mother lay ill, and would die before Brookings reached St. Louis. Those given to psychological interpretation might suggest that Brookings left home to escape the approaching tragedy of his mother's death. Nevertheless, St. Louis itself, reeling with its newfound prosperity in the aftermath of the Civil War and the opening of the West, should not be underestimated as an attraction to the young, ambitious Brookings. The city offered an opportunity for excitement, independence, and wealth.[6] In nineteenth-century America, psychological needs were often compatible with the entrepreneurial drive for success.

Robert Brookings, upon arriving in St. Louis, immediately enrolled in an accounting course at the local business school. He then joined his brother Harry in the woodenware business. Harry was employed by the Cupples dry-goods firm, which conducted an impressive woodenware business in the new western market between the Mississippi River and the Pacific. The owner of the firm, Samuel Cupples, was a devout Methodist, but he was best known in business circles as an overbearing, hard-driving entrepreneur. Cupples and Harry Brookings, who was later described by his brother's authorized biographer as "genial in his personal relationships, but ruthless, devoted to fleshpots, and inclined to stand on housetops and crow," must have set a sharp contrast to the tall, good-looking, gregarious but temperate Robert S. Brookings, who neither smoked nor drank.[7] Nonetheless, Samuel Cupples, perhaps because he was without children of his own, took a quick liking to the younger Brookings. He soon promoted the young man from bookkeeper to the firm's traveling salesman.

Traveling through a territory that ranged from Cheyenne and Denver to San Francisco, and down to New Orleans, Brookings spent the next four years mostly on the road, coming home only one month each year. Stopping in towns such as Ft. Benton, Montana—where, it was said, every fifth house was a saloon and every tenth a brothel—Brookings sent back orders for clothespins, bowls, kitchen utensils, rolling pins, ropes and twine, and a variety of other items found in late-nineteenth-century grocery stores. Competition in the wholesale woodenware business was particularly fierce in these days, as Chicago and St. Louis fought for control of the market. Within four years, Brookings had built Cupples and Company into a dominant outlet in the Midwest. Store owners were won over by the outgoing, serious young salesman, who read Plutarch's *Lives* in his spare time, had taught himself German, and played the fiddle on request.

Brookings's success astonished many, including Samuel Cupples. Thus, when the twenty-one-year-old salesman threatened to leave Cupples in order to start a business with his brother, Mr. Cupples, by this time a severe asthmatic, quickly offered the two brothers an equal partnership. Later Brookings would say, "I went to work for Samuel Cupples at seventeen. Four years later, Mr. Cupples became my partner."[8] By the end of the decade, the new partnership in the woodenware business dominated wholesale trade in the United States. Mostly under Brookings's direction, the firm established offices in all the major distributing centers between New York and San Francisco. In the woodenware business, Chicago wholesalers had been surpassed by the young entrepreneur from St. Louis, Robert Brookings.

Brookings built his empire on traditional late-nineteenth-century business practices, which sought to establish dominance in the market by watching costs, cutting prices, and driving out the weaker competition. As he later recalled, "Had the strong concerns not used their strength by selling temporarily in certain sections at unprofitable prices in order to kill off a weaker competitor and broaden our market, we would not have been considered progressive. Today they would put us in jail for the things we all did then."[9] Nonetheless, Brookings realized that eliminating the competition was not enough unless this achievement was backed up by a strong internal organization. Like Carnegie in steel, Brookings operated his company as a closed partnership, but, again like Carnegie, he rewarded loyal managers with offerings of company stock, a policy that drew them into a tight partnership. Brookings knew all too well, from his own experience, the threat posed by an industrious employee who might be tempted to take off on his own to compete with Cupples and Company.

Throughout these years while Brookings was building his business, he continued to seek self-improvement. For a while he lived in the home of the daughter of the famous physician, William Beaumont, so that this elderly matron, prominent in St. Louis society, could teach him the manners of the class to which he aspired. She cultivated and refined his tastes for art and music, instructed him in the appreciation of fine furniture, silver, china, linen, and rugs, and taught him the social graces of a young gentleman. Soon, he began to give parties, which became great social events for the St. Louis bourgeoisie. He joined the St. Louis Choral Society, traveled to Europe, and asked the dean of the local institution of higher education, Washington College, to draw up a reading list for him in literature, history, and economics.

Still, Brookings's social life had something of a superficial quality. His desire to be accepted among the St. Louis elite was apparent to all. His shyness, sometimes hidden in a compulsive need to talk incessantly, indicated a man who was insecure about his own intellectual and social standing. After ten years in St. Louis, he still spoke a rough Maryland vernacular, and no amount of drill could prevent him from saying, "You was." Although he entertained on a grand scale, he remained aloof. Furthermore, hidden behind his social activity was a secret dream of becoming a musician, a concert violinist.

In the summer of 1884, Brookings astounded St. Louis society by taking leave of his business to travel to Berlin, where he hoped to begin a new life as a violinist. He spent over a year in Berlin. There he met Nicholas Murray Butler, then a twenty-two-year-old student and later president of Columbia University. They became fast friends, joining one another for trips to the opera, museums, and the city's famous beer gardens. Through Butler, Brookings came to know Berlin's business, intellectual, and artistic elite, including Joseph Joachim, Germany's best-known musician. Brookings must have felt a sense of trepidation and anxious anticipation the day Joachim asked the young American to play for him, and deep disappointment when Brookings had finished and Joachim politely expressed the opinion that his talents were only those of a good amateur. Brookings stayed in Germany the rest of the year, hiking throughout Europe. History might have been different if he had been told he had genuine musical talent.

Brookings returned to America in 1885 with an Amati he had purchased as a remembrance of his *Wanderjahr*. Now determined to make a fortune, Brookings in the next decade fanatically pursued his pecuniary interests. Not long after his return to business, he faced the fiercest challenge he had encountered since joining Cupples and Company, the formatio · of the National Cordage Company in 1887. This cordage trust was the result of a successful attempt to organize the manufacturers of twine and rope into a single giant combine. The founders of the National Cordage Company sought to do what Rockefeller had done in oil—monopolize the industry. Within a year they controlled forty-nine manufacturing plants accounting for 60 to 70 percent of the mill capacity in the industry nationwide.[10]

Brookings realized immediately that Cupples and Company, whose business consisted largely of the sale of rope, twine, and brooms, was seriously threatened by this new monopoly. He responded accordingly: Cupples and Company went into the manufacture of cordage. Brookings purchased a half interest in a small cordage factory in Brooklyn, New York, and then provided the necessary capital to enlarge the plant. He thereby ensured a steady supply of products for his wholesale business. In the end, the inability of the National Cordage Company to control the independent manufacturers, and the insatiable demand for liquid capital created by overinvestment in modern machinery, entailed failure for the monopoly. The company's sensational financial failure in 1893 helped precipitate one of the worst depressions in the history of the United States.[11]

But if the Depression of 1893 spelled failure for the National Cordage Company, to Brookings it appeared as an opportunity to expand. Like Carnegie in steel, he understood that a depression presented a unique opportunity to build. Land and labor were cheap, and for those who had money, now was the time to spend it.

Brookings, since his first days as a bookkeeper, had kept close watch over his accounts. In carefully scrutinizing his books, he saw that the drayage costs of transporting goods from the railroad terminal to the Cupples warehouse had risen dramatically since he entered the business. Slowly, as he dwelt on this problem, a plan came to him to build a single terminal for the distribution of wholesale goods brought into St. Louis by rail. Keeping the plan a secret, even from Samuel Cupples, Brookings gradually bought up land around Seventh and Spruce Streets, in the heart of the city. After he acquired the land, he entered into secret negotiations with city officials and railroad representatives to build a huge station that would be both a railroad terminal and a warehouse for the major wholesalers of St. Louis. Once city officials and the railroad had agreed, Brookings revealed his plans publicly. His proposal met with immediate resistance from other wholesalers, who opposed the idea of abandoning their buildings in order to relocate the wholesale and grocery district a quarter-mile west of the existing location. Through quiet persuasion and sheer economic pressure, Brookings finally persuaded the wholesalers to join in the great enterprise of building Cupples Station. Brookings himself borrowed money from the Seligman Brothers in New York to finance the project. Completed in the mid-nineties, the giant structure became the marvel of St. Louis and the business world, winning acclaim from all quarters. *Scientific American* praised Cupples Station as "the most complete development of a typically American idea."[12]

The eight-story brick building, valued at $3 million, occupied thirty acres. Its operations employed 2,000 workers who served some thirty-odd companies. Loaded train cars were brought directly into the station, where the goods they carried were unloaded into forty-eight immense hydraulic lifts for transport to the designated floors. The Cupples Station was soon receiving and shipping more freight than any other terminal in the country. The station was managed not by the wholesalers, but by Brookings and Cupples. In this way, by charging the traders on a pro rata basis, Brookings ensured the efficient and honest operation of the terminal, while earning additional income for his own firm. By 1895, the man who had once forsaken business for music had accumulated a fortune of over $6 million.

During these years Brookings tried but found it difficult to relax. He purchased an estate in the Ozarks, to which he would retreat on weekends to hunt, play golf and polo, and give grand parties. Still, he worked as hard as he played. He achieved success, but in his triumph Brookings so overtaxed himself, both physically and emotionally, that in 1895 he suffered a breakdown and was forced to enter a sanitarium. It was his old friend and mentor, Samuel Cupples, who suggested that now was the time for Brookings to give up his entrepreneurial pursuits for philanthropy. On Cupples's recommendation, Brookings became the president of Washington College. Thus began a second life for Brookings.

At the time Brookings assumed the presidency, Washington College was an underenrolled, underendowed institution located in a single downtown building in St. Louis. The school was best known for its manual training program, which combined intellectual pursuits with carpentry.[13] Brookings devoted himself entirely and unsparingly to building this school into a first-class university: he personally selected and purchased a site outside of St. Louis in Forest Park to build a new campus; he supervised the construction of that campus's Tudor-style buildings; and he gradually built an ample endowment for the school.[14] To further ensure its financial success, he and Samuel Cupples donated their interest in Cupples Station to the new Washington University. Furthermore, Brookings funded the construction of an administration building, while Cupples did the same for an engineering building. Brookings persuaded Adolphus Busch, the beer producer, to finance a building to house the new chemistry laboratory.

Some members of the Washington University board of trustees complained of Brookings's monologues at meetings, but few doubted his devotion to the university and his energy. When Henry S. Pritchett, president of the Carnegie Foundation, in his influential survey of medical education in the United States reported that the medical school at Washington University was simply inadequate, Robert Brookings was at first outraged, but in the end he was persuaded that Pritchett was correct in his evaluation. Brookings then spent over a year studying the major medical schools in Europe and the United States, before he felt confident enough to revamp the medical program. He began by hiring Dr. David L. Edsall, professor of medicine at the University of Pennsylvania, to become dean of the medical school at Washington University. With Brookings's support, Edsall recruited the best professors in the nation to come to St. Louis to build a first-rate medical program.

An important event in Brookings's life occurred as a result of his association with Pritchett; through Pritchett he was introduced to Andrew Carnegie. Brookings and Carnegie soon became close friends. When Carnegie and his wife traveled to St. Louis to attend a conference on international peace, they accepted an invitation to stay at Brookings's home. The two men, both incessant talkers, made a unique pair. As self-made men who sought to build a better world, they had much in common. Carnegie, the older and more widely known of the two, introduced Brookings to national philanthropic circles. At Carnegie's invitation, Brookings became a founding member of the Carnegie Corporation and a trustee of the Carnegie Peace Foundation. Soon he was also a trustee for the Smithsonian Institution, an active participant in the National Civic Federation, and a consultant to the Taft Commission. Thus, Brookings was a natural choice to become a founding trustee for the Institute for Government Research when, in 1916, Jerome Greene asked him to accept this responsibility.

Brookings's growing awareness of national and international issues was further expanded when Andrew Carnegie invited him to participate in presenting to Kaiser Wilhelm II of Germany a memorial signed by seventy American representatives in honor of the twenty-fifth anniversary of the emperor's reign.[15] In June 1913 Brookings traveled with Carnegie to Berlin, where they personally presented the memorial addressed to "our strongest ally in the cause of peace." The meeting with the kaiser deeply influenced both men. Kaiser Wilhelm became for Carnegie and Brookings the "Hero of Peace."[16] The outbreak of war in Europe a year later shattered Carnegie's belief that international peace was possible in his lifetime; and Brookings declared that "no one can make me believe that the Kaiser wanted war."[17] Yet, while the war brought disillusionment to Carnegie, it brought further opportunities for Brookings.

Brookings's involvement in the Wilson administration during the war convinced him that the future lay in economic research. His participation in the war effort came about through a fortuitous set of circumstances. He was not a well-known national figure in either politics or business, but he had participated in the Taft Commission as a consultant. In this role he became acquainted with Hollis Godfrey, a disciple of scientific management and a prime mover in the war-preparedness effort. Shortly before the outbreak of war, Godfrey recommended Brookings to the Wilson administration as one of seven men who "would do the most for their country" if America entered the war.[18] Four months after the nation declared war, Wilson appointed Brookings to the War Industries Board (WIB), the principal economic coordinating agency of the war.

In many respects Brookings, now 66, was a perfect choice for the WIB. Although the retired millionaire from the Midwest had relatively few close contacts in Eastern financial circles, he was well known among midwestern manufacturers and was recognized as a friend of Andrew Carnegie. Brookings consciously projected the image of a self-made businessman—worldly, practical, and successful—but he was in fact far from the stereotype. Behind the image lay a man who once had seriously considered leaving business

2. Andrew Carnegie and Robert S. Brookings in Berlin, June 1913. (Courtesy of the Brookings Institution Archives)

in order to pursue a career as a concert violinist and who had been relentlessly driven to amass a fortune as quickly as possible so he could retire from business to devote himself to other endeavors. He lacked a formal education, yet he was convinced that the future lay in university-trained professionals. His own ideas concerning economics were often inconsistent and vague; nevertheless, he alone founded what would become one of the most prestigious economic research institutions in the United States.

The two other men Wilson selected to join Brookings on the WIB were also unusual choices for the board: Bernard Baruch, a Wall Street financier who seemed to have an uncanny sixth sense about the stock market, and Judge Robert Lovett, a mugwump Democrat from Texas and chairman of the Union Pacific Railroad. Like Brookings these two men were generally outsiders to established business circles; each came at least originally from the South; and each enjoyed his new status derived from his position in government. "One could not enter his club," Brookings later reminisced about these years in wartime Washington, "without meeting someone who had something to tell, and in the smoking rooms after dinner, [the war] offered a never ending source for discussions."[19] The awakened sense of his own importance in government inevitably led Brookings to clash with the egotistical Baruch, who also experienced the exhilaration of power.

In the fall of 1917 the economy experienced difficulties that threatened the total war effort. There were severe shortages and bottlenecks, and the price index, prepared by Wesley C. Mitchell, showed that prices for all commodities had risen from a base of 100 the previous April to 170 in March 1918. Finally, at the urging of Baruch, Wilson expanded the powers of the WIB to fix prices and to set priorities in the production and manufacture of war goods. Wilson selected Brookings to head the price-fixing committee, and Baruch to head priorities. The two men confronted one another immediately. Brookings saw Baruch as nothing more than a speculator, a view shared by many in business who knew Baruch. Furthermore, Brookings believed that an excess-profits tax was needed to control undeserved earnings, while Baruch opposed a tax on business earnings. Both men agreed on price fixing, but Baruch saw in Brookings a "ladylike old bachelor" who talked too much to get things accomplished.

By the spring of 1918, a concerted movement was underway to oust Brookings from his position as chairman. William Hard, writing for the New Republic just a year earlier, had expressed the common complaints about Brookings as an administrator. Hard wrote, "Now Mr. Brookings is a very fine person, of high intelligence; but by universal consent, he lacks . . . speed."[20] One WIB staff member loyal to Baruch, Chandler Anderson, attended only one meeting chaired by Brookings before concluding that he had "no decision of character or continuity of purpose and is fussy and tiresome to a degree with a ceaseless flow of pointless and commonplace remarks." Chandler cattily described Brookings's method of conducting a meeting as involving the delivery of "a long rambling speech largely autobiographical" that accomplished little.[21]

Contrary to Anderson's and Baruch's perceptions, Brookings proved to be an efficient administrator in an agency that lacked the actual power to control prices. One historian has described the bargaining sessions as poker games that required "bluff and finesse" on Brookings's part. In these sessions only industry representatives knew all the facts concerning costs and inventories. Brookings could only cajole and threaten; he could not command. Yet he maintained his integrity. For instance, he withdrew from negotiations with lumber interests because he had substantial lumber holdings in the Northwest.[22] Nevertheless, the work of the WIB should be judged a failure, especially when the board's record is compared to the outstanding record of the government in controlling inflation during World War II.[23] The success of the WIB lay not so much in its specific record, but in the model it provided for business-government cooperation during the 1920s and early 1930s.

Brookings later wrote that he left the WIB convinced that there were two key social problems to be solved in the world, "the emancipation of the masses from economic slavery imposed by an unfortunate development of an unsound aristocracy" and "the elimination of war."[24] As a practical businessman he proposed specific remedies to bring social stability to the United States and the world. He sought an enlightened capitalist world order, able to combat both socialism and communism. Brookings saw himself as a reformer, not a radical, a Wilsonian seeking a form of corporate capitalism that would alleviate class tensions and prevent war. Immediately following World War I, Brookings turned his attention to the problems of class conflict, an issue that loomed large in the public mind following the seizure of power by the Bolsheviks in Russia. In a series of editorials for the *Washington Post* and the *New York Times*, Brookings proposed that workers be given equal representation on the board of directors of all of the nation's major corporations. This was the way, he declared, to bring "real economic democracy" to the nation. Brookings's proposal was by no means original.[25] As early as 1904, another St. Louis businessman, Nelson Olsen Nelson, had proposed a cooperative restructuring of industrial ownership in his factories. Furthermore, other Wilsonians, including Brookings's old foe Bernard Baruch, endorsed similar schemes in the postwar years to bring a kind of participatory democracy to

America. The idea of placing workers on the boards of corporations was in fact more radical than anything Social Democrats in Germany had advocated before the war, and at times Brookings could sound as radical as any prewar German Marxist. For instance, he observed that large corporations in modern society had, in effect, reduced workers to "the position of a commodity to be purchased at the market price."[26]

Of course, Robert Brookings opposed any form of socialism. He remained an enlightened businessman who sought to create a form of capitalism resistant to social instability. He did not propose to transform corporate capitalism into a worker-controlled state. His proposal for increased worker participation in the corporate economy, moreover, failed to address the central question posed by socialists, "Who was to select the workers who would represent labor on the boards of these major corporations?" Brookings, like most men of his generation and class, always expressed a strong dislike for men primarily interested in securing special privileges for themselves or their class. Brookings presumed that men should stand above class interests, so he looked to "statesmen," those men who were trained to bring high standards of conduct and efficiency to industry and politics. Therefore, Brookings opposed the idea that worker representatives on corporate boards should be rank-and-file unionists elected by their shops. Furthermore, he always maintained a faith that the American corporation ultimately served the people by ensuring "stability essential to the security which promotes the distribution of our national wealth among all people."[27]

But even these views were liberal for the time. The decade of the 1920s would be marked by antiunion activity on the part of many businessmen, who often hid their hostilities toward labor behind the so-called "American Plan," a system calling for the formation of company-controlled employee associations as opposed to outside labor organizations.[28] Brookings's proposals received a hearing in the press, but he was clearly out of step with the thought of most manufacturers in the Harding-Coolidge era. Similarly, Brookings's ideas on international trade were brushed aside. Writing for the *New York Evening Post*, a newspaper that had been bought by Thomas Lamont, a J. P. Morgan partner, to air his internationalist views before the American public, Brookings called for the formation of a European Economic Union (with or without England) to facilitate trade within Europe and between Europe and the United States. Such a customs union, he argued, would lead to lower tariffs, the mass standardization of goods, and economic interdependence and prosperity for all nations.[29] Brookings's dreams of international peace through free trade expressed a Wilsonian perspective that would be carried into the 1920s by enlightened businessmen and financiers, who ironically would be attacked by the Brandeisian wing of Wilsonian Democracy in this same period and in the 1930s. There was a richness in Wilsonian thought that allowed a myriad of interests to claim Wilson as one of their own while denouncing others who also saw Wilson as their mentor.

From his experience in Washington Brookings drew one major lesson: economic problems lay at the crux of most of the world's difficulties. These economic issues were complicated enough, he wrote, without allowing politicians to mess up the works further. "Practically all of the problems which have been submerging the world since the signing of the Armistice," he told a friend, "are economic problems, more or less poisoned by political traditions."[30]

In 1922 Brookings proposed to his close friend Henry Pritchett, who recently had been appointed acting chairman of the Carnegie Corporation (between the one-year term of James Angell and the appointment of Frederick Keppel later in the same year), that the corporation sponsor a research institute to address both domestic and international economic problems. Brookings observed, "The events of the past ten years, particularly those of the years since the war, have gone far to emphasize the fact that many governmental questions are, in essence, economic questions." Brookings therefore proposed that a research institute be formed, "free from any political or pecuniary interest" in order to objectively "collect, interpret, and lay before the country in a coherent form the fundamental economic facts."[31] Pritchett agreed. Shortly after Brookings's letter, and after further negotiation, the Carnegie Corporation offered a five-year grant of $200,000 to seed the new institute.[32]

At the same time, Brookings made plans to establish a Robert S. Brookings Graduate School to train a cadre of skilled researchers who would staff important government positions. He hoped that this cadre would be particularly useful as staff members to important congressional committees. Shortly after receiving the Carnegie grant, Brookings completed negotiations with Washington University to establish a joint graduate program in which students would divide their time equally between St. Louis and Washington, D.C.

The Institute of Economics (IE) and the Graduate School, although separate legal entities for tax purposes, maintained from the outset a "sister" relationship with each other and with the older Institute for Government Research. Staff members from these three institutes frequently shared common responsibilities, and the boards of trustees were interlocked so that a complete consolidation of the three could be facilitated in the future.[33] The two new institutes would instill fresh life in the IGR. The Great War had diverted the early enthusiasm that reformers initially showed for the IGR. In fact, by 1918 only Frank Goodnow, the chairman of the board, and Robert Brookings were regularly attending trustees' meetings.[34] As the Rockefeller Foundation grant, originally received by the IGR in 1916, neared depletion, Brookings undertook to save the IGR by raising an additional $70,000 from friends. At the same time he sought to interject new blood into the IGR board by arranging for Herbert Hoover, Elihu Root, and William Taft to become trustees.[35]

Yet he realized that he was fighting a rearguard action and that the best way to keep the IGR going was to tie its work to a larger enterprise. The first step in organizing the Institute of Economics and the Graduate School was to form boards of trustees, with the expectation that their members would raise money and add prestige to the new institutes. Many of those whom Brookings invited to serve on the boards were men he classified as "conservatives or capitalists"—men such as New York banker Paul Warburg, Associate Supreme Court Justice George Southerland, and chairman of the American Red Cross John Barton. To ensure the nonpartisan quality required to attract money from the Rockefeller Foundation and other potential donors, Brookings insisted that the trustees would not be allowed to intervene in the internal affairs of either institute.[36] In fact, the influence of board members was exerted more subtly than in direct intervention, particularly when it came to choosing a new research director for the Institute of Economics.

Brookings's first choice for the directorship was Arthur Hadley, president of Yale University, but when Hadley declined the nomination in order to rewrite an economics textbook, Brookings offered him instead a chair on the board. At the first meeting of the trustees most of the board showed little understanding of academics. In fact, the new trustees began with a discussion of why a man such as Charles Eliot, president of Harvard University, chose to be a university president at a modest salary of $10,000 a year when he could have received five times that amount as president of a railroad. "Why will men like President Eliot be content with such small salaries?" Brookings asked rhetorically. His own response was that "there is satisfaction in the service that is rendered in professional life which accounts probably for the fact."[37]

With this said, the board turned to the main issue at hand—selecting a director. Leading economists were mentioned and dismissed in turn as incapable of directing the new institute: Wesley C. Mitchell, who had recently begun his study of business cycles, was seen as "a specialist with not broad enough interests"; Thomas Walter Page of the Tariff Commission lacked "pep"; Edwin Gay, the manager of the *New York Post*, former chairman of the Harvard School of Business, and head of the Division of Planning and Statistics during the war, was seen as "absolutely uncompromising." Brookings suggested John R. Commons, even though he was tinged with "socialist leanings," but the other board members distrusted his "administrative abilities," which was a nicely put euphemism for his politics. At this point the board decided to pursue the possibility of selecting a younger economist, "a man who has gone far but not fully arrived." Former Secretary of the Treasury David Houston had exactly this kind of man in mind when he nominated Harold G. Moulton, a young economist from the University of Chicago. Immediately, John Walcott, chairman of the Smithsonian, seconded Houston's choice as a man with a fine personality and very broad views. Both men knew of Moulton's pioneering work on the role of money in a capitalist economy. By the time the meeting adjourned, Brookings had been assigned to contact Moulton.[37]

When they met, Brookings discovered, much to his surprise, that Moulton held some reservations concerning the position. He specifically wanted a guarantee that the new institute would be free from any trustee interference. Although he was sympathetic to business, he did not want to serve as the director of an organization such as the National Industrial Conference Board, which he considered "a very partisan organization supported by the manufacturing interests of the country." Only after Brookings gave his absolute assurances that there would be no trustee interference did Moulton accept the job, which he was to hold for the next thirty years.[38]

Although Brookings continued to take an active interest in his institutes, he played little, if any, role in directing the course of research undertaken by the IE under its new director. In matters of economics, Brookings clearly deferred to Moulton, who, for his part, felt that Brookings's ignorance in economics was at times appalling and showed no hesitation in telling him so. Yet, perhaps in part because of this very lack of formal training in economics, Brookings maintained a broad vision for reforming the world. Often, over the next years, he expressed his concerns that the IE was not moving fast enough in devising practical economic programs, only to be told by Moulton that before programs could be proposed, facts and data needed to be collected and then evaluated, and that this was an arduous, step-by-step process. Furthermore, Moulton and his staff of professionally trained economists knew the limits of reform in a world of scarcity. To give to one group meant taking away from another. Thus the world of the economist was a world of trade-offs.

In spite of Moulton's attempts to "educate" Brookings through an extensive correspondence between the two, Brookings became increasingly reform-minded as he grew older. In 1925, shortly after the founding of the Brookings Institution, Brookings experienced two severe heart attacks. Recovery came slowly, but his recuperation sparked an outburst of renewed activity. A new life seemed to open for Brookings. On June 19, 1927, he married Isabel January, the daughter of a longtime St. Louis friend, a woman over thirty years his junior. The marriage seems to have reawakened his creative instincts. At the age of seventy-five, Brookings published his first book, *Industrial Ownership: Its Economic and Social Consequences.*[39] In the next five years, he published half a dozen pamphlets and two other books.

Brookings, as his contemporaries knew, was neither a profound nor an original thinker, but his writings conveyed the excitement of a man who saw the possibilities of building a better world. His reform proposals were specific, to the point, and free of elaborate theoretical discussion.

At the core of Brookings's proposals was a call for more (and "wiser") government intervention in the economy. Although he continued to maintain that the evolution of the corporation in modern capitalism was inevitable and desirable, he realized that some corporate practices continued to hurt the public, particularly the laboring classes. Therefore, he urged the enactment of a federal incorporation act that would confer upon a governmental body the power to prevent corporate abuse. He argued that this governmental agency, as well as the public, should be given access to corporate books.[40] He concluded that "intelligent public supervision" of corporations was the only way to "protect the public and trade alike from grasping, intractable minorities."[41] Brookings also spoke in favor of agricultural cooperatives, federal unemployment insurance, and a European trading union.

With the stock market crash of 1929, Brookings became even more critical of the current economic system. He expressed dismay and distrust in regard to capitalists. "Our democratic government," he wrote to the dean of Washington University Law School, "through the ever widening influence of our financial groups in and out of Wall Street, has, through the adapting of corporation laws, placed the great bulk of the people in a state of economic servitude."[42] Shortly before his death, Brookings again expressed concern about the growing disparity of wealth in America. Writing to Moulton, he declared that "the right to aggregate capital through incorporation" has "placed capital in a position where it practically dominates labor; and has shown, with some exceptions, that instead of realizing its ethical opportunity for shortening labor hours and increasing labor compensation, [the right to aggregate capital] has not been sufficient to give the great mass of the population that reasonable capital accumulation which would protect them from unemployment and the many menaces of old age."[43] Again, he urged Moulton to guide the Brookings Institution to the forefront of reform. Moulton and his professional staff of economists at the institution, however, remained far less critical of the market economy than did the institution's founder.

In the same year, 1932, that Brookings wrote to Moulton imploring him to have the institution address the problems of inequality in the current system, Adolph Berle and Gardiner Means published their influential book *The Modern Corporation and Private Property*, which argued that within the modern corporation, management had become separated from ownership. The consequence of this revolution, Berle and Means argued, was that managers ran the corporations independently of the control of the owners.[44] In retrospect it appears clear that, ironically, a similar process had occurred within the Brookings Institution, a nonprofit corporation without shareholders. Although the analogy between the managerial revolution within private corporations and that within the Brookings should not be overstated, the fact remains that Robert S. Brookings, the institution's founder, and his personally selected board of trustees had little to say about the running of the institution. Instead, management was in the hands of Harold Moulton, who made day-to-day decisions concerning the research goals, personnel, and general direction of the institution. Moulton needed the annual approval of the board when its members gathered each year in Washington, D.C., but the minutes of the board of trustees during these early years suggest that the approval process was largely a formality.

At the same time, the founder's vision was narrowed by the social scientists, who were less interested than he in reform per se and placed their confidence instead in the ability of the marketplace to ultimately adjust economic and social ills. Brookings, the capitalist, proved to be much more inclined to question the status quo than did the experts who prided themselves on their objectivity. If the founder had been able to dictate institutional policy, the social science research conducted by the Brookings Institution might have been more superficial but more critical of the capitalist system. Instead, the research carried out under the direction of Moulton was designed to evaluate specific economic policies of major national and international importance. Staff economists at the IE did not hesitate to take stands on the important issues of the day. Nonetheless, these men were primarily concerned with promoting the "efficiency" of the current system, not with proposing alternatives to the system. The full implications of this social science outlook, and the ambiguities of "efficiency" as a measure for public policy evaluation, became apparent within a decade after the founding of the IE and the Graduate School.

4·HAROLD G. MOULTON: EFFICIENCY, ECONOMIC EXPERTISE, AND THE FOUNDING OF THE BROOKINGS INSTITUTION

HAROLD G. Moulton, as director of the Institute of Economics and as first president of the Brookings Institution, articulated Robert Brookings's concerns for a better world in the language of the social scientist. Charged primarily with staffing the institution and directing major areas of research, Moulton shaped Brookings's dream of a research institution into a viable organizational reality, and he dominated the institution until his retirement in 1952.

During these years a small staff of economists and political scientists—who numbered no more than thirty men and women at any one time—were associated with Moulton. Organized along the lines of an academic department in a major university, with Moulton serving as a kind of department chairman, researchers were allowed to pursue research of their own choosing with complete independence from trustee interference. The men and women who joined Moulton in Washington to form this enterprise prided themselves on their scholarly objectivity as professional social scientists. Yet, as anyone familiar with academic life knows, departments frequently take on unique characters of their own, shaped by the personalities of their members. Such would be the case with the Institute of Economics and the later Brookings Institution. To understand these institutions and their response to the major economic and political issues of the day, the historian needs to understand the men and women who staffed them.

Brookings and Moulton agreed that "the new institution must be courageous and liberal in its point of view. Conservatism as such has no legitimate place in the institution."[1] With this prescription in mind, Moulton brought to Washington a group of twelve economists including two who were to direct the graduate program, which was seen at the outset as playing second fiddle to the IE. These twelve men and women formed the core of the early institute, but among the early staff three men in particular, Edwin Nourse, an agricultural economist, Leo Pasvolsky, a Russian immigrant concerned with war debts and reparations, and the iconoclast Walton Hamilton exerted a dominant influence on the institute.

Nourse, Pasvolsky, and Hamilton agreed that there was something wrong with the world and that past economic dogma had failed to explain these ills. Although Nourse and Pasvolsky rejected Hamilton's belief that Veblen's institutional economics was "the only way to the right sort of theory," they concurred with Hamilton's estimation that theirs was an age of "cosmic Protestantism voicing discontent against artificial systems and bent upon erecting a true and multiform reality."[2] They were primarily concerned with immediate problems and they believed that they were undertaking a historic step in applied economics, an economics concerned with contemporary policy. They took their mission seriously, but as young men in their thirties and early forties, they brought to the early institute a freewheeling spirit. "It was an exciting conference room in those years," Edwin Nourse later recalled. "But there was also an easy camaraderie that ran from the top to the bottom of the organization."[3]

Nonetheless, if the first staff members imparted a unique spirit to the early institution, their orientation as professional social scientists defined their role within the institution. Central to their identities as professionals was their belief in the importance of being nonpartisan and their optimistic faith in·their ability to make the system more efficient. Yet the exact meaning of "nonpartisanship" and "efficiency" remained ill-defined, waiting for the practical application of the ideal. Underlying the general consensus among the social scientists lurked strong disagreements concerning these terms. The problem was not just a semantic one; at issue was the very nature of the social science enterprise in the 1920s. Within a few years, the "easy camaraderie" of the group gave way to a fierce debate over the nature and purpose of social science research, and this debate, which led to the founding of the Brookings Institution, set the direction for the institution for the next two decades.

The social scientists who came to the Institute of Economics in

1922 saw themselves as standing for the public interest above the prejudices of both the masses and the corporations. On this much they continued to agree, but exactly what was meant by the public interest remained, like nonpartisanship and efficiency, unclear in their own rhetoric, except that it involved a profound suspicion of electoral politics in matters of public policy. These social scientists perceived their task as one of providing technical expertise to a society disrupted by partisan interests. They stood for the public interest of the Republic; yet they held little faith in the people, the masses, whom they saw as easily swayed by self-interest, to preserve this Republic. Thus the elitism of the mugwump tradition prevailed, carried into the twentieth century not by gentlemen in evening clothes but by academics in tweed.

The economists who came to the Institute of Economics were not unique in their distrust of partisan politics. Most economists in the postwar era, although they felt less threatened by democracy than had social scientists of an earlier generation, remained equally cynical. The most eloquent expression of this distrust of partisan politics came in John Maynard Keynes's widely read *Economic Consequences of the Peace*, which acerbically accused politicians of destroying the conference at Versailles. American economists were no less hesitant in showing their disgust toward politicians. Wesley C. Mitchell, who was just beginning his pioneering study of business cycles, frankly said that "it is bad for social theory to get involved in politics."[4] Partisan politics posed a vast barrier to the "reconstruction" of economic society that was so frequently talked about in the economic profession in the immediate postwar years. Raymond Bye, an economist at the University of Pennsylvania, wrote with his typical audacity that if there were economic troubles in the world at that time (and surely there were), they were largely attributable to "statesmen" who had consistently disregarded the advice of economists. "For the economist alone," he wrote, "is ready to show that [existing problems] may be solved when politicians are willing to listen to advice."[5] In maintaining this skepticism toward partisan politics, in believing that capitalism could be made more efficient without a radical restructuring of class relations, and in continuing to regard expertise as the means to a more efficient system, economists in the postwar years provided a continuity in reform thought from the nineteenth century to the twentieth century.

Yet while the economists who came to Washington to work with

Moulton shared this general professional distrust of popular democracy, a sharp difference separated postwar economists from those prewar reformers associated with the "efficiency and economy" movement. Specifically, the meaning of "efficiency" changed during the intervening years. When the administrative reformers at the IGR and the economists at the Institute of Economics spoke of efficiency, they imparted different meanings to the term. In the Progressive period administrative reformers, such as William F. Willoughby, primarily used "efficiency" in the sense of managerial and administrative competency. In the postwar years, the IE economists expanded the definition to include at least two separate meanings. First, economists regarded efficiency in the sense of opportunity costs, or resource input compared with produced income. Frequently, opportunity costs were measured in terms of dollars spent and income obtained. At the same time, the more liberal-minded economists, particularly Walton Hamilton, who was associated with the Graduate School, provided a second meaning to "efficiency" by discussing the human cost incurred and the human satisfactions and benefits produced.[6] Both considerations, opportunity costs and human costs, expanded the meaning of the term beyond the narrow confines of administrative reform into areas of broad public policy.

The differences over the meaning of "efficiency" involved more than simply the proper definition of a word. At issue was the direction of future work at the IGR, the IE, and the Graduate School.

For the staff at the IGR, under Willoughby, creating a more efficient society meant pursuing administrative reform of the federal bureaucracy. By equating administrative efficiency with nonpartisanship, political scientists such as Willoughby refused to involve themselves in larger policy issues. Instead, Willoughby insisted that the Institute for Government Research existed for the sole purpose of rendering all possible assistance in making government administration more efficient and more economical. He wrote one concerned congressman that "it would be a mistake for [the IGR] to seek to concern itself in any way with matters of policy."[7] Policy, he assured the congressman, is "best left to Congress."

To those economists who came to the Institute of Economics and to the Graduate School in 1922, Willoughby's views appeared antiquated and simplistic. Like Willoughby, these economists saw themselves as objective social scientists, nonpartisans who stood above the political debate. Yet economics necessarily involved making choices concerning the efficient allocation and distribution of scarce goods and resources. This meant that economists must address larger policy issues. Economists, therefore, struck a middle course between confining their interests to administrative reform, on the one hand, and proposing a major, and radical, transformation of the economic system on the other. The market economy was a given; the question was how to make specific policies more efficient in terms of opportunity costs and human satisfactions. Entailed in the IE outlook was a belief that economists must address the issues of the real world, not the problems of an abstract visionary world that did not exist.

The differences between the administrative reformers at the IGR and the economists at the IE and the Graduate School were not at first apparent. Yet such disagreements could not be suppressed for long; slowly, a fierce fight, one that extended into the general social science community, erupted. The fight initially concerned the question of whether the IGR should expand its interests beyond administrative efficiency. In the process of the debate, however, the economists at the Graduate School and those at the Institute of Economics entered into a profound discussion concerning the meaning of efficiency and the public interest as it pertained to their work. The outcome of this debate, which was eventually subsumed in a controversy over academic freedom, set the tone for the Brookings Institution for the next two decades and explains the institution's involvement in Indian reform in the 1920s and its relationship to the New Deal and the Fair Deal.

At the age of thirty-nine, Harold G. Moulton came to Washington with a reputation as an original, independent-minded economist, an innovator within the established empirical tradition. Like so many others in this generation of social scientists, Moulton came to the East from the Midwest. Born in 1883 in the farming community of LeRoy, Michigan, he was the next youngest of seven children. The Moulton children were indeed remarkable. All five of Harold's brothers, including his well-known brother Forest, a mathematical genius, would later be listed in *Who's Who*. In his early years, Harold was actually considered slow, and perhaps because of these familial perceptions Moulton became fiercely competitive.[8] After graduation from a one-room high school, Moulton attended Albion College for one year before accepting an athletic scholarship to the University of Chicago, which had opened its doors in 1892 under the direction of President William Harper.

Moulton, it appears, came to Chicago largely because of its famous coach, Amos Alonzo Stagg, who had gained a reputation for success on the athletic field and for his sports philosophy of "rugged Christianity" that taught the principles of "fortitude, self-discipline, and self-reliance."[9] Moulton played baseball for Stagg for the next three years, maintaining a creditable batting average of .300 throughout his career. In his later life, Moulton emulated his coach's puritanical abstinence from alcohol and tobacco and prided himself on his athletic fitness; and when he took a secretary to lunch, he always invited his wife to join them.

While at Chicago, Moulton fell also under the influence of the chairman of the economics department, J. Lawrence Laughlin, another man who stressed the practical and moral aspects of life. Laughlin fired the young Moulton with "a desire to go to the essence of the problem and to be very realistic and practical in doing so."[10] A conservative who refused to join the American Economic Association until 1904 because of Ely's "statism," Laughlin furiously attacked the "radicals" who argued for the free coinage of silver; he charged that protection-minded senators who advocated high tariffs were acting as the agents of large corporations; and he condemned the building of the Panama Canal as "a futile waste of money."[11] Completely concerned with the practical, Laughlin had no use for "metaphysical nonsense," yet he remained no less a moralist. Under Stagg and Laughlin, Moulton's personality became set. He was competitive, confident, and at times obstinate. Moulton's yearbook captured this quality in an epigram placed beneath his picture:

> In arguing, too, this person owed his skill
> For e'en though vanquished, he could argue still.[12]

By his senior year Moulton had decided to pursue graduate studies in economics.

Moulton's graduate work under Laughlin manifested the same concern with the practical and the politically relevant that he had displayed earlier. Furthermore, Moulton did not hesitate to take sides on an issue. His prizewinning dissertation, published as *Waterways versus Railways* (1912), ostensibly was a cost-benefit analysis of canal versus railroad transportation, but it was also a critical examination of the economic issues behind a movement that had sprung up at the turn of the century to revive America's canal system. This waterway movement gained momentum when, in 1907, the state of New York appropriated $101,000,000 for the improvement of the Erie Canal.[13] In the same year, Theodore Roosevelt gave official sanction to the nationwide movement when he appointed an Inland Waterway Commission, which further encouraged the numerous waterway associations. Chicago businessmen, observing the Illinois phase of the new canal boom, proposed building a deep-water canal from the Great Lakes to the Gulf of Mexico.

After extensive research, much of it in Europe, Moulton concluded that canals were simply more expensive, less practical, and less efficient than railroad transportation. More interesting than this economic analysis of canal transportation, though, was his critique of the politics behind the movement. He boldly indicted the entire waterway movement as politically motivated. Nearly as much money had been appropriated for improvements of small creeks in favored congressional districts as the entire amount approved for construction of the Panama Canal.[14] Moulton further charged that any appropriation for waterways carried with it a large amount of political patronage that was doled out to construction companies in exchange for "cash contributions to campaign funds, and . . . direct influence upon the voting of laborers engaged upon public works. Thus, the party machine is strengthened."[15]

Moulton went on to accuse the leaders of the canal movement of being self-serving demagogues, and their followers of being irrational dupes. The popularity of the canal craze, he said, showed that only "a very small fraction of our population . . . can be regarded as having attained any considerable degree of rationality. The great majority is not capable of understanding and assimilating the multitude of our considerations and problems that are constantly arising."[16] Skeptical of the masses' ability to make rational decisions, he saw a paradox in modern society: As society becomes more complex and seemingly more enlightened in general, existence becomes more strenuous and popular delusions become more prevalent. This paradox, Moulton concluded, placed a new responsibility on the few, the objective-minded social scientists, to act as a constructive force in American society.

After earning his degree in 1913, Moulton accepted Laughlin's offer to teach the introductory course in money and banking, with the expectation of taking over the advanced course when Laughlin retired. Moulton now turned his scholarly attention to the classic problem of capital formation.[17] His investigations led him to conclude that the United States had entered into a new stage of capitalism in which a consumption ethic should replace the antiquated puritan ethic. Moulton, in the process, challenged the older views of capital formation, which rested implicitly on the virtues of a rural society. In making this argument, Moulton presented a new interpretation of the role commercial banks played in capital formation. Moulton's theory posited that short-term commercial banking loans were a major source for primary capital formation. Most economists, including Laughlin at the time, held that short-term loans could be effectively applied only to readily saleable goods and inventories, not to long-term investment purposes.[18] Moulton's theory, now accepted by economists in the form of the deposit multiplier, implied that commercial banks actually created money when borrowers deposited their loans in the banking system. The expansion of loan funds, therefore, meant the expansion of primary investment capital. This view of capital investment embodied a challenge to the position of classical economists, who maintained that capital formation rested on the virtues of frugality, saving, and deprivation. Instead, Moulton showed that capital formation occurred when consumers borrowed. In turn a slowdown in consumption meant a decline in short-term borrowing and therefore a decline in capital formation.[19]

Thus Moulton arrived at a consumption theory of capital development, a view he maintained throughout his career. If increased consumption was the key to increased productivity and continued economic growth, as Moulton said, then wages must be maintained and prices *reduced* to ensure increased purchasing power.[20] He further argued, as had Veblen, that prices could best be reduced through technological innovations and managerial efficiency, which would lead to the production of cheaper goods. Innovation and efficiency therefore became key themes in Moulton's economic outlook and were repeated time and again in his writings and speeches.

Yet for all of Moulton's audacity in putting forward his theory of capital investment (many economists took issue with it at the time), he remained within the mainstream of economic thought. He described his economics as "nonpartisan" but "progressive." Like most other economists of his day, Moulton believed in the primacy of the institutional marketplace, the necessity of a balanced budget, and the importance of the gold standard.[21] Throughout his long career he maintained a fear of the inflationary consequences of deficit spending. In the early 1920s he felt that the best means of cutting government expenses was in "a thorough-going reduction of military expenditures."[22] For a while he even held membership in the American Peace Society, a liberal organization with an internationalist perspective.

The selection of Moulton to head the new research center, the Institute of Economics, placed him on the cutting edge of the applied social sciences. During the war, the success of statistical analysis, particularly as conducted by the War Industries Board and the Shipping Board, had caused wide discussion within the social science community on the need to establish a national economic research bureau to continue the work initiated by the federal government. As the war neared its end, for instance, Edwin Gay, director of the Bureau of Planning and Statistics, an independent wartime agency directly under President Wilson, issued a call for a "Peace Industries Board" to conduct economic research in the postwar period. A similar concern for continued research was echoed shortly afterwards by Irving Fisher, a Yale economist, in his presidential address before the American Economic Association in 1919. Such sentiments led in 1920 to the establishment of the National Bureau of Economic Research (NBER), funded by the Yale-based Commonwealth Fund.[23] Nevertheless, the NBER limited its research goal solely to the collection of data relevant to national income analysis.

Thus, the founding of the Institute of Economics by Brookings a year later marked a progression in applied economics. As envisioned by Moulton and Brookings, the new research institute was intended to enlarge the research agenda beyond the confines of national income analysis to include a broad range of topics such as industrial relations, agriculture, and international trade. Brookings and Moulton agreed that the new institution must be courageous and liberal in its point of view.[24]

The trustees and the financial sponsors of the Institute of Economics deliberately abstained from direct involvement in its internal affairs; they did not attempt to influence its day-to-day operations or its research agenda. Although the trustees acted as a review committee of the IE's work, approving major research projects at their annual meeting, approval was essentially a formality. A proposed project was never turned down by the board during Moulton's reign. Essentially, direct contact between the board and the research institute was conducted through correspondence between Robert S. Brookings and Harold Moulton.

Moulton, as director of research at the institute, played a key role in determining research projects. With its small staff of economists, the institute did not have an elaborate procedure for approving or evaluating projects. In a sense the research conducted by the IE, and the later Brookings Institution, was for the most part an aggregation of separate projects undertaken by individuals working independently. Before a project was initiated, a proposal was submitted to Moulton, who gave the final go-ahead to begin work. Once a manuscript describing the results of a project was completed, the author submitted his work to an ad hoc review committee consisting of three IE staff members specifically selected by Moulton. If the author felt that the committee's suggested revisions were such as to change the substance of the manuscript, the author was allowed to append a chapter to the published work stating this point of view and the nature of the difference between the committee and the researcher. Because research was supposed to be empirical and not theoretical, however, such differences over substance did not usually occur. Furthermore, a selection process that brought only certain types of economists to the institute reinforced the amiable relations among the staff during these first years.

In selecting the economists to staff the new IE, Moulton drew from the best in each field. Included in his research team were Thomas Walker Page, former chairman of the Tariff Commission; the young Isador Lubin, previously an economist for the War Industries Board; and industrial specialists A. E. Suffern, C. H. Chase, and Helen Wright. Constantine McGuire and Cleona Lewis undertook their pioneering studies of the international economy, while George G. Wright, George Weber, and L. R. Edminister examined international commercial policies. At the outset Moulton targeted three areas of particular importance for IE investigation: agriculture, war debts and reparations, and industrial relations. He assigned to these areas his best economists, Edwin Nourse, Leo Pasvolsky, and Walton Hamilton.

"The present condition of the American farmer," Moulton wrote to the trustees, "is perhaps the insistent question before the American public today."[25] Moulton accurately saw that the farm issue would be one of the decisive factors in the campaign of 1924. Agriculture had prospered during the war, but in mid-1920 farm prices declined precipitously. By the end of 1921, wheat was selling for $0.93 a bushel when it had been selling a year and a half before at $2.58. Corn prices dropped by $1.45 in the same period. As a consequence, long-term debt for farmers rose from $3.2 billion in 1910 to $8.4 billion in 1920. By 1923, long-term agricultural debt reached a high of nearly $11 billion.[26] Because Moulton deemed it essential that immediate attention be given to the farm question, he encouraged Nourse in particular to pursue research in this area. Nourse's reputation as the nation's leading agricultural economist had been enhanced when he prophetically warned in 1920 of an impending crisis in agricultural prices. Then chairman of the Department of Agricultural Economics at Iowa State University, Nourse foresaw that the contraction in European demand, the increasing foreign competition, and the shrinking domestic market were signs of impending danger, ignored by most other specialists in the field.[27] To remedy this crisis Nourse proposed farm cooperatives as a means to rationalize the agricultural market. He saw in the agricultural cooperative the major advantages of large-scale business organization, which promised to transform the farmers' demands for equity into a concern for efficiency.

Nourse always kept a scholarly detachment in his published work; nevertheless, he remained an activist in the cooperative movement. When Aaron Sapiro, a California lawyer, tried to direct the cooperative movement along the lines of forming not only producer cooperatives but centralized marketing cooperatives, Nourse vigorously opposed him because he feared monopolistic disruption of the marketplace.[28] Similarly, Nourse was not reluctant to express his opposition to the McNary-Haugen bill, which would have established parity for farmers through government purchases of commodity surpluses. Instead, Nourse felt that the farmer's interests demanded the freeing of "world-wide commerce and industry to restore the purchasing power for his products. Reparations and interallied debts are the crux of the problem," he declared.[29] McNary-Haugenism, as viewed by Nourse, offered government intervention in the domestic marketplace, while ignoring the more crucial need of the American farmers to find international markets for their goods.

Nourse's belief in free trade and in the ultimate efficacy of the market was shared by the other economists at the Institute of Economics. A general set of economic principles, which many at the time would have described as "liberal," defined the outlook of the institute during these years. Under Moulton's direction, the IE earned during the 1920s a reputation as a leading advocate of free trade. During a ten-year period, from 1923 to 1933, the institute published over fifteen studies on the tariff problem. Moulton gained enough of an international reputation in the field so that J. M.

Keynes personally solicited articles from him on the tariff problem for the *Manchester Guardian*.[30] Closely related to this work on the tariff issue was the institute's study of the economic problems arising from war debts and reparations following World War I. The reparations crisis had come to a head in January 1923, when the Reparations Commission declared Germany in willful default on coal deliveries. Two days later French and Belgian troops marched into the Ruhr. In an attempt to deal more peacefully with the problem, the Reparations Commission set up an international committee to consider the question of Germany's capacity to pay. At the head of this committee was the American Charles Dawes, director of the Bureau of the Budget. Dawes, who had become acquainted with Moulton when the Bureau of the Budget had been temporarily located at the Institute for Government Research building on Connecticut Avenue, selected Moulton and the IE to assist the expert committee to study the German reparations problem. Two IE staff economists, Cleona Lewis and Constantine McGuire, worked with the committee, which submitted its final report on April 9, 1924.[31] The report argued that the economic restoration of Germany should be a prerequisite to any further rescheduling of German payments, and it recommended that the German budget be reorganized in order to allow the payment of specifically assigned reparations payments. Furthermore, at the request of the Treasury Department, Moulton counseled the American delegation in its negotiations with the French. To ensure that others in government did not miss the message, the IE issued twenty thousand copies of its *Germany's Capacity to Pay* in pamphlet form.[32] The economists at the IE presciently warned that unless Germany prospered—and this meant that the Allies should relax their demands for war reparations and that the United States should ease tariffs—economic depression and political crisis would engulf all nations.[33]

During the 1920s the IE, no matter how thorough its work on war debts, drew sharp attacks, especially from the Hoover wing of the Republican Party and from isolationists of both parties. Isolationists, at times appealing to a coarse chauvinistic and Anglophobic sentiment in the electorate, accused the institute of being an un-American, pro-German, free-trade propaganda agency serving international bankers.[34] Such fervor was hardly dampened by the reply of the IE that "it is impossible for the United States to maintain, much less expand, our domestic markets unless we maintain at the same time our export market."[35] Such advice smacked of "finance imperialism" to the isolationists. Although American business expanded dramatically into foreign markets during the decade of the twenties, despite the high tariffs and war reparations, isolationist sentiments continued to remain a powerful political force throughout the period.

In a certain respect, the Institute of Economics welcomed these attacks. Such opposition confirmed that the institute spoke for the public interest, not special elements within any party. When Secretary of Commerce Herbert Hoover, speaking at a press conference, charged that Moulton's work on the French debt problem had led to a lowering of the U.S. claims and that Moulton represented a liability to the United States to the extent of $10 million a year in perpetuity, the "nonpartisan" nature of the IE was once more confirmed.[36] Hoover resigned from the board of trustees when the IE continued to press for lower tariffs. Later, in 1930, Harold Moulton joined other economists to protest the Hawley-Smoot tariff. The institute's internationalism was based on objective economic analysis, but underlying this objectivity often lurked strong emotional feelings. No man better characterized this mixture of outward objectivity and subjective attachment to the internationalist cause than did Leo Pasvolsky, Moulton's collaborator on a number of studies.

Forced to flee Russia with his family at the age of twelve, Pasvolsky spent the early years of his life in America with other anti-Czarist refugees in New York City. While attending night school at City College and pursuing graduate work in political science at Columbia University, Pasvolsky edited the *Russian Review*, an anti-Czarist journal published in English. Pasvolsky actively participated in the political debates that raged through émigré circles at the time. One story had it that Pasvolsky debated Leon Trotsky during the latter's short stay in the States in 1916.[37] When the liberal revolution did come under Kerensky a short time later, Pasvolsky's journal greeted the revolution as "Russia's rebirth," and urged the United States to extend loans to the new government to ensure the future of the revolution. But with Lenin's coming to power in February 1917, Pasvolsky's optimism soured. He initially held that the Bolshevik experiment would fail because "communism is impossible without the application of compulsion in the economic life of the country, but economic production is impossible with the application of such compulsion."[38]

Later, while covering the Paris Peace Conference for the *Brooklyn*

Eagle in 1919 and the Washington Arms Conference for the *Baltimore Sun* in 1921, Pasvolsky changed his original views of the Soviet Union. While he remained fervently anticommunist, he urged the United States to recognize the state of the Soviet Union. "The paths of Russia's and America's historic destiny," he wrote, "have converged and their common path is the road of world peace." He felt that the first step in reestablishing political relations with Russia would be to correct the "tragedy of Versailles" by inviting Russia to join the League of Nations.[39] Pasvolsky saw himself as a nonpartisan economist; yet he acknowledged such a profound passion for free trade and international cooperation that he was willing to accept a communist Soviet Union into the family of nations. Thus, a fine line separated Pasvolsky's role as an objective social scientist and his role as an advocate of certain policies involving free trade, internationalism, and the recognition of the Soviet Union.

In truth, in the outburst of activity at the Institute of Economics in these early years of its existence, little time was allowed for economists to sit back and contemplate the nominal meanings of nonpartisan and partisan. In one sense, institute economists found verification of their nonpartisan status in the trustees' refusal to intervene directly in the institute's work. Nevertheless, special interests frequently tried to apply pressure on the board to influence institute studies. The most notable example of this pressure came when Walton Hamilton and his colleague at the Graduate School, Helen Wright, were preparing to publish a critical study of the bituminous coal industry in which they recommended that the coal industry be consolidated into a single public corporation. In their manuscript, which was published in 1928 as *The Way of Order in the Bituminous Coal Industry*, Hamilton and Wright urged that the federal government establish an industrial board composed of fifteen directors, five chosen to represent consumers such as railroads and public utilities, and an equal number each from the coal miners and the coal operators.[40] The entire corporation would be overseen by a new federal regulatory agency, staffed by economists and charged with maintaining proper management of the industry.

When the coal operators learned of the manuscript through editors of McGraw-Hill, which was printing the book, they reacted immediately. Coal operators began pressuring the executive committee of the IE board of trustees to have Hamilton and Wright modify their findings. A concerted letter-writing campaign, led by "the West Virginia coal crowd," attacked Hamilton's book as "radical and socialistic." This was not the first time that coal operators had attempted to influence an IE study. Three years earlier leaders of the coal industry, after reading Isador Lubin's manuscript on miners' wages and the cost of coal (which also had been sent to them by an editor at McGraw-Hill), had applied pressure on board members to have Lubin change his interpretation. The board had resisted intervention at the time, but now, three years later, they confronted the same group of coal operators, who were particularly aroused by Hamilton and Wright's proposals. This was to be the first major test for the board and its policy of nonintervention. Moulton advised Brookings to tell the operators that the institute was neither for nor against them, but "we are concerned only in finding out what will promote the *general welfare*."[41] In the end, the trustees remained steadfast in their commitment to a policy of nonintervention in the research activity of the institute. The episode, however, seems to have reinforced Brookings's perception that Hamilton was a little too quick in passing judgment.

In many ways Hamilton did present the image of a radical. Described by a colleague as the most extreme and articulate exponent of Veblen's institutional economics, Hamilton combined economics with social psychology, history, politics, and law in his writings. He had been trained originally as a medieval historian at Vanderbilt and then at the University of Texas under Alvin Johnson, who was later director of the New School for Research and who persuaded Hamilton to turn to economics. Because of his background, when Hamilton became the first dean of the Robert S. Brookings Graduate School, he insisted that students in economics should be trained in the principles of the other social sciences and the liberal arts.[42] Earlier, as a professor at Amherst College, Hamilton had established an interdisciplinary program for adult workers that combined economics with philosophy, history, and practical government.[43] In applying this concept to the Graduate School, he sought to accomplish more than training mere technicians. He sought to educate economists who would be imbued with a broad vision.

The Graduate School, which opened its doors under the direction of Hamilton in 1924, with a pledge of $50,000 a year for a period of seven years, soon became a center of intellectual ferment in the social sciences. With a staff separate from that of the IE, consisting of Helen Wright, Walter Shepard, and Leverett Lyon, the Graduate School quickly developed a national reputation for its innovative and exciting program. Hamilton reached out to the social science community in developing the school's reputation. Some staff members of the new school and the IE, including Moulton, Nourse, and Hamilton, had actively participated in the establishment of the Social Science Research Council in 1923. Now, Hamilton used his extensive contacts to invite an exciting array of speakers to lecture to the Graduate School.[44] Students would hear Harold Laski on "Politics and Economic Theory" and William Dodd on "Economic Reconstruction of the South," and courses were offered by Charles Beard, Carl Becker, and Arthur C. Cole on American history. Well-known progressive legal scholars like Felix Frankfurter and Roscoe Pound lectured on contemporary problems of jurisprudence, while philosophy courses were given by Morris Cohen, Alexander Meikeljohn, and Clarence Ayers. Franz Boas discussed the nature of culture and society, and economists John R. Commons, J. A. Hobsen, and Paul Douglas presented new perspectives on economics.[45]

Hamilton insisted that the school should prefer the brilliant student, even though such a youth might be erratic when compared to the one who was almost always certain to do "good" work. He also astutely observed that the presence of women in the graduate program would ensure the quality of student work, and raise "the morale of the student body." Hamilton agreed only reluctantly that a Ph.D. should be given: "If a degree must be granted, it must be a concession to the ways of American education."[46] Still he insisted that student work should be relevant and should include recommendations for reform. Thus he encouraged his students to probe into areas beyond the traditional scope of academic economics. For instance, Max Lerner investigated the image of the business titan in English literature.[47] Carl Brent Swisher began his lifelong study of legal history, which he was to pursue subsequently as a professor at Johns Hopkins University. Mordecai Ezekiel, later an innovator in statistical measurement, studied the meaning of social welfare in a capitalist society.

Yet the very success of the program led to inevitable opposition from the more conservative elements in the IGR, which were led by W. F. Willoughby. Hamilton had too broad a vision to see in Willoughby anything other than a dull, persistent mechanic. Willoughby, who was still directing the herculean task of completing monographs on each of the government agencies—a project that would eventually run to over fifty volumes—strongly disliked the nature of Hamilton's graduate program. After three years during which only one student presented a dissertation on a government agency, Willoughby concluded, quite correctly, that students were more interested in "theory" and "politics" than in what he called "applied government."[48] In 1926 Willoughby angrily wrote the school's founder, Robert Brookings, that Hamilton was deliberately ignoring the "great field of public administration." Willoughby, who had known Brookings since their work on the Taft Commission in 1910, carried considerable weight with the man who had founded and financed the school. And Willoughby's letter was well-timed. Brookings himself was having considerable doubts about the Graduate School. Now seventy-five years old, Brookings told Moulton that he felt ill at ease around the graduate students, many of whom treated him as a pompous old man. Furthermore, he felt that the school had become a training ground for professors and thus had diverged "a long way in its results from the direct service I have always had in mind."[49] He now believed that the granting of Ph.D.s "lowered rather than increased the prestige that we have primarily had in mind." Finally, on April 21, 1926, Brookings acted on his own. He instructed Moulton to form a committee to prepare a report to the trustees for their upcoming spring meeting on the possibility of consolidating the three institutions, the IGR, the IE, and the Graduate School, into a single institution. Moulton's committee, which was composed of Leverett Lyon, Edwin Nourse, and Walton Hamilton, in the end followed Brookings's wishes and urged the consolidation of the IGR and the IE and the dissolution of the Graduate School.[50] Only Hamilton dissented from the report.

Specifically, Hamilton pointed to the list of 120 students who had attended the school. The list was indeed impressive. A generation of scholars and government officials had received their start at the Graduate School. They included Isador Lubin, John U. Nef, Stacy May, Paul Thomas Homan, Frank Tannenbaum, and those mentioned earlier, Max Lerner, Carl Swisher, and Mordecai Ezekiel. Many of these former students, Hamilton pointed out, had already made substantial contributions in their fields. They had been trained to be policy makers, not mere technicians. They had left the Graduate School, Hamilton assured Brookings, with a broad vision of society.

Moreover, Hamilton felt that a larger issue was at stake. The questions raised by Willoughby went to the very heart of the nature of nonpartisan expertise in public policy. For Hamilton public policy ultimately was always political in nature. "The School," he wrote, "is concerned with 'politics' which is to be very broadly interpreted." Whether a certain policy should be pursued or not, it seemed to Hamilton, was the first question to ask before one set out to examine the administrative efficiency of the governmental agencies charged with carrying out the policy. And any answer to this question of whether a policy should be pursued or not ultimately raised political issues of who gets what and how much. Because the IGR under Willoughby refused to confront these questions, Hamilton concluded, the IGR was not an institute of policy or even of government. Instead the IGR was a "bureau" concerned only with the reorganization of government departments and with the mechanics of the budget. Within these narrow confines "it takes agencies for granted and avoids questions of reason for existence and function."[51] The IGR approach, Hamilton bluntly declared, myopically ignored the larger policy questions facing society.

This contention led to Hamilton's second point: Policy evaluation necessarily entails certain political assumptions concerning the nature of the public interest. Hamilton realized that the claim of representing the public interest, a claim on which the IGR and IE based their definition of nonpartisanship, was far more complicated than Moulton had suggested when he had written to Brookings that the coal operators "take it for granted that we are either for or against them. This is because they have not yet come to appreciate that there is a *general welfare* point of view to which a disinterested, investigative institution is devoted."[52] Moulton had assumed that because an institution was disinterested it represented a "general-welfare" view, and that furthermore this view stood above class interests. Such an assumption ignored the possibility that Hamilton's proposal to incorporate the coal industry might in fact be contrary to the immediate economic interests of the coal operators and in fact be more beneficial to the class interests of the coal workers. Moulton's view of disinterested research denied that in certain circumstances the special interests of a group or class might actually benefit the public interest of the entire society. Hamilton proposed, to the contrary, that what would immediately benefit the coal workers would benefit all of society in the long run.

An avowed follower of Veblen, Hamilton saw the issue of general welfare as an institutional problem revolving around the intelligent control of industry. He consistently emphasized his belief that the study of economics should be concerned with controlling society's industrial institutions. During the Depression Hamilton would declare, "If our industries are to be instruments of national well-being, we must employ a varied program of economic control."[53] The efficacy of control depended on the ability of the aware, able, and dedicated leadership of experts to devise programs that adapted society's institutions to accommodate the public interest. In defining the public interest Hamilton realized that economists needed to be more than disinterested nonpartisan specialists. Instead, because certain value assumptions would be interjected into any definition of the public interest, Hamilton insisted that economics develop a broad political perspective of society. Thus Hamilton argued that the Graduate School, by emphasizing the liberal arts, which Willoughby and Brookings took for "theoretical" nonsense, was satisfying the primary goal of the program—the training of a cadre of economists to enter government as policy makers.

Hamilton lost the debate. In the process the issues raised in the discussion concerning the meaning of nonpartisanship and the public interest would be ignored. The trustees, when they convened for their annual meeting in 1927, simply approved the consolidation of the IE and the IGR into a single institution to be called the Brookings Institution and to be headed by Harold Moulton. The decision to merge the IE and the IGR included the understanding that the Graduate School was to be disbanded in favor of a smaller training program for advanced graduate students. Hamilton was offered the opportunity to join the new Brookings Institution, as were other faculty members, but he politely resigned to become a professor at the Yale Law School, which, in the 1920s, had emerged as the most exciting and controversial law school in the nation.[54]

Much to the displeasure of the board and Harold Moulton, however, the controversy failed to subside. Students at the Graduate School, when they learned of the board's decision, immediately organized a series of meetings to protest the action as threatening "academic freedom." In focusing on academic freedom they perhaps missed the central issue, the nature and purpose of nonpartisan research, but the cause of academic freedom, especially following the repression of many academics during World War I, was bound to attract attention. Moulton tried to fend off the students by suggesting that the matter be taken to the American Association of University Professors, but the students, led by Gustav Peck and George B. Galloway, refused to be diverted and instead wrote a scathing attack on the consolidation plan for the *Survey*, a liberal magazine concerned with social-welfare issues of the day. Now that the debate had been brought into the wider social science community, Charles Beard, who had resigned his position at Columbia University during World War I over the issue of academic freedom, volunteered to investigate the students' charges. Because Moulton believed that the editors of *Survey* were "more interested in staging a public controversy than in educating the public," he replied directly to Beard, instead of through the editors, supplying him with relevant documents concerning the case. Upon reviewing the documents, Beard telegrammed the editors that he was totally satisfied that the consolidation of the IE and the IGR, and the disbanding of the Graduate School, had not infringed upon academic freedom.[55] That the editors did not print Beard's telegram only confirmed Moulton's low opinion of their intentions. Moulton let the matter die through neglect. Gradually the students' protests dissipated into more immediate concerns of finishing degrees and finding jobs. Still, nearly thirty years later when the Brookings Institution held a fifty-year anniversary dinner celebrating the school, many graduates refused to return to their alma mater. Bitterness lingered, foretelling the estranged relationship between the Brookings Institution and the liberal community in the next decade, the 1930s.

The controversy between Willoughby and Hamilton had done little to clarify the meaning of nonpartisanship, which the Brookings Institution, now under Harold Moulton, continued to equate with pursuit of the general public interest. Moulton also continued to maintain that the institution should be "liberal" in its economic outlook, but he became increasingly absolutist in his belief that there were certain economic truths concerning the primacy of the institutional marketplace and a balanced budget and that economists, free from political motivation, should uphold these truths. Ironically, the staff members at the IGR, as it continued to be called within the Brookings Institution, broadened their interests slightly, to include policy recommendations as well as administrative surveys. This concern appeared in the IGR's influential study of the Bureau of Indian Affairs in the late 1920s. The institute's work with the Bureau of Indian Affairs was undertaken with the major purpose of improving administration and personnel practices, yet in the course of its study the IGR staff expressed a reluctant willingness to enter into some questions of policy. In this respect, Hamilton had pushed the IGR into new areas. Nevertheless, the nagging question remained: Could the improvement of administrative efficiency within government alone serve the general interest and thereby ensure human satisfaction?

5 · LEWIS MERIAM, EXPERTISE,
AND INDIAN REFORM

THE BROOKINGS Institution resumed activity with full vigor following the controversy over the Graduate School. In 1929 Moulton made plans for a new headquarters to be located at 722 Jackson Place, diagonally across the street from the White House. When completed in 1931 the limestone building displayed the prosperity of the 1920s. It contained an oak-paneled library, beam ceilings, residential rooms for guests, and a Round Table Room that became one of Washington's most celebrated meeting places. Moulton's imprint was clearly in evidence: the building included a small gymnasium and purportedly one of the best squash courts in Washington. The funds for this exquisite building had been provided by Robert Brookings's new wife, Isabel Valle January.

Meanwhile, the work of the Brookings economists continued to flourish. The Institute of Economics, now incorporated as a separate division within the Brookings Institution, undertook crucial investigations into the agricultural depression and technological unemployment. Edwin Nourse, appointed director of the IE, favorably reviewed the marketing and credit operations of the Federal Farm Board, a recently established agency in the Hoover administration. At the same time, Isador Lubin completed his study *The Absorption of the Unemployed in American Industry*, which argued that, contrary to the traditional view, technological unemployment was not inevitable and could be corrected through continued economic growth.[1]

Much of the work of the Brookings Institution during this time, as evidenced in these studies, sought to bring efficiency and economic stability to the corporate economy. Nevertheless, the meaning of efficiency, even after the bitter debate between Willoughby and Hamilton, remained ambiguous. The relationship between administrative efficiency, which weighed financial costs against benefits, and economic efficiency, which measured human satisfaction and benefits, was left unresolved. The staff of the institution still assumed that administrative efficiency produced, at least in the long run, human satisfaction. This assumption narrowed the reform vision of the Brookings Institution. The tension between managerial efficiency and human satisfaction became all too apparent in the Brookings Institution's involvement in the reorganization of the Bureau of Indian Affairs in the 1920s. In many ways, this instance of participation in social reform, the most enduring work undertaken by the institution in this period, can be viewed as a prelude to the Brookings Institution's response to the Great Depression in the next decade.

The reorganization of the Indian Service shows that the Brookings staff acted as more than a medium for corporate ideology. In fact, the role of the institution in Indian reform illustrates how a variety of humanitarian concerns have been translated into technical problems by nonpartisan specialists in the twentieth century. Administrative reform frequently leads to real progress for a society dependent on large-scale organizations. This progress is at best incremental in nature, however, reflecting gradual change within an administrative context rather than an innovative programmatic change within public policy. To those reformers who seek radical transformations and to those groups at the bottom of society who expect more than "efficiency and economy" in government, administrative reform may appear only to perpetuate the inequalities of a class-ridden and racist system.

Shortly after the controversy over the future course of the Brookings Institution, Secretary of the Interior Hubert Work decided to commission an investigation into the condition of the Indians in the United States. This request came after a decade of vehement criticism from outside reform elements concerning the conduct of the Indian Service and its treatment of native Americans. (The Indian Service was that division of the Bureau of Indian Affairs directly involved in working with Indians.) Reformers, led by John Collier, had long charged that inefficiency, incompetence, and corruption were keeping the Indians in a state of abject, disease-ridden poverty.

3. Pima Indian homes of mud and arrowweed near Casa Blanca, Arizona, 1926. (Indian Survey photograph, courtesy of the Brookings Institution Archives)

Confronted by this sentiment, which appeared to be attracting a wider audience, Secretary Work finally turned to the Brookings Institution, in particular to Lewis Meriam of the IGR, for a candid, objective, and nonpartisan evaluation of the Indian Service.

Meriam spent the next five years, from 1927 to 1932, attempting to upgrade the Indian bureau. With the cooperation of the Rockefeller Foundation and the continuing support of the Hoover administration, Meriam proved to be instrumental in helping to reorganize the agency. The reorganization, which was accomplished in 1931, increased the power of skilled specialists in the Indian bureau. Later, under the Roosevelt administration, the organizational changes would be followed by a radical change in Indian policy, and John Collier would be appointed as commissioner of the Bureau of Indian Affairs.

The report prepared by Meriam after his initial investigation of the Indian bureau, *The Problem of Indian Administration* (1928), marked a major turning point in Indian policy. One historian of Indian education has described the Meriam report as "the symbol of a definitive response to the failure of fifty years of assimilation policy."[2] Yet scholars, as well as some of Meriam's contemporaries, have missed the central message of the report: Conditions among the Indians could be improved through better administration and better personnel in the Indian Service. Meriam and his associates were less interested in changing current Indian policies than with ensuring that existing policies were implemented efficiently through

4. Sunny Brook Public School, Potawatomie Agency, Kansas, 1926. (Indian Survey photograph, courtesy of the Brookings Institution Archives)

a properly organized administration run by well-trained specialists. Thus the Meriam report did not look ahead prophetically to a New Deal for Indians.[3] Rather, it harked back to the approach of the pre-war "efficiency and economy" movement. Lewis Meriam and his associates were "efficiency experts" in the best tradition of the IGR.

The emphasis on efficiency embodied in the recommendations of the Meriam survey contrasted sharply with the program presented by the critics of the Indian Service. Collier and his group of reformers advocated a radical shift in policy away from individual land ownership toward tribal incorporation of Indian land. They also believed that the Indian tribes should be given their own governments, police forces, and judiciary systems. Although the Meriam report mentioned the possibility of experimentation in these areas, it did so only in passing. It focused primarily on the importance of increasing revenues, improving the caliber of personnel, and re-arranging the administration of the Indian Service, and avoided any recommendation that suggested a radical shift in Indian policy. Given the Indian bureau's intransigence toward change, however, the report appeared innovative to many because of the administrative improvements it proposed.

Administrative reformers such as Meriam and popular reformers such as Collier agreed on one basic point in particular—the need for expertise in government and for the elimination of partisan politics

in administration. Furthermore, both groups believed that inefficient bureaucracy thwarted representative government. If government was to succeed, highly trained specialists must replace corrupt
and partisan bureaucrats. Thus, technicians and activists alike
shared with earlier reformers a profound faith in the effectiveness of
expertise.

As individuals, however, Meriam and Collier were separated by
temperament and social role. Although they could agree on certain
long-range goals, they disagreed just as readily over the means for
achieving these goals. Meriam was not personally inclined toward
activism; he preferred to work with the higher echelons of government. This attitude was reinforced by his social position as a staff
member of a nonpartisan, independent research organization, the
Brookings Institution. His political power derived from his authority as a social science technician. Yet Meriam did not naively
dismiss the need for an activist movement such as Collier's to
bring about reform. He astutely observed that "the Indian Service
must be reformed, and it cannot be reformed unless the public is
aroused."[4] Nonetheless, he left to the activists the major role in
arousing the public. Meriam's work must therefore be understood
in conjunction with Collier's activity.

Collier himself was a complex man. One contemporary described him as "the most keen, cool, far visioned practical student
of the Indian problem today." Yet another close associate who knew
Collier equally well characterized him as having "a sincere and lofty
idealism, and unrestrained personal ambition, a messiah complex
and a trained knack for politics."[5] Born in Atlanta, Georgia, in 1884
to a distinguished family, Collier originally traveled to New York
to attend classes at Columbia University. Once in New York, he
became interested in immigrants and community organization. In
1907 he joined the staff of the Peoples Institute, a social service organization working with immigrants on New York's east side.
Through his work he developed a deep respect for the immigrants'
culture, a respect that found theoretical coherence for him in Mary
LaFollette's and E. C. Lindemann's concept of "cultural pluralism."
Cultural pluralism became an integral part of Collier's world
outlook,

Like many southerners, Collier believed that industrial society
with its insidious materialist underpinnings undermined ethnic culture and individual creativity. He felt that through community organization, however, ethnic groups could counter the negative

effects of industrialism by banding together to protect their own separate identities. The community would preserve ethnic pluralism against the homogenizing effects of industrialism. However, the defeat of the New York reform movement following the war, and the ensuing Red Scare of 1919, disillusioned Collier. It was at this point that he became aware of the problems facing the Pueblo Indians.[6]

Collier first encountered the Pueblo Indians in the winter of 1919, when he traveled to New Mexico to visit his close friend Mabel Dodge, who had settled in Taos with her husband to form a writer's colony. Collier discovered in the Pueblo Indians an unassimilated people who had remained ethnically pure throughout two centuries of Spanish and Anglo domination. Shortly after his first visit to New Mexico he wrote, "The Indian problem embodies a world wide problem, whether material civilization—machinery and the dictates of machinery—and selfish individualism shall dominate man or whether man shall dominate them, subordinate them, and use them."[7] He believed that renewed conflict over this issue was inevitable between whites and Indians, and he was proved right when Senator Holm O. Bursum introduced legislation that ensured the continued encroachment of white settlers on Pueblo land.

The Bursum bill reflected in many ways a classic situation in American history: confrontation between poor whites and Indians over land. The population of New Mexico had increased from 100,000 to 360,000 between 1910 and 1920. Around the Pueblos lived many Mexican and Anglo settlers who owned small ranches or farms. Most of these settlers were in debt.[8] Initially, the Pueblos had allowed them to homestead and buy the land, but suddenly these land actions were called into question by a Supreme Court decision in the case of *Sandoval vs. the United States* (1913). Concerned with the legal status of the Pueblo Indians, the court ruled that the tribe had been under the control of Congress since 1849, and, therefore, the Pueblo Indians were not citizens and could not have owned the land they claimed to have leased or sold to the white settlers. In short, the court in effect nullified land sales by the Pueblos. When Albert Fall became Secretary of the Interior under Harding, he saw a perfect opportunity to bolster Republican Party support in New Mexico through the enactment of a law favorable to white land interests. Thus the Bursum bill was introduced, with its threat to deprive the Indians of over 60,000 acres of their land.[9]

Collier relied mainly on two groups to mount a campaign against the bill, Indians and women. Through his efforts, a Council of All-Pueblo Indians was called in the fall of 1922. Indians throughout New Mexico gathered in San Domingo to attend this first council held since 1680, when Indians had rebelled to drive out the Spanish. At the two-day meeting, the participants agreed to organize against the bill. Under Collier's direction, the Indians issued a proclamation addressed to the American people. "We, the Pueblo Indians," the proclamation began, "have always been self-supporting. . . . Today many Pueblos have less than one-half acre per person when twelve acres is considered necessary for a white man to live on." How can we give up more land? they asked. "Why have the Indian Office and the lawyers paid by the government to defend our interests framed a bill contrary to our interests?"[10] Many Americans would begin to ask the same questions as the Indians took their cause to the public.

The Federation of Women's Clubs responded immediately to the Indians' cause. The federation's Commission on Indian Welfare, headed by Stella Atwood of Riverside, California, played a key role in the campaign against the bill. Mrs. Atwood, a social worker who had become interested in Indians while serving on the Selective Service Board, had been introduced to Collier following his first visit to New Mexico in 1919. After she was informed of the dangers of the Bursum bill, she not only organized the federation against the bill, but she was also able to offer financial support to Collier's activities. In May 1923 she officially hired Collier as a research agent for the federation's Commission on Indian Welfare.[11]

With an active membership of 3,000 women, the federation proved to be a formidable opponent of the Indian Service. "Composed of the better half of such American women as have been accustomed to use their leisure for purposes of public and personal improvement," wrote Vera Connolly in Good Housekeeping, the Federation of Women's Clubs confronted the Indian Service with "the righteous wrath of American womanhood, of consecrated women, aroused to deep indignation and bonded together in a crusade to obtain justice for the oppressed."[12] The women of the federation gave the reform movement a moral tone not easily matched by the Indian Service.

Collier and his fellow reformers believed that the Indian Service represented "the perfect example of bureaucracy's menace to civilization, tyrannical and omnipotent over Indians, helpless before its own routines."[13] Because the Indian Service was inefficient, he said, it was inevitably antidemocratic. "The experience of responsible democracy," Collier would later write, "is, of all experiences, the most therapeutic, the most disciplinary, the most dynamogenic, and the most productive of efficiency." Efficiency demanded expertise. Collier's faith in specialized knowledge, considering that he so profoundly disliked industrial society, was contradictory. This belief in expertise was, nevertheless, shared by other reformers. "The problem of the Indian," wrote a close friend of Collier, "is not for political opportunists and civil service clerks, it is for specialists. . . . Above everything it calls for specialists."[14]

Joined by the Indians and the Federation of Women's Clubs, Collier organized the first truly mass movement on the behalf of American Indians in history.[15] Using techniques of mass propaganda, the campaign reached a broad audience including liberal groups, professionals, intellectuals, school children, and most importantly, the educated middle class. The movement gained added weight from the support of such nonpolitical groups as the American Anthropological Association, the Association for the Advancement of Science, and the American Ethnological Society.[16] Lead articles on the subject regularly appeared in the *New York Times* and the *New York World*, as well as *Survey* and *Sunset*, a West Coast muckraking magazine edited by Walter Woelke.[17] In 1923, the separate segments of the militant Indian reform movement coalesced into the American Indian Defense Association, with a membership of 1,700.

When the opposition of the Pueblos to the Bursum measure became known through public pressure, Senator W. J. Borah took the unusual step in 1923 of recalling the bill from the House of Representatives. Returned to the Senate Committee of Public Lands and Survey, the bill faced an uncertain future. When Congress reconvened the next year, Collier undertook a national tour with sixteen Pueblo Indians to draw attention to Secretary Fall's machinations and to rally support for the Jones-Leatherwood measure, an alternative proposal that would create a three-person federal commission to settle contested land claims. The Indians visited Philadelphia, New York, and Chicago; in Chicago they earned the endorsement of Harold Ickes, who later supported Collier for the post of commissioner of Indian affairs.[18]

Such efforts led to the defeat of the Bursum bill, but the fight between the Indian Service and the reformers was far from over.

Following the defeat, the Bureau of Indian Affairs launched a concerted campaign to discredit its critics. Collier observed that the Indian Service had "never been more dogmatic, more irresponsible. . . . Brutalism toward field representatives and disregard and suppression of their recommendations has never been more extreme."[19] Denouncing the reformers as "decadent Greenwich villagers from New York," the bureau launched an offensive against the Pueblo Indians and the Federation of Women's Clubs.

First, the Indian Service engineered the removal of Stella Atwood as chair of the federation's Commission on Indian Welfare. Using Collier's own tactics, Clara D. True, a supporter of the Bursum bill, appeared with a delegation of seven "progressive" Indians at the biennial convention of the General Federation of Women's Clubs in Los Angeles in 1924. The delegation represented the bureau's answer to the Council of All-Pueblo Indians, the All-Pueblo Progressive Council of Christian Indians. Financed totally by the Bureau of Indian Affairs, and directed on the floor by the able Clara True, the "progressive" forces were able to defeat Stella Atwood for the chair of the Commission on Indian Welfare. They defeated also a resolution aimed against the commissioner of Indian affairs.[20]

On the Indian reservations, the bureau pursued a policy of transferring or removing "any disloyal employee . . . who is known to be giving aid and comfort to the enemy at this time."[21] The issue finally came to a head when C. J. Crandall, superintendent of the Northern Pueblos, arrested the governing board of the Taos Pueblos over an internal religious controversy. Collier secured their release and then organized a delegation of twelve Indians to travel to Utah and California to state their case before the public. In California the Indians appeared at the Commonwealth Club, the Oakland Forum, and the Berkeley Playhouse.[22] The commissioner of Indian affairs in turn denounced the group as Soviet-financed agitators.[23]

By 1925, the need for an objective approach was evident, and a call for an investigation of the Indian Service was being raised in many quarters. Reflecting this growing sentiment, *Scientific American* urged an independent study. While the "average Indian seems to be physically inferior to the white man," the journal declared, psychiatric tests conducted during the last war had shown that "morally the red man is equal to the white." Thus, to ensure that Indian blood is "not debased and with it an inferior [hybrid] strain admitted," common sense dictated that the Indian race must be protected and preserved. Indians, therefore, should be given at least a rudimentary education, medical aid, hospitals, and asylums. Such a program should be devised in an "intelligent and scientific way" by a scientific commission.[24] Working from different assumptions, the Board of Indian Commissioners, an advisory board to the Bureau of Indian Affairs, also called for a study into Indian conditions. In 1926, Collier joined the chorus when he proposed that the Institute for Government Research conduct such an investigation.[25]

John D. Rockefeller, Jr., had become interested in the Indian question in the early 1920s. In 1926 he offered financial support to Secretary of the Interior Hubert Work, Fall's successor, for a survey of Indian affairs. Through Thomas Jesse Jones, a long-time advocate of Negro civil rights and close associate of the Rockefeller group, Lewis Meriam was recommended to the Rockefeller Foundation as the best man to conduct such a project. Acting on Jones's recommendation, Kenneth Chorley, director of the Spelman Fund, met with Meriam to discuss the possibilities of undertaking a study. Following the meeting, Chorley advised Secretary Work to commission the IGR to review Indian conditions, and on June 17, 1927, Work did so. Prior to entering the arrangement W. F. Willoughby, the director of the IGR, had assured Work that the survey would not "take sides for or against the Indian office." Instead, the institute would look to the future "to indicate what remains to be done . . . to improve the conditions of the Indians."[26] It was agreed that Meriam would be released from his regular duties for a year so that he could oversee the study.

Lewis Meriam seemed ideally suited to the task. He was the model scientific expert. He prided himself on his objective, rational approach to solving social problems. In this sense, he well represented the Brookings Institution's image as a nonpartisan research institution. "I have worked so long with the Institute for Government Research," he wrote a friend in 1929, "that I have an institutional rather than an individual point of view." He added rather candidly, "I can in no way . . . separate the actions of Lewis Meriam, a private citizen and those of Lewis Meriam, the technical director of the Indian survey."[27] In his personal life, Meriam had been a lifelong Democrat. His willingness to separate his professional work from his political beliefs was a characteristic shared by other social scientists in the modern era. The social scientist was assumed to be a dispassionate and objective man, concerned with relevant social questions, yet independent in thought and willing to break with tradition. This ideal had already become an integral component of social science thought. Meriam's concern with objectivity, relevance, and independent thought manifested itself throughout his early career. Graduating from Harvard in 1906 with a bachelor's degree in English and a master's in government and economic studies, Meriam found a career in government first at the U.S. Census Bureau as a statistician and editor, and later as an assistant chief of the Children's Bureau after it was organized in 1912 under Julia Lathrop.[28] His stay in the Children's Bureau was marked by ambivalent relations with Lathrop. While he admired her ability to lobby in Congress, he felt her methods often bordered on blackmail.[29] In fact, Meriam detested Lathrop's political behavior; he firmly held to the belief that good politics should emerge from rational discussion.[30]

In 1916, Meriam was approached to join the staff of the newly organized Institute for Government Research, and he accepted. Among other assignments with the IGR, he worked as a staff aide to the Congressional Joint Committee on the Reclassification of Salaries, which drafted the landmark Classification Act of 1923. Following this assignment, Meriam was asked by the governor of North Carolina to serve as an adviser to his Salary and Wage Commission. Meriam's belief in better personnel as a means of reforming government would be seen also in his work for the Indian Service.

Meriam realized from the beginning that the Indian problem needed to be seen in a context that included social, economic, and legal conditions. Such a study would be unprecedented. The last attempt to survey the Indian situation had been Henry Row Schoolcraft's *Information Respecting the History, Conditions, and Prospects of the Indian Tribes of the United States* (1855). With 350,000 Indians organized into 200 different tribes scattered through twenty-six states, Meriam obviously could not complete his study alone. The IGR had made it clear to Secretary Work that Meriam would staff the survey with "persons highly qualified as specialists in their respective fields, scientific in their approach, not sensationalists, and free from preconceived views and opinions." Because of this last qualification, anthropologists would not be appointed to the survey's staff.[31] A Yale-educated Indian, Henry Roe Cloud, however, was appointed to act as a liaison to the tribes to be surveyed.

Serving with Cloud on the survey was the chairman of the history department of the University of Oklahoma, Everett Dale, a specialist in general economic conditions. Dale had worked as a cowboy and a ranchman for five years before earning an M.A. and Ph.D. from Harvard. Another staff member, chosen for his expertise in education, was W. Carson Ryan, professor of education at Swarthmore College. Ryan had been education editor for the *New York Post* in 1920–1921. With an extensive background in government (he had been president of the Federal Employees Union in Washington, D.C.), he had participated in education studies in Canada, Puerto Rico, Newark, and the District of Columbia. Ryan was later to play a central role in the reorganization of the Indian administration.

Meriam also brought to the staff two women he had met while at the Census Bureau. To serve as specialist on the conditions of Indian migrants to urban communities, Emma Duke was hired. She had worked in the Census Bureau from 1900 to 1907 and in the Children's Bureau from 1912 to 1920. The other woman on the staff was Mary Louise Mark, a professor of sociology at Ohio State University who had met Meriam while she was at the Bureau in 1911. She became the survey's specialist in family life and the activities of women. Other staff members were hired as experts in law, agriculture, health, and research methods.[32] As a journalist observed at the time, these men and women were "sober, scientific specialists."[33]

Field work began on November 12, 1926, and the Meriam survey team completed its report, *The Problem of Indian Administration*, in February 1928. The report was hailed as "the most important single document in Indian Affairs since Helen Jackson published her *Century of Dishonor* fifty years ago." Writing seventeen years later, historian Randolph C. Downes concluded that "the Meriam Report was a masterpiece of reform propaganda in the best sense of the word."[34] The report detailed the deplorable living conditions of Indians. "An overwhelming majority of Indians are poor, extremely poor," the report began, "and they are not adjusted to the economic and social system of the dominant white civilization." *The Problem of Indian Administration* went on to indict the Indian Service in 872 pages documenting the charges that many Indians literally were dying because of neglect, Indian children were abused in government schools, and tuberculosis and trachoma were so prevalent that the survey members feared the spread of these diseases to whites. Contrary to the position of the Indian Service, the survey concluded that, with Indians having an average annual per capita income of only $100, there was "altogether too much evidence of real suffering and discontentment to subscribe to the belief that Indians are reasonably satisfied with their condition. The amount of serious illness and poverty is too great to permit real contentment."[35]

In general, the report's recommendations for improving the Indian Service in economic, health, and education areas centered on increased appropriations and increased expertise for the service. The Meriam survey urged that "a national emergency should be declared requiring increased appropriations by Congress."[36] More specifically, the report recommended that the first priority of Congress should be the appropriation "at the earliest possible moment" of an additional $1 million to improve the quantity, quality, and variety of the diet of Indian children. In regard to education, the Meriam team believed that the Indian Service could attract better teachers by raising salaries. It was also suggested that new positions could be created in vocational and industrial education.[37]

Meriam particularly recognized the need for reorganizing the administration of the Indian Service. He wrote Collier that "I have always regarded the complete reorganization of the headquarters [as the] key to the whole situation because it controls everything else."[38] He understood at the very outset that the Indian Service would be extremely difficult to reform because of "its age, its size, its diversity of subject matters, its dispersion over twenty-six states with more than two-hundred tribes, its political ties, [and] its low state of efficiency."[39] His hope for reorganization rested in his proposal to establish a scientific and technical division for planning. This unit, to be called the Division of Planning and Development, would serve as a general staff charged with designing and implementing policy and accountable directly to the commissioners. The division would serve two general purposes: First, it would provide an organizational means to support reform of the bureaucracy. Second, the planning staff could evaluate the problems of the Indian Service without reference to old organizational lines. Thus, by creating a new agency within the bureaucracy, Meriam hoped to subvert the old bureaucracy, while providing a base for the new "technical men" so that they "could not be thwarted in all their efforts by the old bureaucratic permanent employees who have so long dominated the service."[40] The Meriam report urged that $250,000 a year be appropriated to establish such a division.

Substantiating many of the complaints previously voiced by the reformers, *The Problem of Indian Administration* received a favorable reception among this group. In a review for the *Survey*, Collier commented, "To the Indian and friends the report is enormously important. It destroys forever the official pretense that Indians are rich and are growing richer." The report "gives facts," and it "gives judgments," the more persuasive from its "studied coldness of expression." But, Collier asked, "Who and what condition is responsible?" The Meriam report had not provided an answer to this fundamental question. Collier further observed that, while providing facts and some recommendations, the report did not examine the operating principles of the Indian Service.[41] Critical of the land allotment system, Collier and the American Indian Defense Association urged a radical shift in Indian policy away from individual land ownership to corporate tribal ownership.

The Meriam survey was also critical of the allotment system established under the Dawes Act of 1887. "It almost seemed," the report conjectured, "as if the government assumed that some magic in individual ownership would in itself prove an educating factor." The report nevertheless recommended that the allotment system continue to be pursued, although with extreme conservatism. It mentioned the possibility that the government might experiment in corporate ownership of tribal property, but this suggestion was made only in passing.

Still, the recommendations received a less than enthusiastic reception from the Indian Service. Although Assistant Commissioner E. B. Meritt wrote to Meriam pledging to implement the report's recommendations as "rapidly as possible and to require the promptest of action," the fact was that most Indian bureau officials, including Meritt, found the recommendations "academic, untenable, and unworkable." Furthermore, the survey's recommendations were opposed by the Board of Indian Commissioners, by the missionary societies, and, ironically, by an agency the IGR had helped organize, the cost-conscious Bureau of the Budget.[42]

The people from the Rockefeller Foundation welcomed the Meriam report as a significant step in Indian reform. Thomas Jesse Jones, educational director of the Phelps Stokes fund, typified foundation sentiment in a letter he wrote to Meriam shortly after the report was released. "As a program for the improvement of the Indian," Jones wrote, "the Indian investigation has never been surpassed; . . . your presentation is sympathetic, fearless, clear, and comprehensive. In a word, you have realized the standards of the best practical statesmanship."[43] Jones believed that the program, now that it had been proposed, needed to be implemented as soon as possible. He wrote Kenneth Chorley, now head of the Rockefeller Foundation, that "students of the American Indian situation are unanimous in their conviction that the administration of Indian Affairs needs a thorough reorganization."[44] Ensuring that further action would be taken on the Meriam Report, in September 1929, the Rockefeller Foundation awarded $50,000 to the Institute for Government Research and asked the institute to provide a staff of experts to the Commissioner of Indian Affairs. Meriam was the obvious choice to direct this next stage in the reform effort.

Meriam realized that any attempts at reorganizing the Indian Service would largely depend on a sympathetic president, secretary of the interior, and Indian commissioner. He welcomed, therefore, the election of Herbert Hoover and the subsequent appointment of Lyman Wilbur, former president of Stanford, as secretary of the interior. With these men in office, Meriam hoped to secure "the appointment of a new, able, and progressive Commissioner of Indian Affairs."[45] When Commissioner Edward Burke offered his resignation, Meriam was encouraged. Shortly after Burke's resignation, Edgar Meritt, the assistant commissioner, stepped down from his post. Conditions for reform seemed optimal.

With the removal of Burke and Meritt, Meriam attempted to take full advantage of the reputation he had gained as an expert on Indian affairs: he sought to intervene in the selection of the new commissioner. Secretary Wilbur had come under considerable pressure to make a political appointment to the position. The former Commissioner of Indian Affairs under Woodrow Wilson, Cato Sells, appeared to be a front-runner since he had bolted his party to campaign for Hoover in Texas during the election of 1928. The other political favorite, E. L. Rogers, was being pushed for the post by Representative Knutsen of Minnesota.[46] To counter these political influences, representatives of such liberal reform groups as the Indian Rights Association, the Eastern Association of Indian Affairs, and the New Mexico Association, along with Meriam, Thomas Jesse Jones, and Kenneth Chorley, submitted a list of five names to be considered for the appointment.[47] From this list Wilbur chose Charles J. Rhoads to be the new commissioner. Rhoads, a Philadelphia banker and president of the Indian Rights Association, was Meriam's first choice for the job.[48] When Rhoads seemed hesitant to accept the post, Kenneth Chorley sent him a telegram urging him to do so.[49] For assistant commissioner, Wilbur selected another man from the list, J. Henry Scattergood, also an active member of the Indian Rights Association in Philadelphia and the treasurer of Bryn Mawr College. Following the selection of these two men, Wilbur announced the beginnings of a what he called a "New Deal for the Indians." He predicted that under the new policy Indians would become a self-sufficient people within the next twenty years.[50]

Meriam foresaw accurately that reform within the Bureau would be greatly aided by the support of John Collier and the popular reform movement. Collier greeted the Rhoads and Scattergood appointments as a progressive step in Indian affairs.[51] Although Meriam felt that Collier was perhaps a little too dedicated, and perhaps a little too narrow, he respected him. Thus, while attending the meeting of the National Conference of Social Work held in San Francisco in the summer of 1929, Meriam broached with Collier the subject of forming an alliance. Meeting with a favorable response, Meriam initiated a series of lengthy conferences with Collier, his associate Charles Elkus, and M. K. Sniffen, who was secretary of the Indian Rights Association. From these meetings a consensus was reached to work together on a commonly agreed program and "let the minor things ride."[52] Following these meetings, Meriam urged Rhoads and Scattergood to work with Collier. He commended Collier as "being exceptionally well-informed, able, and progressive, and influential with the progressive element in the Senate." Moreover, warned Meriam, Collier could be "a doughty antagonist."[53]

The alliance between Collier and the commissioners did not last long, however. New to their offices, Rhoads and Scattergood in the end proved unwilling to break with the reactionary forces in the Indian Service and the Congress. Almost at the beginning of the alliance, serious difficulties developed over the bureau's relationship to Congress. The first foreseeable signs of difficulty appeared when the chairman of the Subcommittee on Indian Affairs of the Appropriations Committee, Louis Cramton of Michigan, rejected an Indian arts and crafts proposal drafted by Collier, and the commissioners, assuming that the bill was dead, failed to offer any resistance.[54]

At the same time, the Klamath tribe sent a delegation to Washington to lobby for a bill incorporating Klamath property. Despite the fact that Rhoads had recommended to Congress the enactment of such a bill, the delegation was informed by minor officials in the bureau that the Indian office would never endorse an incorporation bill. Provoked by this phlegmatic attitude, the Klamath delegation turned to the Senate Investigating Committee and specifically charged their district superintendent with neglect of duty and fraudulent practices in relation to federal projects on the reservation. Collier and Meriam advised the commissioners to promise to make a full investigation of the charges. Influenced by Scattergood (or so Meriam believed), Rhoads did not heed their advice.

Rhoads was called before the Senate committee, to whom he pleaded unfamiliarity with the situation: "I am coming here more to learn than to tell you how it works. I am altogether new to this." Scattergood undermined Rhoads's testimony, however, when he took the stand and proceeded to defend the superintendent. Not leaving well enough alone, Scattergood publicly threw his arm around the superintendent and congratulated him on "routing all his enemies." Later, following a Senate investigation, the commissioners would be forced to remove the superintendent from his position.[55]

The final break between Collier and the commissioners came over the supplemental appropriation for food and clothing for Indian boarding schools. When the measure was brought to the attention of Cramton, the congressman, who had always denied the facts of the Indians' insufficient food supply, called Rhoads and Scattergood into his office for a conference over the request. Claiming that the appropriation for food and clothing would set an unwanted precedent for future appropriations, Cramton proposed a compromise measure that would cut this allocation in order to increase funds for labor-saving equipment such as electric dishwashers, washing machines, and other devices. Rhoads and Scattergood accepted this compromise without informing Collier and Meriam.[56]

When Meriam and Collier discovered the shift in the appropriations bill agreed to by the commissioners, they felt betrayed. Both had the impression that the change had been made to save Cramton's face. Collier felt that he had been particularly used. "We saw them daily, sometimes all day," he recalled, "but we were uninformed and misinformed."[57] Rhoads pleaded with Collier and Meriam "not to give any publicity to the situation." Nevertheless, Collier was directed by his executive committee to write a press release exposing the compromise. He wrote the release, but before he issued it to the press, he agreed with the commissioners to withhold the story if the commissioners would make an adequate presentation in the Senate hearing on the appropriation bill. Unfortunately, there was a slipup that caused the story to appear in the noon editions; all friendly relations between Collier and the commissioners ended abruptly. Collier returned to his old role as a hostile critic and became a prosecuting witness for the Senate committee investigating Indian affairs.[58]

Meriam regretted losing Collier's support. He felt that Collier had been right on the Klamath Indians and the issue of supplemental appropriations. Moreover, he felt that the commissioners would "get much further if they kept him [Collier] on their team." He wondered if his own usefulness was over. Following the split with Collier the commissioners immediately lost all interest in the legislative program. When they refused to back a proposal for an Indian claims bill because of opposition by the Department of Justice and the Bureau of the Budget, further bad relations inevitably ensued between reformers and the Indian Service.[59] With the defection of Collier, Meriam found himself without active support from the reform movement.[60]

Under these circumstances Meriam's proposal for a Division of Planning and Development met with increased bureaucratic resistance. Initially Rhoads had appeared to favor the proposal. On June 18, 1929, he telephoned Meriam to assure him that he "desired and planned to carry out the recommendations of the Meriam Report with reference to the establishment of a department of planning and development, manned by technical experts."[61] Meriam's proposal, however, was opposed by his old adversaries, the Bureau of the Budget, Cramton, and longtime administrators in the service.

The commissioners, particularly Scattergood, relied increasingly on the advice of veteran administrators. Meriam concluded, in a letter to Guy Moffett of the Rockefeller Foundation, that "neither Commissioner Rhoads nor Commissioner Scattergood ever shared our deep conviction that an independent staff agency was essential for reorganization work." Considering the recommendation as "perhaps desirable but possibly academic," the commissioners had "no such conviction on the subject as would lead them to take the issue to the President."[62] Confronted by an economic crisis of the greatest magnitude, Hoover turned his interests to other matters. In any case, Hoover had proved to be no great advocate of reform, having supported Representative Cramton throughout the appropriations struggle.

The failure to establish a planning division made it necessary for Meriam to pursue a piecemeal strategy. "We were forced," he said, "more or less to muddle along, taking advantage of . . . opportunities as they presented themselves."[63] He set out to help the commissioners get the "right kind of people" into key positions. In this way, he hoped to lay the foundation for administrative reorganization.

The first appointment recommended by Meriam was the most crucial, as he later observed, because "it broke the ice and led to many more."[64] The opportunity to insert an opening wedge in what seemed to be the bureaucratic monolith came with the appointment of Robert Lansdale as field representative to the commissioner. Because he was forceful as well as tactful in recommending changes, Lansdale became the leader of the reform forces within the bureau. As a former executive secretary for the Montclair Council of Social Agencies in New Jersey, he felt he understood from experience how organizations operated. Through his conscientious work in the Indian Service, he not only gained the confidence of Rhoads, but also established a rapport with the older employees. The commissioner was so pleased with his work that he increased Lansdale's staff to include two other social workers.[65]

The next important appointment came in education. Meriam's report had clearly shown that a radical change in Indian education was needed. When Meriam began his work with the Indian Service, the director of education was H. B. Peairs, a man who had many excellent qualities but whose ties with the bureaucracy prevented him from reorganizing his department. At Meriam's suggestion Rhoads established an informal advisory committee on education consisting of Thomas Jesse Jones, Dr. W. Carson Ryan, and Mabel Carney.[66] When Peairs decided to retire early, this committee was in a position to recommend W. Carson Ryan for the directorship. Through an open competitive examination Ryan became director of education on August 20, 1930.[67] Ryan set out immediately to energize the liberal forces in the department.

He established three important new positions for the administration of Indian education: those of a supervisor of elementary education, a supervisor of home economics, and a director of guidance and placement. Cooperating with the Civil Service Commission, he raised the standards for school personnel. Principals were required to have college degrees. New teachers were hired in native arts, vocational trades, and home economics. Social workers and school counselors were introduced into the system.[68] In an attempt to break down the isolation of the Indian schools, Ryan instituted annual regional conferences for superintendents so that they could share experiences and educational techniques. Furthermore, he established a Division of Guidance and Placement, with regional offices in Minneapolis, Kansas City, Albuquerque, Phoenix, Salt Lake City, Los Angeles, and Berkeley.[69] Perhaps most importantly, Ryan implemented a new policy encouraging Indian children to attend public schools.[70]

Ryan's efforts in education were supported by two other divisions, the Division of Agricultural Extension and Industries, headed by A. C. Cooley, and a revitalized Health Service, under M. C. Guthrie. With increased funding, Guthrie expanded his staff to include six traveling doctors, thirty-four field nurses, and sixty-three hospital nurses. The Health Service initiated an extensive program for the prevention of trachoma and tuberculosis, and it supplemented such efforts in preventive medicine by cooperating with state and local public health agencies. Guthrie also insisted that more attention be given to the collection and tabulation of vital statistics.[71]

In education, health, and agricultural extension, Meriam's appointees found much of their work being hindered by a group of administrators who had been with the service for a long time. The stronghold of this group was the Division of Administration, at the head of which was B. S. Garber, a longtime employee of the bureau known for his frugality. All matters of administration, including personnel, went through the Division of Administration before they came to the other division heads. Ryan, for instance, discovered that before he could hire any new employees, their appointments had to be approved by Garber. Meriam's specialists often found their expertise being subordinated to considerations of routine administration.

From his vantage point of working directly under Commissioner Rhoads, Robert Lansdale perceived that breaking Garber's power in the Division of Administration was the key to reorganizing the Indian Service. His close association with the commissioner enabled him to impress Rhoads with the inefficiency of an organizational arrangement in which department heads did not have full responsibility over their agencies. Lansdale's objective came closer to realization as a new breed of technical men gradually began to push out the older administrative men. By the spring of 1931, retirements and transfers out of the service were up 25 percent from 1929, when

Meriam began his work. Initially, as noted earlier, Rhoads resisted moves to reorganize the Indian Service. But Lansdale's continued pressure, along with Garber's own arrogance, finally forced Rhoads to accept reorganization. On March 9, 1931, a reorganization order was issued.[72]

"In my judgment," Meriam wrote to Collier shortly after the signing of the reorganization order, "the reorganization is the best single thing which the Commissioner had done since he took office."[73] What made the order particularly significant, Meriam continued, was "the fact that it puts the new men, Carson Ryan, Bob Lansdale, Cooley . . . in almost complete control of the headquarters office. Garber's old control had been largely broken." In the new order Garber was subordinated to the role of chief clerk of administration, and "the old administrative division which used to rule the roost drops down to its proper place as a facilitating service."[74]

In 1932, Meriam returned to the Institute for Government Research. Although he would be consulted on Indian matters as late as 1936, his major activity would be directed toward the reorganization of the federal government and in evaluating social relief measures proposed by Congress. He believed that he had accomplished his major goal in ameliorating the Indian problem—the reorganization of the Indian Service. The reorganization had been accompanied by other developments that appeared to benefit the Indians. The Hoover administration had nearly doubled appropriations for the Indian Service, from $15 million in 1928 to $28 million in 1931. The food allowance in boarding schools had been raised from 11 cents to 37.8 cents per day, and the clothing allowance from $22 a year to $40 a year. The work force had increased nearly 300 percent with the addition of 2,000 employees. Agency salaries had increased 25 percent. The Indian Service began cooperating on a closer basis with state social service and health agencies.[75]

Nevertheless, many of Meriam's contemporaries as well as later historians condemned the Rhoads administration as a failure. For instance, F. Running Bear, the executive counsel of the American Indian Association, praised the "unselfish spirit of Commissioner Rhoads," but deplored the fact that "his administration . . . had resulted in a greater, more comprehensive bureaucracy than before." He pointed to the fact that 46.9 percent of the bureau's total expenditures went for salaries, wages, and personnel expenses. Critics could point also to the failure to enact any important legislation. Rhoads's only success had been with the passage of the Leavitt bill, which relieved Indians from liens on their land totaling millions of dollars.[76] Yet his legislative proposal covering arts and crafts, land claims, and new experimentation in federal-state relations for Indian affairs (the Swing-Johnson bill, 1931) had not received congressional approval.

Meriam had failed in a more important respect. A fundamental assumption of the Rhoads administration had been the long-standing belief that Indians should be assimilated into American life. Meriam himself conceded a potentially significant lapse when he observed that the "investigation of the problem of the Indian Administration made by the IGR had not considered the fundamental question as to whether the country's policy with reference to the Indians was based upon an adequate understanding of the nature of the Indian himself." The IGR had "proceeded upon the assumption that the existing American policy with reference to the Indian, namely that of teaching him the white man's way of living, was sound."[77] Thus Meriam and the IGR had missed an opportunity for real reform of Indian policy.

Yet to call Rhoads's administration or Meriam's assistance to the Indian Service an utter failure is too harsh, for this judgment neglects the nearly insurmountable problems created by previous administrations. Significantly, Collier was impressed enough with Meriam's work to write him asking whether he would be interested in the post of commissioner, if Roosevelt were elected in 1932. In the same letter, Collier suggested that Meriam arrange a meeting with Roosevelt to discuss the problems of Indians, in the same way that the IGR had met with President-elect Harding in 1922 to discuss the problems of a national budget.[78]

Meriam replied that the best man to meet with Roosevelt would be George Foster Peabody, a liberal of long standing from New York. Meriam further advised that Peabody could best be approached through Thomas Jesse Jones of the Rockefeller Foundation. Meriam told Collier that he supported Roosevelt's candidacy, "for it is time we had a more liberal person in office," and that he hoped Roosevelt, once in office, would appoint a new commissioner. Meriam felt no hesitancy in recommending the removal of Rhoads and Scattergood from office. Still, he suggested that Roosevelt be approached with not just one name, but a list of names, pointing to a "type instead of an individual" who would best serve the Indians as commissioner. He added that his own name should probably not be included in the list because he lacked administrative experience.[79]

Meriam admitted to Collier, however, that he had "never felt less certain about my future, but I am not thinking about it. It does not do any good." Without offering to elaborate, he confided that "I am reasonably certain that the Indian work has hurt rather than improved my standing within the walls of Brookings whatever it may have done outside."[80] Perhaps Meriam's role had become somewhat too activist for the Brookings Institution, but whatever difficulties he may have had with the institution were soon worked out. His reputation among liberals and with Congress proved over time to be a great asset to the Brookings Institution.

In 1937 Meriam was selected to act as a liaison between the President's Committee on Reorganization and the Brookings Institution, both of which were working for Congress on executive reorganization. Ironically, by this time Meriam had moved away from liberalism in his own politics, now fearing the increased power of the president, particularly in fiscal matters. Although he had favored increased appropriations for Indians in 1931, by 1938 he shuddered at the consequences of deficit spending brought about by the various relief measures of the New Deal. In particular, he emerged as a vocal critic of social security and compulsory health insurance. The administrative reformer had become a fiscal conservative.

6 · THE INSTITUTION IN THE NEW DEAL: THE
NONPARTISAN IDEAL IN THE LIBERAL STATE

I N THE midst of the most severe political and economic crisis that
American capitalism had experienced since the depression of the
1890s, in a decade that called desperately for new policies and programs to sustain economic recovery and alleviate the suffering of
thousands of unemployed workers, the Brookings Institution, under Harold Moulton, failed in its mission to act as an innovator in
public policy. This failure was a peculiar result of the institution's
perceived obligation to stand for the public interest of society against
partisan political forces that seemed to subvert the free workings of
the marketplace. Thus after a brief flirtation with Roosevelt during
the first chaotic days of his administration, the Brookings Institution became increasingly distant from the New Deal, while remaining strident in its defense of the market economy against the intrusion of the government. The institution declined to play the role of
a mediator between the state and liberal capitalists who sought cooperation with the government in order to rationalize the economy
and to mollify the masses. Rather, the Brookings Institution's obstinate defense of the market against state interference in the economy,
as proposed by New Deal reformers, prevented it from acting as a
liaison between government and the liberal elements in the business
class.

Some historians have suggested that business came to terms with
Roosevelt by the late 1930s.[1] Yet the Brookings's continued opposition to New Deal policies, and Moulton's subsequent crusade
against Keynesian economics, indicates that not everybody with a

business orientation made peace with the liberal state. The marriage between business and government proposed in the Progressive period, and consummated by Hoover in the following decade, ended in dissolution decreed by Franklin Roosevelt in the 1930s. To many, including the staff at the Brookings Institution, this divorce between government and business was for the best.

Still, certain businessmen sought to restore government-business cooperation. These businessmen, labeled corporatists by some historians, were assisted by a small group of social scientists who envisaged a corporate liberal state that allowed government to cooperate with business for the benefit of both.[2] By the late 1930s corporatist efforts centered on three areas: government reorganization designed to strengthen the executive branch of the federal government, a modified Keynesian program that accepted fiscal deficits but not a meaningful redistribution of wealth, and increased government planning through the National Resources Planning Board.

The Brookings Institution, whose policies were articulated by Moulton, fought each point in the liberal program—government reorganization, deficit spending, and national planning. The institution regarded the liberal program as a crude attempt to politicize the economy by those who failed to appreciate the delicate workings of the market. This opposition to the corporatist program presents an anomaly for those historians who interpret recent America in corporate liberal terms. A corporatist interpretation would expect an agency such as the Brookings Institution to act as a mediator between liberal capitalists and the state by assisting the Roosevelt administration in developing a political and economic agenda.

Yet contrary to the corporate liberal interpretation, capitalist institutions are not monolithic. Each institution develops a unique character that is determined by its history and the men who serve the institution. Of course, this character is framed within the social-political setting of the society within which the institution operates, but nonetheless institutions take on their own personalities. In the case of the Brookings Institution, its character was shaped by men such as Harold Moulton who adhered vehemently to a belief that the proper role of the staff social scientists was to serve and protect the public interest. This view of the nonpartisan expert was elitist in nature, but this perspective also prevented the institution from obsequious service to class interests. Furthermore, this idealization of nonpartisan expertise, developed at the turn of

5. The Brookings Institution building, 1931–1959: 722 Jackson Place, N.W., Washington, D.C. (Courtesy of the Brookings Institution Archives)

the century by economists such as Richard Ely and promulgated by mugwump reformers, is crucial to understanding Moulton and his institution during the 1930s. Moulton's training in economics only strengthened his belief that the public interest would best be protected by a market economy, which, if functioning at its optimum, should be able to correct economic ills and to ameliorate, as far as possible, social inequalities. The view of social scientists as defenders of the public interest, it seems, prevented the institution from acting as a positive force in the highly politicized Roosevelt administration. Moulton nevertheless continued to see himself as a liberal. He asserted that "our basic purpose is to help bring about a more efficiently functioning economic system. This is what I call reconstructive liberalism."[3] In this respect the staff of the Brookings Institution continued to meet the standards of the professional mugwump tradition: they were nonpartisans who distrusted political motivation.

There were ironies to be seen in this tradition, however, as it was carried into the decade of depression. Whereas once the mugwumps had sought to weaken Congress and strengthen the chief executive, now the Brookings Institution sought to preserve congressional power. Where once the institution had urged economic innovation in theory and in practice, now it would defend economic dogma. Now the marketplace became a fixed and rational entity. Social scientists in the past had promulgated a faith in man's ability to control economic forces. Now, Moulton felt obliged to declare that "in the long run the decisions of the marketplace are the truest guide to economic production and development." From this principle, which Moulton considered a basic truth of modern civilization, he concluded that men could exert little influence over the underlying mechanism of the marketplace. "It follows," he said, "that the ill consequences of depression cannot be averted. The most that can be hoped is that the slow process of education may bring increased moderation in good times."[4] In the past, social scientists had expressed some distrust of the masses, but they had remained confident of the expert's ability to control the course of economic society. By the 1930s even this limited sense of the power of man's rationality would be questioned in Brookings Institution publications.

The view that man ultimately had little control over capitalist society, at least to the extent of doing any good, directly challenged the New Deal program and the assumptions of most of the social science community. Men such as Charles Merriam, a Chicago political scientist, Louis Brownlow, director of the Public Administration Clearing House, Beardsley Ruml, an idea man for philanthropic and liberal business circles, and even Frederic Delano, chairman of the board at the Brookings Institution, maintained a traditional social science faith that man could intervene in society to further mankind's progress. These men were willing to accept FDR's crisis leadership and the New Deal program.[5] They were willing to enter into politics, to interpret the facts, and to plead a cause, while the Brookings Institution sought to maintain its distance in order to remain objectively nonpartisan. To those social scientists who favored the New Deal, the Brookings Institution's attitude seemed to be only a presumptuous pretense masking an implicit political outlook. Frederic Delano, however, eventually came to accept these criticisms, which in time precipitated a crisis within the Brookings Institution leading to Delano's resignation. Delano reflected the deep division in the applied social science community itself, as well as the Brookings Institution's growing isolation from the mainstream of contemporary thought.

Much of the tone of the Brookings Institution was set by Harold Moulton. At no other time in the institution's history, in fact, would one man exert such a powerful influence over both the trustees and the staff. Hugh Johnson went so far as to charge that the institution had become a "pressure bureau to publicize the ideas of Harold Moulton."[6] Johnson's charges were made in response to Moulton's criticisms of the National Recovery Administration (NRA), an agency headed by Johnson, but nevertheless there was something to the accusation. Of course the rest of the staff were too intellectually independent to simply kowtow obediently to any one man or any single doctrine, but all the same Moulton's thinking on current issues found its way into many of the Brookings's studies during this time. Supremely confident of his abilities, Moulton bowled over his lesser opponents, won over his equals with sheer intellectual power, and condescended to his betters. For instance, after only two meetings with John Maynard Keynes in 1924 and 1931, Moulton concluded that this eminent British economist simply did not understand the basic principles of economic reasoning.[7] One primary idea had become central in Moulton's thinking: "Be moderate, particularly when it comes to government spending." The strength of his own personality pushed this concept forward until it became part of the character of the institution. Those who could

6. Lewis Meriam, Leverett Lyon, William F. Willoughby, and Edwin G. Nourse. (Courtesy of the Brookings Institution Archives)

not accept Moulton's outlook departed to join the New Deal, leaving Moulton largely with colleagues of the same mind as himself.

Moulton rejected out of hand the New Deal premise that the purchasing power of the masses could be increased by putting men to work on relief projects. Such projects in fact, he believed, threatened to create a destructively unbalanced budget and eventually inflation. He was not a believer in laissez-faire economics, however. Nor did he accept the doctrines promulgated by monetarists such as Ludwig von Mises and Friedrick von Hayek.[8] Moulton believed that ultimately purchasing power, not money supply or interest rates, determined economic conditions. Government did have a role to play in the economy, but the burden of productive growth lay principally with business and its ability to increase the purchasing power of the masses. The most important role that government could play was the creation of favorable conditions so that business could regulate itself. From the outset of the Depression, Moulton urged the establishment of a government board, modeled closely on the War Industries Board, to support self-regulation among American businessmen.

Moulton was not a profound thinker, but he was consistent, careful, and frequently insightful. For these reasons he earned respect among the Brookings trustees. Furthermore, Moulton gave continuity to the board, which experienced constant flux during the Depression years. From the founding of the institution in 1927 to America's entrance into World War II in 1941, thirty-six different men served on the board of trustees, with only three of these, Harold Moulton, Jerome Greene, and Leo S. Rowe, serving for the entire period. Some who left the board resigned to take care of their own businesses during the Depression. In 1930 Frank Goodnow and Raymond Fosdick, founding members of the IGR, resigned because of age.[9] Death took many as well. Of the nineteen founding board members, seven had died by 1935, including Robert S. Brookings in 1932. George Eastman died in the same year. During these years of upheaval, it fell to Harold Moulton to provide experience and coherence in board meetings. In the process Moulton's prestige among board members was enhanced. He represented tradition, and in this instance tradition imparted power.

Similar changes in the composition of the staff added further to Moulton's influence. In 1933, the Brookings maintained a staff of only fifteen members. A year earlier Moulton had encouraged the retirement of six staff members from the old IGR, including W. F. Willoughby. With the start of the New Deal, many of the younger economists left the institution to enter government. Isador Lubin joined the Roosevelt administration in 1933. Lewis Lorwin, another labor economist, also departed, in 1935, to work in government.[10] Moulton throughout the decade of the 1930s hired only six new staff members to replace those who left, but many of these also moved on within two or three years. Thus much of the work fell to a group of senior staff members, Nourse, Pasvolsky, Lyon, Meriam, and Moulton. What was most lacking at the institution during these years was not experience, but the transfusion of new blood that is necessary for the continuing vitality of any organization.

While the institution experienced extensive changes in its board and staff, a financial crisis threatened the very existence of the Brookings organization. That the institution survived this period can be attributed to Harold Moulton, who now found himself playing yet another role—that of fund raiser. The Depression cut heavily into the institution's financial stability. Both traditional foundation support and new contributions dwindled. In early 1931 a ten-year grant from the Carnegie Corporation ended and Moulton was informed that he could expect no further assistance. In the same year a seven-year grant from the Laura Spelman-Rockefeller Foundation also ran out. To make matters worse, Robert Brookings, who had contributed over $1 million, warned that the institution could expect no further endowment money from him.[11] If Moulton had ever thought he could persuade him otherwise, Brookings's death the next year ended that hope.

In these dire circumstances Moulton sought other sources of money. Moulton thoroughly disliked "going around, cup in hand," as he later described it, but nevertheless, he realized that he could no longer count on adequate endowments from established sources. With the income from the institution's investments amounting to little more than $30,000 a year, Moulton accepted the fact that the institution must fight for its survival. First he changed the Brookings Institution's investment practices to raise income. He began investing funds in the construction and operation of office buildings in the Washington area. (Moulton would discover at least one advantage to the growth of government.) At the same time he began to invest in preferred stocks rather than in bonds.[12]

In addition, institutional expenses were cut and new areas of research were developed. Now less emphasis was placed on foreign affairs and more on domestic policy. Moulton directed the staff to undertake "efficiency and economy" studies for a number of state governments on a contractual basis—work once rejected by the Brookings economists as mundane and, therefore, relatively unimportant. In the next decade, the institution would undertake work in North Carolina (1930), Alabama, New Hampshire and Mississippi (1933), and Iowa (1934). Such work paid the bills and also enabled the Brookings to play a key role in reorganizing the governments of these states.

Nevertheless, Moulton saw such work as an underutilization of talent. Some Brookings men, indeed, had shown themselves capable of handling much larger projects. For example, the director of the state surveys, Arthur Millspaugh, before joining the institution in 1929, had served as Persia's financial adviser from 1922 to 1928. In this capacity, which qualified him as the second most powerful person in the nation, he had helped reorganize Persia's fiscal system, succeeded in nearly balancing the national budget, and introduced a tax system that would continue into the 1970s.[13] Yet only four years after his service to the Shah of Persia, Millspaugh found himself acting as an adviser to the governor of Mississippi on how best to strengthen the executive house in a state quite suspicious of strong governors.

Never tiring in his efforts to sustain the Brookings, Moulton also devised a scheme to attract railroad money by initiating an in-depth study of the nation's transportation system. In early 1931 he undertook a national speaking tour of major cities to lecture on transportation problems. After completing the tour he traveled to New York, where he met with the editor of the *Railway Age* to discuss his proposal for a comprehensive transportation study. The two men, joined by a representative of a major New York bank, conceived of the idea of the National Transportation Committee to sponsor the study. In the fall of 1932 such a committee was duly formed, consisting of Calvin Coolidge, Bernard Baruch, Alfred E. Smith, and Alexander Legge.

The funds for the study of the nation's rail system came from principal investors of railroad securities, insurance companies, and savings banks—and, as Moulton later recalled, "four universities (brought in for window dressing)." The principal investigator for the project was Charles Dearing, a Brookings transportation economist. The final report concluded that the efficient movement of traffic by the cheapest agency or combination of agencies cannot be "realized under an uncoordinated regulatory system such as we now possess."[14] The committee agreed that railroads should effect their own consolidation without government interference, but it repeatedly clashed over the issue of railroads versus motor transportation. On one side stood Bernard Baruch, who urged increased taxation of trucks and buses to lessen the attraction of automotive transportation. He was confronted by New Yorkers Al Smith, a partner of John J. Raskob and the DuPonts (major stockholders in General Motors), and Robert Moses, a former member of the Bureau of Municipal Research, who, by 1932, was already dreaming of building a New York highway system. At times the clashes between the committee members became so heated that they nearly came to blows. This dissension among capitalists should have suggested to Moulton and others that industrial self-regulation was unlikely and that governmental involvement would be needed to improve the transportation situation.

It was not until late 1932 that the institution's financial problems were eased somewhat through a large grant from the Maurice and Laura Falk Foundation. The head of the Falk Foundation, J. Steele Gow, a conservative steel magnate, had met Moulton through the foundation's close contacts with the Social Science Research Council. In one of their meetings Moulton proposed to Gow that the

Falk Foundation sponsor a project that would focus on America's economic capacity for recovery from the Depression. Pleased with what he saw as Moulton's "conservative character," Gow readily agreed to finance the study if Moulton would promise two things: first, to remain president of the Brookings Institution while the study was being conducted; and second, to personally direct the study to its conclusion.[15] In the past, Moulton had hesitated before making such promises. Now he was willing to accept such strings provided that they did not interfere with the quality of the study.

Contrary to Gow's perceptions, in 1932 neither the Brookings Institution nor Harold Moulton was what could accurately be described as conservative. If anything, Brookings economists at the outset of the Depression were slightly in the forefront of current economic thinking. Moulton believed that the price mechanism of a capitalist economy remained the primary tool for distributing national wealth, but for this reason he also believed that the government should intervene to break up cartels, which artificially restricted prices. Nevertheless, he opposed a deficit spending policy.

On the whole, a sense of fiscal moderation pervaded the economic profession during the first years of the Depression.[16] Senator Robert Wagner discovered this when he polled leading economists throughout the country in the spring of 1932 concerning his proposal for a billion-dollar public-works bill. Many of the economists endorsed Wagner's bill, but with great hesitation and with a great number of qualifications. For instance, Edwin Dickinson of the University of Illinois told Wagner that government should "tighten its belt, balance its budget and appropriate directly for the relief of the needy such sums as are absolutely necessary."[17] A chorus of other economists including Walton Hamilton, J. M. Clark, Irving Fisher, Stacy May, and Frank Knight expressed similar concerns about a balanced budget. Even as late as 1933, after Roosevelt had assumed office, Jacob Viner, a well-respected economist, declared that the only hope of relief was for the nation to cut expenditures further and to return to a "drastic balanced deflation."[18] And Alvin Hansen summarized the feelings of most economists when he warned that government deficits and public works, a stopgap at best, would only harm the capital market.[19] In the nation's most protracted depression it seemed that economists were unwilling to break with established truths. In many ways the general public proved more willing to experiment. Accordingly, as one economist noted, "The economist . . . has little prestige with the American public, even on those subjects in which he alone has expert knowledge, and the public prefers to take its economics from newspaper editors, politicians, and bankers."[20]

Even Franklin Roosevelt showed himself to be a fiscal conservative in the early stages of the New Deal. During the presidential campaign of 1932, Roosevelt attacked Hoover's fiscal irresponsibility, promising to eliminate government waste and return the nation to a balanced budget. His promises to balance the budget should be seen as more than political rhetoric, even though once he was in office he would be forced into deficit spending practices in order to finance his relief measures. The president's concern with balancing the budget was evident in his appointment of Lewis Douglas, who was prevailed upon to resign his seat in Congress to become director of the Bureau of the Budget. Douglas was asked to attend all Cabinet meetings, and he had a standing appointment in Roosevelt's bedroom each morning between 9:00 and 9:30 to discuss the business of the day.[21]

Furthermore, one of the first measures of the Roosevelt administration was to ask Congress on March 10, 1933, only six days after the inauguration, to pass an economy act that would reduce the compensation of federal employees and cut veterans' benefits. Roosevelt's concern with increasing governmental deficits was expressed in urgent terms: "With the utmost seriousness I point out to the Congress the profound effect of this fact [the increase in deficit spending] upon our national economy. It has contributed to the recent collapse of our banking structure. It has accentuated the stagnation of the economic life of our people. It has added to the ranks of the unemployed. Our government's house is not in order and for many reasons no effective action has been taken to restore it to order."[22] Such sentiments not only endeared Roosevelt to fiscal moderates within his own party, men like William Douglas, John Garner, and Bernard Baruch, but won him the support of many outside the party who would later break with him, among them Harold G. Moulton.[23]

The acrimony that characterized the relations between the New Deal and the Brookings Institution developed gradually, largely because the direction the Roosevelt administration would take was not at first clear. In fact, initially all signs pointed toward a close working relationship between FDR and the Brookings. In many respects Lewis Meriam's work with Indians, and the Institute of Economics' studies on agriculture and the coal industry in the 1920s, foreshadowed the kinds of problems faced by the New Deal in the 1930s. Furthermore, Moulton had opposed Hoover's bid for re-election, largely because of his failure to lower tariff rates imposed by the Hawley-Smoot Act and his plan to build the St. Lawrence Seaway.

During the campaign, Moulton contacted Roosevelt through FDR's uncle, Frederic Delano, chairman of the board at Brookings, to offer the services of the institution. Moulton felt that the reorganization of federal agencies would be a major step in cutting government expenses. He wrote to Delano, assuming that his remarks would be conveyed to FDR, that "the task for us would probably be facilitated if the democratic Party [sic] were elected."[24] Shortly afterward, Moulton received word from Roosevelt that the Democratic candidate was definitely interested in government reorganization, an interest dating back to his days as assistant secretary of the navy when he had testified in favor of Willoughby's reorganization plans. "Quite frankly," Roosevelt wrote, "we need help. Because I know of the splendid work that has been done by you and the Institution . . . I hope that you will be able to give us some assistance in the preparation of a fairly definite plan between now and early March."[25] Moulton then assigned a Brookings group to examine ways in which government could be reorganized and expenses cut, and Roosevelt selected a former congressman, J. Swager Sherley, to act as liaison with this staff.

Working on the principle that the key to retrenchment lay in the financial administration of government, members of the Brookings group began holding meetings with government officials. In a series of memoranda, Charles Hardy and Paul David outlined the current financial practices of the Bureau of the Budget. Moulton and Arnold Bennett Hall, who had recently joined the staff and later was to become president of the University of Oregon, began regular meetings with the new director of the budget, Lewis Douglas, and the secretary of commerce, Daniel C. Roper. Moulton and Hall strongly argued that the Bureau of the Budget be strengthened and expanded into an office of general business administration, directly under the President.[26] Once in office, Roosevelt temporarily dropped immediate plans for government reorganization, but the issue would be raised again in Roosevelt's second term.

Moulton's contacts with top administration people also allowed him the opportunity to promote his plans for self-regulation of business. Shortly before the inauguration, Moulton again wrote to Delano. Next to the banking situation, he observed, the condition of industry required the most immediate attention. "The only answer I can see," he declared, "is to set up a 'War Industries Board.'" Of course, Moulton continued, the situation had been different when the WIB was formed. Then, the problem was to promote production, whereas in 1933 the problem was to control it. Still, "in both cases there must be and was a necessity to regulate."[27]

Moulton's proposal for a new planning board was not original. Throughout the 1920s, a number of economists including Paul Douglas, Stuart Chase, and Rexford Tugwell continued to discuss various planning schemes stemming from their experience with wartime socialism. At the Brookings Institution, before the disbanding of the Graduate School, frequent discussions had been held concerning planning in the Soviet Union and in Mussolini's Italy.[28] For instance, following a trip to the Soviet Union in 1927, Tugwell had come to speak to the students at the Graduate School on the success of Russia's planned society.[29]

Now, in 1932, the Depression brought a new sense of urgency to these discussions. Before Moulton wrote his letter to Delano he must have been aware of Charles Beard's plan, endorsed by the editors of the liberal *Forum*, which called for the repeal of antitrust legislation and urged Congress to establish syndicates first in agriculture and housing, in order to lay the foundation of what he called a National Economic Council. By 1932 others saw planning as the wave of the future. For instance, the American Historical Association's Committee on Social Studies predicted that "the economy of individualism will be superseded by a cooperative economy based on popular consent."[30]

Certain businessmen also espoused planning as a way out of the Depression. For example, Owen Young of General Electric felt little hesitation in generalizing that "every advance in social organization requires the voluntary surrender of a certain amount of individual freedom by the minority and the ultimate coercion of the majority." The Chamber of Commerce simply declared, "We have left the period of extreme individualism."[31] Gerard Swope, also a General Electric executive, perhaps best articulated these planning sentiments for business by proposing the formation of trade associations throughout industries. While Swope's plan harked back to the more moderate associationalist views prevalent in business during the twenties, Beard represented the leftist end of the planning spectrum. Nevertheless, there was widespread agreement that planning of some sort was necessary for recovery and that antitrust legislation should be repealed, or ignored.

Moulton's suggestion for the revitalization of the WIB, therefore, was right in line with current thinking among enlightened businessmen and social scientists. Indeed, his proposals gave further impetus to the planning movement. Working closely with a former congressman from New Jersey, Meyer Jacobstein, who had recently been hired by the Brookings Institution to act as a liaison with Congress, Moulton enunciated a detailed plan of his own that called for close cooperation between government and industry. His plan was no doubt an amalgam of ideas and proposals brought forward by the Chamber of Commerce, businessmen such as Swope, organized labor, and government officials. As Walton Hamilton, by then a professor at Yale, later remarked, "The term 'self-government in industry' had a sonorous sound, an instantaneous appeal, and just the right touch of vagueness to appeal to everyone."[32] Through the "self-regulation of business," Moulton sought to encourage managerial efficiency, while maintaining current wage rates. Significantly, his plan, in contrast to those of others, did not project any widespread price-fixing mechanism, although it did embody the ideal of trade cooperation and class reciprocity. Specifically Moulton called for the formation of an agency, something like the War Industries Board, that would oversee the formation of self-regulated trade associations in certain key industries. At this point, Moulton accepted price fixing by selected industries through self-regulation. In a sense, then, his program was more limited than that of the WIB or that subsequently embodied in the NRA.

By March 6, 1933, Moulton was ready to take his plan to the Roosevelt administration. His first step was to send a memorandum, "A Plan for Economic Recovery," to Raymond Moley, a former professor from Columbia who had become a member of Roosevelt's "Brain Trust." Moulton's memorandum would later be described by historians as a "program for industrial loans," but a careful reading of the proposal shows that it was much more than that.[33] The memorandum was in fact a proposal to establish an agency to oversee and encourage self-regulation in specific industries. It also developed detailed arguments against other proposals dealing with public works, banking devices, and monetary policy. Moulton conceded that Hoover had taken positive steps in solving the economic crisis by attempting to balance the budget and by establishing the Reconstruction Finance Corporation, but he argued that more drastic measures were now called for. "The heart of the problem is to set the wheels of industry moving," and the "ultimate key" to an improved economy could be found in increasing the purchasing power of the masses.[34] Moulton advocated, therefore, that government secure unified or collective action on the part of all businesses in a number of *selected* industries. He stressed that he did not envisage the extension of collective action to all manufacturers or to small businesses. The first step in establishing self-regulation would be the creation of a National Board for Industrial Recovery with powers similar to the WIB. Congress, Moulton added, should confer on this board the authority to suspend antitrust laws. At the same time this board would establish production schedules and would formulate employment and wage policies in key industries. To guarantee production, the government would extend loans to these selected industries.

Shortly after Moulton sent this memorandum to Moley, he drafted a legislative bill incorporating the basics of his proposal. Early in April, Moulton took this bill to Senator Robert Wagner with the suggestion that he sponsor it in conjunction with other recovery measures he was supporting. Meanwhile, Jacobstein submitted a memorandum to FDR that summarized Moulton's bill. To further ensure FDR's support, Moulton asked Frederic Delano, who had been consulted during the drafting of the bill, to speak directly with his nephew concerning the proposal. At the same time, Moulton and Jacobstein initiated a lobbying effort of their own by holding a series of conferences with Ray Moley, Paul Warburg, and Bernard Baruch. In late April they extended their discussions to include various cabinet members, such as Secretary of Commerce Daniel Roper, Secretary of State Cordell Hull, Secretary of Agriculture Henry Wallace, Postmaster General James Farley, and Secretary of Labor Frances Perkins. Jacobstein also attempted to rally labor support by discussing the plan with Sidney Hillman, a ranking official of the Amalgamated Clothing Workers Union.

At FDR's suggestion, Robert Wagner finally established a committee in May to explore the entire recovery program. Present at the first meeting of the committee was a group of individuals from business and government who had submitted various proposals for industrial recovery, including Harold Moulton and Meyer Jacobstein.[35] At the end of the conference, Moulton was selected along with David Podell, a lawyer, and W. Jett Lauck, an economist, to draft a bill for industrial recovery. This initial bill built the foundation of what was to become the National Industrial Recovery Act, but in the process Moulton's original proposal would be broadened to include all industry and to provide for price fixing.

While this group was meeting, two other committees had been formed at the Commerce Department and the Agriculture Department to draft recovery measures. The committee from Agriculture, headed by Jerome Frank, was working on a public works bill. On May 5, three days after the first meeting of the Wagner group, representatives from Frank's committee met with Moulton in his office to collaborate on consolidating the two measures. The final compromise reached included a proposal to extend credits to industry, shorten work hours, and outlaw price cuts.

At this point Moulton and Jacobstein were clearly making progress with their proposal. But the addition of the committee from Commerce to the Wagner-Frank group suddenly changed the tone of the discussions. The combined group turned to considering the need of establishing base prices for production costs to apply to each trade association. The concept of base prices represented a direct challenge to both Moulton and Jacobstein, who felt that setting such prices would allow certain industries to profit artificially by the industrial codes. Ultimately prices should be set by the market, they said, but they were unable to convince the others of their position. Feeling that they had no recourse, Moulton and Jacobstein dropped out of the proceedings. At nearly the same time, Moley invited Hugh Johnson, a former WIB official and close associate of Bernard Baruch's who wanted an expanded program, to draft the final version of the bill. Johnson's draft was subsequently passed as the National Industrial Recovery Act, which established the National Recovery Administration.

When the NIRA became law, Moulton at first claimed great credit, but actually profound differences separated his proposal from the final bill. He eventually came to regret in particular that the bill had been expanded to include all industries, when he had proposed that only certain key industries be specified for supervision by the national agency. Moreover, he believed that the Johnson bill invested the president with too much power, particularly in the area of foreign trade. Moulton maintained that in order to maintain price levels, Roosevelt would have to restrict imports, and that this restriction would limit the ability of European countries to buy American cotton and other farm produce. Most important to Moulton, however, was the threat that the NRA, through its base-price system, would pose to the operation of the free market.[36]

Moulton's criticism of the base-price system was a harbinger of future difficulties within the NRA, which almost from the beginning was plagued with internal dissension. Leon Henderson, a liberal economist who took over the Research and Planning Division of the NRA in 1934, made his group the center of opposition to price controls.[37] He was joined in this fight by Leverett Lyon, who had become deputy administrator of the Trade Practices Section. Like Henderson, Lyon desired open price provisions, cost discounts, and uniform price differentials instead of rigid price controls.[38] Confronted by continued opposition from other NRA officials and business lobbyists, Lyon offered his resignation after a short time in office in order to return to the Brookings Institution.

By the autumn of 1934 the dispute over price controls had become a political issue in Congress. Under pressure from that body, as well as from labor and consumers, Roosevelt appointed a review committee headed by Clarence Darrow to investigate problems within the NRA. The final report of the Darrow Committee caught many by surprise. Darrow charged that the NRA was in fact promoting monopolistic exploitation of the market by large business. Furthermore, he affirmed the criticisms of the base-price system that had been voiced by the Federal Trade Commission, the Agricultural Adjustment Administration, and certain congressmen. With the Darrow report in hand, Congress finally undertook a major review of the National Industrial Recovery Act, which had been in operation less than two years but which was coming up for reconsideration.[39]

It was at this point that the Brookings Institution stepped directly into the fray. In a series of studies conducted under the direction of Lyon, Brookings economists examined the NRA closely, and they reported on it in highly critical terms. Their criticisms followed the line that had been set by Moulton in 1933. First, the economists concluded, the NRA had been unnecessarily expanded to cover the entire range of business activity, instead of being confined to a select group of major industries. In the process of this expansive evolution, the agency had developed into a "sprawling administrative colossus without clearly defined policy." The NRA bureaucracy could not even discharge its responsibilities for price setting and compliance with codes.[40] As a result the operations of the NRA were ineffective as a recovery measure. While admitting that the NRA's effect on the economy could not be measured precisely, Lyon and his associates pointed to indications that the agency had in fact retarded "the expansion of income for labor and capital alike." It seemed clear to the Lyon group that the NRA, by setting high commodity prices and high wage rates, had worked against increases in man hours worked and units of goods produced. That economic conditions were not propitious for a sizable expansion of wages in key industries seemed obvious to the Brookings economists and they said so.[41]

Opponents of the NRA immediately seized upon the Brookings studies to bolster their arguments. The chairman of the powerful Senate Finance Committee, Pat Harrison of Mississippi, who had seen parts of Lyon's report, *The National Recovery Administration*, in proof, read unfavorable portions of the study into the *Congressional Record*.[42] Two months after the publication of the report in book form, the U.S. Supreme Court ruled that the National Industrial Recovery Act was unconstitutional.

Lyon's study of the NRA signaled a growing uneasiness on the part of the Brookings Institution toward the Roosevelt recovery program in general. Although Moulton had welcomed FDR's election in 1932, by 1934 there was a prevalent feeling at the institution that Roosevelt was playing politics with the economy, as seen in his willingness to appease all interest groups and his continued policy of deficit spending. The Brookings Institution, on the other hand, believed that its mission was to represent the public interest and to offer a course of action based on objective economic study. This concern with objective truth was expressed in the Brookings Institution's "capacity" studies, undertaken at the request of the Falk Foundation. The capacity studies would be the most important theoretical work that the institution undertook during the Depression. The series consisted of four books: *America's Capacity to Produce* (1933), *America's Capacity to Consume* (1934), *The Formation of Capital* (1935), and *Income and Economic Progress* (1935). The purpose of these books was clearly stated in the first volume: "Only on the basis of real understanding of the motivating forces in economic progress can the nation's accomplishments in the years ahead be commensurate with the opportunities within our reach."[43] Until the National Resources Planning Board undertook its major studies of consumer incomes and expenditures in 1938, the Brookings capacity studies remained the major guide to the economy for policy makers, liberal and conservative alike.

When completed, the first two volumes, which were concerned with production capacity and consumption capacity in the 1920s, drew two major conclusions about the causes of the Depression and the way toward recovery. First, the masses of people, because of their low standard of living in the 1920s, had not been able to accumulate savings of real significance. Secondly, it followed from this conclusion that the bulk of the nation's savings was in the hands of a small fraction of the population, those in higher income brackets. The third volume of the studies, *The Formation of Capital*, authored by Moulton, showed in anticipation of Keynes that money saved was not necessarily spent for capital goods. In the 1920s too much capital had been diverted toward speculation or toward the gaining of ownership and control of industries, instead of being invested in new capital construction.[44] In fact, the growth of the stock market and the accelerated movement of industrial mergers had diverted capital from productive avenues of growth toward speculation.

The conclusions of the capacity studies led the Brookings investigators to the belief that the distribution of income throughout society should be made more even. This recommendation was not as radical as one might think, for the studies made a sharp distinction between equality of wealth and a fair distribution of income. In so doing, they expressed opposition to any panaceas that promised to equalize wealth in America. Some differences in wealth among people were natural. On the other hand, however, it would not be appropriate for the United States to have a class-ridden society. At the basis of American capitalism the Brookings Institution saw a reciprocity of class interests, for "we all work for one another and the employers and the employees are the same people." Employment and production were complementary concepts: "One generates the other, one is not independent of the other."[45] The best way to distribute income fairly, therefore, was not by passing class legislation but by lowering production costs through increased managerial and technological efficiency. In effect, if prices were lowered, real wages would be increased and income fairly distributed. "The highway along which continued economic progress must be sought," the studies proclaimed, "is the avenue of price reductions. When this road is followed the benefits of technical improvements are conferred automatically upon the divisions of the population."[46]

Here was the essence of the good society as Moulton saw it: class reciprocity, an equal exchange of benefits from one class to the other. The nonpartisan expert stood above class interests, imparting the technical wisdom that established the basis for efficient management and technological advance. Moulton distrusted politicians, particularly Roosevelt, because they were given to passing legislation aimed at benefiting one class over the other. For this reason partisan politics was a disruptive force in American society. Moulton saw Roosevelt's support of relief appropriations and extensive public works programs primarily as an attempt to win voters. Such programs had created a federal deficit estimated at $7.3 billion. By 1934 Moulton was not alone in his feelings that Roosevelt was motivated solely by politics and that this fact accounted for the deficit. That same year Lewis Douglas resigned as director of the budget over the issue of deficits. Furthermore, many Republicans would charge that the sizable Works Progress Administration allocations under Harry Hopkins were political in nature.[47] Moulton was upset by his awareness of this political component that appeared to be built into relief spending. Yet he recognized that anti–New Dealers, in accusing the Roosevelt administration of political motivations, were themselves acting for partisan reasons. Moulton tried to keep the institution above the partisan fray; inevitably he was drawn into it.

Yet, even as late as the election of 1936, Moulton refused to provide direct ammunition to Roosevelt's opponents. The institution's critical studies of the Agricultural Adjustment Administration were a case in point. While Lyon was working on his study of the NRA, Edwin Nourse of the Brookings had undertaken a far-reaching, multivolume study of the AAA. Supported by the Rockefeller Foundation, the project culminated in *Three Years of the Agricultural Administration Act*, published in 1937. Nourse had invited Joseph S. Davis and John D. Black to work on the project with him. Black, a Harvard economist, proved to be especially useful because of his long experience working with the AAA from the time he had originally proposed the central concept behind the act, the acreage-allotment system.[48] Ironically, among the investigators Black was to become the most critical of the AAA during the course of the study.

The authors of the study felt that they could provide neither a "yes" nor a "no" answer to the question of whether the AAA program had produced favorable results. In fact, Nourse, Black, and Davis could not agree among themselves as to the full implications or consequences of the act. Black, in spite of his association with the AAA, registered specific complaints against the agency in a separate, concluding chapter. He directed his criticisms particularly at the marketing agreements the government had entered into with farmers in order to guarantee prices for their crops. Nourse, on the other hand, concluded that the Triple A had had "a positive effect of substantial magnitude, though not as great as anticipated." The results of the agricultural adjustments program had been "on the positive rather than negative side." The experience of acreage limitation, he felt, showed that such a measure is "practical in emergency situations." Nourse warned, though, that experience did not support the administration's implicit belief that these controls could be "made practicable as a means of holding the course of production over the years." He pointed to the many abuses in the soil-conservation-payments program, which particularly helped Southern cotton planters. Also, he challenged the economic logic of the ever-normal granary plan, which attempted to regulate farm production through government purchases of surplus crops. Ultimately, he upheld the price mechanism as the best means of maintaining agricultural production.[49]

The study was completed early in 1936, an election year, but was not published until 1937. Moulton, although leery of Roosevelt's program, feared that the results of the study would be seized upon by partisans on both sides. "Such a misuse of the material," Moulton told a trustee, "would detract from the constructive service which the book is designed to perform with reference to the future of American agricultural policy."[50] The delay in publishing softened the impact of the book. By the time the study appeared the Supreme Court, in a 6-to-3 decision, had ruled that the AAA's processing tax was an unconstitutional "expropriation of money from one group for the benefit of another."[51]

The Supreme Court decision required the AAA to return immediately $200 million in processing taxes to agricultural middlemen, a move that was bound to create even greater federal budget deficits. Spenders within the administration, including Lauchlin Currie at the Federal Reserve, Leon Henderson and Aubrey Williams at the Works Progress Administration, and a group of economists at the Treasury Department, urged the enactment of an undistributed-profits tax as a means of activating idle pools of capital and increasing government revenues. But Roosevelt began to look toward balancing the budget as the election of 1936 approached, especially since Republicans were already raising the issue of deficits within the Roosevelt recovery budget. Working with Daniel Bell, who had replaced Douglas as director of the budget, Roosevelt retreated to Warm Springs, Georgia, in November 1935 and proceeded systematically to slash budget requests. He halved the request of the Civilian Conservation Corps, cut road-building funds, speeded the discharge of employees from the now disbanded NRA, and took $150 million from Ickes's Public Works Administration. In January 1936, he renewed his efforts to cut funds from the Reconstruction Finance Corporation ($660 million), the Farm Credit Administration ($80 million), and the Federal Housing Administration ($750 million).[52]

While Roosevelt undertook these budget cuts, and planned more severe ones, a political polarization along class lines was in progress, a trend that was to culminate in the election of 1936. Following the demise of the NRA in 1935, Roosevelt undertook a course of legislation that was bound to provoke an already estranged business community. He openly attacked his opponents in big business, those "economic royalists," by pushing through a corporate income tax and a modest tax on undistributed profits. Roosevelt also called for Congress to enact a social security bill, the Wagner "fair labor practices" bill that pledged government protection to labor's rights in collective bargaining, a banking bill that extended federal control in banking, and a public utilities bill to control the power utilities. The results of this program became evident in the election of 1936, which gave Roosevelt all but two states. There was a sharp shift in upper-class votes (representing the top quarter of income wealth) from the Democratic Party to the Republican Party, while Roosevelt won the support of the lower class (representing the bottom quarter of income wealth). Of the voters who switched from the Democratic Party in 1932 to the Republican Party in 1936, 71.7

percent came from the upper class. Similarly, Democrats gained the support of 77.5 percent of those who were poor or on relief in 1932.[53]

Roosevelt's budget cuts following the election did not reflect his lower-class support, however. Now he slashed appropriations of the very agencies that had helped bolster Democratic support among the lower classes—PWA, WPA, Civilian Conservation Corps, Farm Credit Administration, and the Federal Housing Authority.[54] Roosevelt felt that he could afford to undertake these budget cuts because the economy appeared to be on its way toward revival. By early 1935, production had already risen 57 percent as compared with the Depression low of July 1932, and from the middle of 1935 through December, production had risen another 13 percent. By the end of 1935 wholesale prices had advanced 33 percent and the cost of living had risen 18 percent from Depression lows.[55]

This economic recovery only heightened fears of runaway inflation among Roosevelt's opponents. The president's adversaries were quick to point out that the recovery was based primarily on increased consumer spending rather than on increased capital investment, and thus it represented a reversal of what they perceived as the traditional pattern of past economic recoveries. In the past, they said, increased consumer demand had followed, not led, capital investment. With the failure of the capital market to be revived, banks held in excess reserves more than $3 billion, while demand deposits had risen $4.8 billion, from $22.4 billion in 1935 to $27.2 billion in 1936—all of which threatened to unleash an uncontrolled inflationary cycle.[56] A new vehemence now became evident in demands that FDR return to a balanced budget. Business blamed Roosevelt for the lack of capital investment. How could a reasonable businessman have confidence in a debt-ridden government? "A comprehension by government . . . of the psychology of business," businessmen insisted, "is essential to the stability of employment and a rising standard of living." This understanding was government's first duty, "rather than experimentation with the detailed control of business or the radical reduction of true business profits." More conservative business critics went so far as to accuse the New Deal of making the American people into "bureaucratic serfs." S. Wells Utley, vice president of the National Association of Manufacturers, summarized the thoughts of the more rabid business elements when he declared, "By his persistent advocacy of 'socialistic' experiments, his extravagant waste of money, his reckless expansion of public credit, his policy of inflation and tinkering with currency, his bureaucracy, his catering to class hatred, . . . Mr. Roosevelt has endangered our entire heritage of political and economic freedom."[57]

But businessmen were not alone in their concern over the prospect of runaway inflation. Many liberals expressed similar anxieties. As the liberal *Nation* reported in 1936, "Talk of inflation is once more in the air." Many liberals felt that government deficits could not "continue without a day of reckoning." Analogies were frequently made between the United States and Weimar Germany, the only difference being that the threat in the first case came from the "uncontrolled expansion of credit," rather than from "worthless fiat money." By the spring of 1937, even Marriner Eccles, one of the most consistent advocates of deficit spending, came out in favor of returning to a balanced budget in order to combat inflation.[58]

Finally, on April 7, 1937, acting on the best advice offered by both conservatives and liberals, Roosevelt ordered the curtailment of expenditures. Just as his attempt to restore a balanced budget appeared to be nearing success, with many observers predicting that 1938 would be a particularly good year, economic disaster struck.[59] The rapid decline in income and production during the nine months from September 1937 to June 1938 was without precedent in American economic history. During these months industrial production fell nearly 30 percent. Decline in nondurables was even more drastic—over 50 percent.[60]

Shortly before this recession began, Roosevelt had created political difficulties for himself when he attempted to reform the Supreme Court and to reorganize the executive office. Both the courts and government bureaucracy had for some time presented a significant conservative opposition to his administration, opposition that FDR sought to eliminate through structural changes in government. The Brookings Institution, which had a long tradition as an advocate of government reorganization, now reversed field and became the leading voice in the social science community against FDR's plans. In the process, the institution found itself allied with Roosevelt's most reactionary opponents. The Brookings Institution's attacks on Roosevelt's reorganization plan happened to coincide with open opposition to Roosevelt on the part of business. Liberals mistook the coincidence for collusion.

On the surface Roosevelt's reorganization program should have been one of the least controversial proposals he made during his four terms in office. Yet it elicited a torrent of questions concerning the balance of power between Congress and the executive. The actual fight was less a conflict over constitutional theory in regard to balance of powers than a naked political struggle.[61] The hysterical reactions displayed by Roosevelt's opponents manifested the paranoid state many of them had reached after five years of FDR rule. Seeing the worst in the New Deal, these conservatives compared it with the rise of totalitarianism in Europe and termed Roosevelt a "dictator." For the staff at the Brookings Institution, FDR's plan did not represent the rise of fascism, as his political opponents warned, but it did pose a threat of the complete politicization of fiscal policy.

By 1937, the Brookings Institution had already dismissed the New Deal economic program as a dismal failure. In the summary volume of the Falk capacity study, *The Recovery Problem in the United States*, released in early 1937, Moulton as the principal author concluded that "the conflicting and confusing character of the early Roosevelt program tended on the whole to retard the recovery program." Never before had Moulton been so bold in publicly denouncing the New Deal. What Roosevelt's program had accomplished, he went on to say, was only to increase the public debt. He mordantly pointed out that a greater degree of recovery had been achieved in both Great Britain and Sweden than in the United States, and that neither had increased its public debt in the process (Moulton did not tell his readers that both Britain and Sweden had moved toward more state planning, however). Yet from the British and Swedish experience he concluded that it was possible "to have recovery, even from a world depression, without vast outlays of public debt."[62]

When Roosevelt attempted to reorganize the executive office in 1937, Moulton found himself in a position of confrontation with Roosevelt, a position that the Brookings Institution had historically avoided in regard to presidents. But because the reorganization issue seemed so crucial to the future of American government and fiscal policy, Moulton was willing to take a bold stand against the president. At issue was Moulton's anxiety that "government officials, rather than directors of private financial corporations, are coming to occupy the positions of dominant importance in directing the flow of the national income and level of productive resources of the nation." He warned that government, under the Roosevelt regime, was making private lending institutions into "merely intermediate institutions collecting funds from the saving public and turning them over . . . to government lending agencies."[63] Roosevelt's reorganization scheme threatened to hasten this process by completely politicizing the budgetary process, which had up to then kept a brake, albeit a rather ineffective one, on FDR's spending.

In the debate over the reorganization plan, both sides, FDR and his opponents in Congress, called on their own experts to bolster their arguments respectively for or against the bill. The reorganization fight further split the social science community. On one side stood FDR's presidential committee, staffed by Louis Brownlow and Charles Merriam from Chicago, and Luther Gulick, head of the Institute of Public Administration, formerly the New York Bureau of Municipal Research. Opposing the president was Harry F. Byrd's Select Committee on Government Organization, which had hired the Brookings Institution to conduct its own investigation of government reorganization. An air of cooperation between the two committees existed at the beginning of their work. In fact, shortly before the committees were formed, Moulton had invited Louis Brownlow to speak at the dedication of the new Brookings building on Jackson Street—on the topic "Cooperation in Social Science Research."[64] But the air of cooperation quickly dissipated, with each side accusing the other of having become a tool of the politicians. Because Moulton had long been suspicious of Brownlow's and Merriam's ties to the Democratic machine in Chicago, such accusations came easily.

In the Senate, Roosevelt's political nemesis was Senator Harry F. Byrd of Virginia. Byrd, who had earned a reputation as an administrative reformer when as governor of Virginia he reorganized the state government along scientific lines, always claimed to be the true Progressive. "Roosevelt changed, but I did not," he told the *U.S. News and World Report* later, in the 1950s.[65] Byrd's claim rested on his complete commitment to efficiency and economy in government. His counterpart in the House was the chairman of the House Committee on Government, James Buchanan, a Texas conservative who also maintained that government should run smoothly and frugally. It was Buchanan's chief adviser, Colonel Wren, who suggested that the Brookings Institution conduct the research for Congress on the issue of government reorganization. Wren believed that the institution would agree with his view that past attempts at reorganization had failed because reformers had tried to do too much at one time. Approached by Byrd and Wren to undertake the study, Moulton accepted the task out of "moral obligation."[66]

Byrd offered the Brookings Institution only $20,000 to conduct the project. Frugality began at home in this case, but one major consequence of underfinancing the study was that the institution would not hire the best staff possible. Although Fred Powell, director of the project, utilized some men of outstanding caliber, including Charles Dearing and Lewis Meriam, many of those hired, as a younger participant later recalled, were simply "tired and old." In contrast, the president's committee hired a highly competent staff directed by Joseph Harris.[67]

The Brownlow committee was particularly concerned with the opposition the Office of the Comptroller General and the Civil Service Commission had presented to Roosevelt since he first took office in 1933. The comptroller general had continually slowed down the release of funds for a variety of programs central to the New Deal. Gulick accordingly told Roosevelt at the outset of the study that the committee would confront "the arrogation of policy powers by the comptroller general." Thus it came as no surprise that in its final report the president's committee recommended that the Office of the Comptroller General be abolished and that auditing authority be taken away from Congress and vested in the Executive Office. Further, it proposed that the Civil Service Commission be abolished and replaced by a single administrator appointed by the president.[68] These two proposals were enough to spark a controversy between the president's committee and the Brookings Institution.

Interestingly, in the past the Brookings Institution had also urged that executive budget powers be strengthened. F. W. Powell, shortly before beginning work for Congress on reorganization, had written Moulton that "if we had a proper Budget Bureau (which should not be in the Treasury Department), immediately under the President, . . . we would have accomplished the first step in government reorganization."[69] Such thinking was consistent with W. F. Willoughby's earlier work on government administration, as well as the institution's research on the state level of government, initiated in the Depression years. In state studies for Alabama, Oklahoma, and Virginia, the institution had consistently recommended that the state executive office be strengthened. Furthermore, Willoughby had advocated that the Civil Service Commission be replaced by a single administrator. Yet in its final report the Brookings Institution completely reversed its previously held position. The Brookings staff attacked Brownlow's recommendations for centralizing the budget process in the Executive Office.

Why? An obvious answer to the switch in positions is that the institution was catering to the sensibilities of Congress on the matter of executive power. After all, Congress was paying for the institution's report, and "he who pays the piper. . . ." The institution had extended the extraordinary courtesy of allowing Colonel Wren, a staff member of Congress, to set up an office at Brookings while the project was being conducted. Yet such an answer is too simple. Whatever their opinions of Roosevelt, the staff prided themselves on being objective social scientists and would have been affronted by any charge that they were consciously partisan. Their primary concern was that the president was overextending his powers. In the past they had favored a strong executive, but now, fully aware of how a man like Roosevelt could take advantage of his position, they resisted the Brownlow committee's proposals. Nevertheless, it should also be pointed out that the staff at the Brookings Institution tried to avoid an open conflict over this matter.

From the beginning of the study, Moulton felt that it was important for "the doctors," as he described the two committees, to agree on final recommendations. Any disagreement, he believed, would be used by opponents of reorganization to defeat a proposal no matter what its worth.[70] For this reason, Moulton designated Lewis Meriam to act as liaison between the two committees. But the president's committee resisted close cooperation. Brownlow's first meeting with Moulton took place only after the president's committee had submitted its report in January 1937. By this time a resolution of the differences between the two committees had become impossible. Brownlow initially had requested that the institution not study the Office of the Comptroller General at all. Although Moulton refused, he did agree to send the institution's report on financial administration to the Brownlow committee before a final report was given to Congress. But even this concession proved to be impossible to fulfill. A week later, Byrd insisted that Moulton deliver the Brookings report. Moulton delayed, writing to Brownlow to implore, "We ought to hold our conference as early as possible." Another week passed before Byrd again wrote to Moulton requesting the report. By this time Moulton had no other choice than to submit the report without conferring with the Brownlow committee. Forced to hand over the report, Moulton stressed that it should be considered tentative until he had a chance to meet with the Brownlow committee.[71] Finally, on March 8, after both groups had submitted their conclusions, the two committees met to discuss their differences.

Underlying their differences were two irreconcilable attitudes toward the presidency. Behind the Brownlow committee's proposals was a conception of the president as the representative of the public interest, and to execute this function properly, the president needed a unified Executive Office. Gulick articulated this concept when he wrote to Herbert Hoover that "there is a deeper significance which goes beyond efficiency and economy; it is the impossibility of developing popular government with genuine popular control of the broad aspects of social policy without the maintenance of a unified executive." In order to have a unified Executive Office, Gulick maintained, it was absolutely essential that the president be able to manage the finances of government through a budget system under his control. Gulick concluded his letter with a quotation from Alexander Hamilton: "All multiplication of the executive is dangerous rather than friendly to liberty."[72]

Whereas once the Brookings Institution had been willing to accept this line of reasoning, it now feared the breakdown of the balance of powers guaranteed by the Constitution. The Brookings's final report agreed that the Budget Bureau might best operate directly under the president, but added that "we think it also desirable, however, for the legislative body to maintain a continuing control through audit and final settlement of account."[73] For this reason the Office of the Comptroller General should be retained. Countering the Brownlow committee's conception of the presidency, the Brookings committee warned that "popular control of government would be destroyed if the executive officers . . . could themselves interpret the meaning of appropriation acts."[74] Here, exactly, was the problem. The Brookings Institution feared executive officers—like Harry Hopkins, for instance—who were interpreting appropriation acts to suit their own political purposes.

This fear of Roosevelt's fiscal policy and what was seen as political subversion of government bureaucracy and fiscal policy became evident in Meriam's appearance before the congressional Committee on Government Reorganization in late 1937. Meriam's statement to the committee was focused on the importance of an effective, independent control of public expenditures through the Office of the Comptroller General. At the heart of Meriam's testimony was his concern over the growth of the Executive Office from 572,000 positions in 1933 to 800,000 by 1936. "This means," he told the hearing, "that hundreds of new administrative officers became responsible for expenditures; and in many instances they were not familiar with the great body of administrative laws. . . . Nor did they always appreciate that in public business one must have legal authority for every action." Furthermore, he added, in the emergency Congress had adopted the practice of making large appropriations directly to the president, and the "result was the President was given great discretion in the allocation of emergency appropriations." In these circumstances the comptroller general had wisely restrained the Executive Office by occasionally disallowing payments on certain items. Meriam observed that before the time of the Roosevelt administration such a disallowment caused no commotion. "Rarely did it become a matter of partisan politics."[75] Now in these highly charged times, Meriam suggested, partisan politics threatened to replace constitutional balance and fiscal prudence.

Meriam's testimony did not go unanswered. James Byrnes, a New Deal supporter from South Carolina, immediately went after Meriam. He ruthlessly pursued a line of questioning concerning the institution's support of consolidated executive control of finances as proposed in Willoughby's classic, *The Reorganization of Government*, and as seen in its recommendations to state governments, as recently as 1936, that financial agencies be centralized under the control of the Executive Office.[76] Meriam's testimony was further challenged by other experts brought to the hearings. George Auld of the American Institute of Public Accountants, A. E. Buck, Charles Beard, Herbert Emmerick, and a chorus of other witnesses came out in favor of abolishing the Office of the Comptroller General as a means of increasing governmental efficiency and strengthening executive powers in fiscal planning.

While the hearings were being held, a hurricane of public opposition was forming against the reorganization bill. Roosevelt's opponents Frank Gannett, Amos Pinchot, and the Hearst press had dramatically and effectively organized a well-financed lobbying effort against what was called the "dictator bill." In April 1938 Roosevelt was forced to call a news conference in order to declare he had no intention of becoming a dictator. "I have none of the qualifications," he joked, "which would make me a successful dictator."[77] His opponents thought otherwise. The reorganization bill headed for defeat as veterans' groups, educators, the Forest Service, and others found reasons of their own for opposing the bill. Finally, more than a hundred Democratic congressmen deserted Roosevelt to defeat the bill. Thus the Brookings Institution, in defending the public interest, had helped score a major victory for Roosevelt's opponents, many of whom were aligned with special interests.

The Brookings Institution's overt opposition to Roosevelt's reorganization caused a crisis on the board of trustees. Frederic Delano, who had replaced Robert Brookings as chairman of the board following Brookings's death in 1932, expressed deep concern that the institution under Moulton's leadership had consistently proposed policies "at variance with the policies of the administration in power."[78] Earlier he had attempted to mediate what he perceived as a feud between the Brookings Institution and the National Recovery Administration by nominating Hugh Johnson as a trustee, only to be greeted with ridicule by Moulton. Tensions between Moulton and Delano had been further exacerbated when Moulton suggested that Delano had "helped the Brownlow Group to edge into the Federal government field, though this had been a major field of the IGR."[79] Finally, on May 17, 1937, Delano submitted his resignation to the board. He believed that the Brookings Institution had been placed in an "embarrassing position by the newspapers" during the reorganization fight. He asserted, moreover, that "it is impossible to expect an institution which has to raise funds to be liberal." Moulton denied that he had the "slightest interest in the success of one party against another." He maintained that the great bulk of the institution's work was regarded by "close observers" as "distinctly liberal and forward looking."[80] Moulton continued to proclaim his nonpartisanship and his concern for the public interest above party affiliation, and the majority of the board stuck by him. Seven days after Delano's resignation, the board appointed Dwight F. Davis, secretary of war under Harding, to the board. During these Depression years a distinctively anti-Roosevelt tone had become apparent in the choice of new appointees to the board, who included, among others, Marshall Field III and Dean Acheson.

Moulton's complaints against the New Deal grew increasingly strident. In his report to the trustees in 1937, he openly warned that the "federal budget situation will present perhaps the most important single problem with which the next administration will have to deal."[81] (Little did Moulton realize that Roosevelt would seek a third term in 1940.) Coinciding with his concern over deficit spending was a conscious anxiety on Moulton's part about the growth of Keynesian economic thought in America. The dispute between the Keynesians and Moulton in large part centered on the recession of 1937. The recession on the surface seemed to contradict Moulton's contention that cutting government expenditures would lead to general economic prosperity. Keynesians such as Lauchlin Currie, as well as economists in the Treasury Department, placed the blame for the economic downturn on the previous cuts in government expenditures and the introduction of Social Security taxes. Such assumptions, Moulton told the Union League Club of Chicago, were simply unwarranted. The Keynesian analysis, he declared, was derived from a study of only part of the national income. "What is important from the standpoint of market purchasing power is obviously total money income, not merely that portion derived from government disbursement." He went on to tell his receptive audience that Roosevelt's earlier curtailment of government expenditures had not been reinforced with "increasing disbursement through private enterprise."[82] Businessmen, Moulton reassured members of the Union League Club, felt uneasy about investing money when government did not present a consistent economic program.

Keynesians won the immediate battle. In the spring of 1938, Roosevelt, concerned with the approaching fall elections, called upon Congress for a "spend-lend" program of $4.5 million. The Keynesian fiscal program now appeared to be in complete harmony with the social and economic objectives of the New Deal. The major step in the Keynesian revolution had been taken by a small group of economists, numbering only twenty to fifty men. In the next few years the Keynesians continued to make further converts. Their biggest coup came when they persuaded Harvard economist Alvin Hansen to join the cause. Hansen and other young Keynesians now called into question the validity of the Brookings studies. Reviewing these studies on the distribution of wealth and its relation to income, they concluded that the volumes lacked proper statistical data, drew unwarranted conclusions from the data, and made incorrect economic assumptions.

Moulton lashed back at the Keynesians in a series of articles, pamphlets, and speeches. A frequent speaker before business groups, he carried a single message: Beware of the "New Economics." In 1938, Moulton challenged Alvin Hansen for the presidency of the American Economic Association, a contest that many saw as representing competing economic doctrines. When Moulton's campaign did not even get off the ground, conservative economists interpreted his defeat as a further sign of the increasing inroads being made by Keynesians.[83]

Having neither the prestige of an academic nor the influence of a government economist, Moulton was at a disadvantage in his fight against Keynesianism. Then suddenly, in August 1939, Moulton was asked by the Roosevelt administration to serve on the reactivated War Resources Board, a civilian agency charged with reviewing plans for industrial mobilization. Moulton's appointment came as a surprise to him. He knew full well, as did all of Washington, that Roosevelt personally disliked him. Yet Moulton's opposition to the New Deal in fact enhanced his qualifications for the board. The War Resources Board was Roosevelt's experiment in public relations in regard to mobilizing the nation for war. It put the isolationists on trial by testing their popular strength if they decided to oppose the board. The re-creation of the board also showed that Roosevelt was concerned with efficiency in mobilization. But most importantly, it indicated that Roosevelt was willing to work with business, if war did come. For this reason Roosevelt selected Edward Stettinius, Jr., of the U.S. Steel Corporation to head the board. Joining Stettinius were Walter Gifford of American Telephone and Telegraph, John Lee Pratt of General Motors, and John Robert Wood of Sears, Roebuck. Karl T. Compton, president of the Massachusetts Institute of Technology, and Moulton were chosen to serve as technical advisers.[84]

Lauchlin Currie challenged the selection of Moulton as the War Resources Board's economist, but Moulton's appointment to the board perfectly suited Roosevelt's intentions. Roosevelt considered Moulton an opponent, but he realized that Moulton was also an internationalist at a time when isolationism was still a political force in the country. As it turned out, Currie need not have worried. The board accomplished little if anything at all. In its final report it called for a new WIB to direct economic mobilization. After receiving the report, Roosevelt dismissed the board and pigeonholed the study.

Moulton's appointment to the War Resources Board was to be his last official position in government under the Roosevelt administration. Moulton did not leave Roosevelt with the last word, however. He returned to the Brookings to continue his attacks on the Keynesian economists whom he equated with Roosevelt's fiscal policies. By 1940, as America approached war, Moulton's feud with Hansen had become a matter of public knowledge. *Time* magazine reported that Hansen advocated placing heavy taxes on savings in order to finance public works and war mobilization. In contrast the conservative school, represented by Moulton, held that government taxes on business should be removed. The anti-Keynesian prescription, *Time* told its readers, was best summarized in Moulton's *Capital Expansion, Employment and Economic Stability* (1940). To be sure, this book "broke no new argumentative ground, or offered any new documentation for economists. But to businessmen it served the useful purpose of asserting learnedly with charts and logical principles what most of them accepted on faith."[85] Thus *Time*, although hardly sympathetic to liberal economic views, suggested that Moulton's contribution to economics was that of simply enunciating the popular prejudices of the American businessman.

During the Depression years the Brookings Institution under Moulton lost much of its influence in the liberal community. Liberals now supported a strong, political presidency, an activist state cautiously involved in the domestic economy, and federal programs financed, if necessary, through deficit spending to meet the basic social needs of its citizens. By opposing each point in this liberal program the Brookings Institution had become isolated from the center of power, the presidency. As America approached war in 1940 the institution seemed to speak primarily to a limited audience of business interests—Chamber of Commerce types—and a select group of conservatives in Congress. Liberals saw Harold Moulton's warnings about inflationary consequences of deficit spending as mere pontifications by the Old Guard. While Moulton spoke of inflation, academic economists and liberal businessmen continued to be more concerned with unemployment and depression. These concerns of liberals would be carried into the World War II era by such newly formed groups as the Committee for Economic Development. The war in many ways heightened the estrangement of the Brookings Institution from the liberal community, which now listened for the most part to young Keynesian economists. Paradoxically enough, these young economists claimed, like Moulton, to represent the general welfare of society.

World War II brought few opportunities for the Brookings Institution to reestablish a positive role for itself in domestic policy.[86] By remaining critical of Roosevelt's domestic program, the institution under Moulton played a largely negative role in wartime economic policy, sniping at the Roosevelt administration for its lack of respect for the marketplace.

Nevertheless, Moulton found some encouragement in the growth of the Republican Party. The party had made great gains in the election of 1942 by attacking government bureaucracy and waste. It increased its representation in the House to 208 members and in the Senate to 37. After the election of 1946, Republicans would control both the House and the Senate.

Although the Brookings Institution kept its conservative audience during the war years, it was not very successful in attracting foundation support. Philanthropic foundations judge the efficacy of research organizations by their actual contributions to government, but the Brookings's effect on government during these years, as noted earlier, was seen by many as negligible. As a consequence, foundation support dwindled. By 1942, the year in which the Republicans had begun their political comeback, operating expenses at the Brookings had fallen nearly $150,000 from the previous year to a total of $312,000.[87] The growth of Republicanism in Congress did little to melt the icy attitude that foundations continued to show toward Moulton's institution.

Once again, as in the early days of the Depression, Moulton turned to service contracts to bolster revenues, while he also made cutbacks in institutional expenditures. Harold Metz was assigned to aid the Senate Appropriations Committee, chaired by Senator Bankhead, in studying the manpower needs of the nation. Charles Dearing went to work for the Office of Defense Transportation. Meanwhile, Moulton postponed any long-term plans for expanding the activity of the institution. The fellowship program, which had replaced the Graduate School in 1927, was closed, and the former residence halls were rented to the National Institute of Public Affairs.[88] The demise of the student program meant that the Brookings Institution had lost even this contact with the academic community, from which it was estranged in any case because of the increasing prominence of Keynesian thought in the academic mainstream.

The war, and later postwar prosperity, gave added vitality to the Keynesian revolution. During the war, Keynesians became entrenched in government as well as in academia. They joined the National Resources Planning Board (NRPB), the National Housing Agency, the Treasury Department, the Agriculture Department, and the Securities and Exchange Commission. At the Division of Price Management, under Leon Henderson, a Macroeconomic Group would be formed to prepare programs for economic stabilization. The big issue of the war years was not whether there should be economic planning, but, as Leon Keyserling, a Keynesian economist, later recalled, "how extensive the planning should be."[89] Thus while the Keynesian revolution proceeded forward, Republicans gained control of Congress.

This was, in fact, to be a revolution with a simultaneous Thermidor. Moulton found a role to play in the Thermidor by continuing to attack Alvin Hansen, who had become dean of the American

Keynesians. Hansen had particularly irked conservatives with his pamphlet *After the War—Full Employment*, published in 1942 by the National Resources Planning Board. In this publication Hansen issued a pointed defense of deficit spending, declaring that "a nation may make itself poor by repayment of the public debt; . . . public debt is an instrument of public policy."[90]

Moulton picked up the challenge. In 1943 he drew Hansen into a public debate with a widely circulated polemic *The New Philosophy of Public Debt* (1943). Responding to Moulton's attacks on the New Economics, Hansen charged that Moulton was "more interested in the retirement of the public debt than he is in the pursuit of a fiscal policy which produces economic stability at full employment." Privately, Hansen was outraged by what he saw as Moulton's deliberate distortions of his views. He felt that Moulton had unscrupulously used quotations from an interview reported in the *Chicago Journal of Commerce*—quotations that Hansen had already publicly disavowed as inaccurate. Hansen wrote to Moulton, furthermore, "You have produced a grossly distorted caricature of my views by rigorously omitting innumerable sentences and paragraphs." Moulton replied that the interview as reported, whether disavowed or not, really reflected Hansen's true beliefs, so he had a right to cite it. Moulton privately wrote the business editor of *Newsweek* magazine that he found Hansen "absolutely dishonest."[91]

The debate between Hansen and Moulton did little to change anyone's mind. During the course of the exchange, Moulton tried to convince Dexter Keezer, a Brookings graduate who had become director of economic research at McGraw-Hill, that many "Keynesian" views, especially those on the propensity to consume and the propensity to save on the part of various income groups, could be found in Moulton's own works that predated those of the New Economists. "If you read *Income and Economic Progress*, you will find a chapter in which I showed how the economic system failed to distribute the benefits of technological progress." There was in fact, he said, a propensity on the part of the rich to save more of their incomes than did lower-income groups. "This basic analysis preceded Keynes as well as the New Deal views," he declared.[92] He did not add that, while he might have been the first to show that the wealthy saved a larger proportion of their incomes, he had not proposed, as did Keynes, that a surplus of capital savings could be released through increased, and if necessary, deficit, spending by the government. Moulton's assertion that the rich saved more of their incomes, however, would later be heard in conservative arguments that greater tax benefits should be given to upper-income groups in order to increase capital spending.

Moulton's attacks on Keynes failed to convert economists like Keezer, but they did win him the support of businessmen and conservative economists. Edwin Gay, former dean of Harvard's Graduate School of Business, for instance, wrote Moulton to offer praise and money to aid in the battle against Keynesians. Republican Party officials wrote for additional copies of Moulton's pamphlet to distribute to party members. Letters of support from bankers, stockbrokers, engineers, and corporate executives encouraged Moulton to keep up the fight.[93]

Moulton's *New Philosophy of Public Debt* was also heralded by Republican congressmen who insisted on placing passages from it in the *Congressional Record*. The publication of Hansen's pamphlet by the NRPB only gave evidence that liberals were planning to turn America into a socialist state. Representative Harold Knutsen graphically expressed the sentiments of many of his fellow Republicans: "For years we Republicans have been warning that the short-haired women and the long-haired men of alien minds in the administrative branch of government were trying to corrupt the American way of life and install a hybrid oligarchy at Washington."[94] Republicans specifically targeted the National Resources Planning Board as a "vicious body, and a menace to the American people." One Republican declared that investigation of the board revealed the "dangerous infiltration into our government of these enemies of our American way of life for the purpose of undermining and destroying this government of ours."[95] Led by Everett Dirksen of Illinois, Congress finally cut the entire appropriation for the NRPB in 1943, and then later complained when personnel from the disbanded board were transferred to other agencies.

The defeat of the NRPB, although the fact was not fully realized at the time, marked a major defeat for those who saw in Keynesian thought an instrument for more direct programmatic planning through public works, public housing, and national resources development.[96] But the ideal of planned capitalism, expressed by liberals in their demand for a full-employment economy, did not die an easy death. In 1945, Senators James Murray and Robert Wagner introduced a full-employment bill before Congress. Proposed initially by Lauchlin Currie, a liberal economist in the Roosevelt administration, the bill was an attempt to enact the New

Economics into law by guaranteeing government's commitment to full employment through mandatory-spending provisions in deflationary times. Still, the abrupt demise of the NRPB meant the disbanding of an agency that could have provided an institutional base for planners. Thus Moulton welcomed the end of the NRPB, but he knew far too well that victory in one battle hardly won the war. His fight against Keynesianism continued, in preparation for the inevitable confrontation in the postwar world.

7 · THE FINAL BATTLE: HARRY S. TRUMAN AND THE FAIR DEAL

D URING THE war Keynesianism, despite setbacks such as the defeat of the National Resources Planning Board, proceeded to root itself in government and economic circles. The ascendancy of Keynesian thought ensured that American policy makers in the postwar period would emphasize government's responsibility to maintain the demand side of the domestic economy. Demand became the barometer of economic policy. The lesson from the Depression, as taught by the "New Economics," was simply: Prosperity rested on the government's willingness to ensure that demand be artificially maintained through monetary expansion, redistribution of income, and increased public expenditures, financed if necessary by fiscal deficits. Thus began a fiscal revolution in American economic policy.

This revolution hardly proved to be a revolution, either in its political consequences or in its intellectual nature. This revolution did not transform class relations, bring new groups to power, or disrupt the economic order. In the end, income distribution in the United States remained constant and the class system was preserved. The "New Economics" did attract a new group of economists to Washington, but this phenomenon was part of a long-term development; the demand for expertise in government had, as we have seen, appeared long before the New Deal.

Keynesian policies, which found a more congenial atmosphere for growth in the United States than in any other Western nation, provided a substitute for the more direct economic controls that were adopted in other countries and that in this country had been advocated by social planners like Charles Beard in the early days of the Depression. The central mechanism of Keynesian economic policy, as espoused in America, lay in transfer payments through social security, unemployment, and veterans' programs. By 1950, national defense spending provided another means for the government to supply capital to the national economy, but the main responsibility for setting wages, prices, and profits still fell on businessmen, workers, and farmers. Only a few economists at the time saw that a reliance on fiscal policy perpetuated maladjustment and obscured the need for genuine economic reform.[1] Thus the capitalist economy emerged in the postwar period only moderately reformed, incoherently regulated, and dependent on government. This was to be "capitalism in an oxygen tent."[2] Capitalism survived having neither experienced a revolution, as liberals claimed, nor having taken the "road to serfdom," as some conservatives warned.

In completing the change in government spending practices that had begun during the New Deal, liberal economists sought to link their recommendations to the New Deal social program. Even before World War II had drawn to a close, liberals were already discussing ways of ensuring fiscal stability, economic growth, full employment, and social security through a program which called for security for all "from cradle to grave." This program rested on the extension of Social Security coverage, an increased minimum wage, slum clearance, public housing, national health insurance, and federal aid to education. More politically audacious than their mentor, Keynes, who considered all political matters a "frightful muddle," American Keynesians became active spokesmen for converting the fiscal revolution into a coherent political and social program.

Their social program would meet with little success in the postwar period, however, as Republicans, having increased their strength in Congress during the war years, confronted Roosevelt's successor, Harry S. Truman, with obstinate opposition. Although Republicans opposed deficit spending, at least in their rhetoric, they did not attempt to repeal the Social Security program or other New Deal measures that contributed to deficits; nor did they oppose increased expenditures for national defense. Nevertheless, the Republican Party fought any further advances in the liberal revolution. Thus while the Republican Party for the most part was willing to accept some of the New Deal program that had been enacted during the Depression, it sought to prevent the revolution from going any further. At the forefront of this reaction was the Brookings Institution under Harold G. Moulton.

Moulton's last years before his retirement in 1952 would be spent attacking Truman's Fair Deal, specifically wage and price controls, government labor policy, national health insurance, and the extension of Social Security. Concerned with the political implications of Truman's legislative program, which he called "an effort to control the vitals of private enterprise,"[3] Moulton articulated the anxieties shared by other critics of the Fair Deal. Brookings publications were subsequently given wide circulation in certain business and professional circles, quoted in congressional hearings, and discussed in newspapers and magazines. The tone of these publications was set, as in the previous decades, by Harold Moulton. He carried into the postwar period the same message that he had given in the war years: Government had drifted into "uncharted seas—if not state socialism." The people, he continued to warn, were "fed up with regimentation" and realized that government had directly handicapped business, "principally in the fields of taxation, of labor laws, and by pursuing a public spending program that holds that a domestic debt is of no real significance."[4] In 1946, at the age of sixty-two, Moulton showed no signs of slowing down. In the last six years before his retirement he averaged fifty speeches a year before civic groups, professional conferences, business conventions, and colleges.

Moulton remained a confirmed optimist concerning America's long-range economic prospects, but he doubted that the nation in the short run could afford the costs of full economic security as advocated by liberals. In his last theoretical study, *Controlling Factors in Economic Development* (1949), which he considered a synthesis of a lifetime of study, Moulton predicted that new scientific and technological developments in food, energy, and industry would create an economy that by the year 2049 could support a population of 300 million at eight times the existing standard of living.[5] He foresaw oceans being farmed, a turbine engine the size of a telephone, and new discoveries of oil beneath the continental shelf, as well as synthetic fuel production. The key to the future lay in capital investment and competition, or the supply side of the economy. The major problem that could hinder America's future development was the likelihood of increased social overhead. Therefore, Moulton demanded that government reject current spending policies, end price supports for farmers, and stop encroaching upon the functions of management.

While Moulton never doubted that the American economy would prove vigorous in the long run, he warned that in the immediate postwar period it was not strong enough to carry the accumulative load for "a greatly expanded security and welfare program which includes a great extension of old age benefits, provision for temporary disability for all ages, an increase in unemployment compensation, and an extensive compulsory health insurance program."[6] Certain that Truman intended to press Roosevelt's New Deal program to its absolute limits, Moulton warned that "the desire for security has become so compelling that increasing numbers of people appear to treasure security above freedom and self-reliance."[7] The Brookings Institution, located directly across the street from the White House, became a principal foe of Truman's Fair Deal. So concerned was Moulton with the course of Truman's economic and social program that he refused even to nod to the president on those few occasions when they passed on the street.

Underlying many of Moulton's economic concerns was a profound distrust of Truman's political motivations. Moulton particularly feared that the New Deal with its false promises of a full-employment economy signified the further intrusion of the unregulated discretionary power of politicians and government bureaucrats into the basic liberties of Americans, specifically their rights of property and contract. In the postwar period, Brookings studies reflected an increased anxiety towards federal government and bureaucracy, concerns that had not been evident in the early Institute for Government Research studies. Postwar studies warned time and again that Truman's program, if enacted into law, would mean the interjection of partisan politics into government administration. This fear of a politicized federal bureaucracy increasingly entered into Moulton's speeches in his final years before retirement. Exactly how such a phenomenon might come about was never enunciated, but it was suggested many times that Truman's program would be run by politically appointed bureaucrats and politically minded officeholders who would pursue their own ideological concerns in opposition to the general interests of society. Clearly a strong antibureaucratic bias had become intertwined with a traditional mugwump hostility toward partisan politics.

This anxiety in regard to bureaucracy indicated an important historical shift for the Brookings Institution away from a view that the state could be depoliticized through the establishment of nonpartisan government administration. Roosevelt had shown that bureaucracy could be politicized or circumvented, as evidenced in his relations with the comptroller general. Acutely aware that bureaucracy itself did not guarantee a depoliticized economy, Moulton now argued that the best means of keeping politics out of economic policy was to limit the role of the president and the function of government in the capitalist economy. Nevertheless, the Brookings Institution maintained in its publications an attitude of suspicion toward democracy and the electorate. Although democracy was the least harmful form of government, it suffered from major flaws because voters were not obliged to consider the economic costs of social programs. Furthermore, electoral politics encouraged competitive bidding among parties to offer more than could be delivered. The Brookings Institution proposed that individual liberty and market rights in a free-enterprise system be clearly identified and distinguished from areas of legitimate federal supervision, and that they thus be removed from political scrutiny and democratic pressure. Moulton and his colleagues did not suggest that bureaucracy or federal involvement in the economy could be dispensed with totally, but they did argue against the further extension of the government into the relations between employees and employers, physicians and patients, or producers and consumers. Public interest had become defined as the economic rights of the individual and the general rights of the marketplace. The men at the Brookings Institution continued to see themselves as nonpartisans seeking to rationalize economic policy and government administration by removing partisan politics from public policy.

Distrust of partisan government received its most radical expression in Arthur C. Millspaugh's *Toward Efficient Democracy*, a book specifically targeted at the political abuses of the New Deal. Millspaugh felt that during the Roosevelt years "the substitution of deficit spending for a balanced budget marked the surrender of government to a party strategy based on special interests and the disintegrating demands of classes, groups, and localities." To remedy this situation, Millspaugh proposed a total reorganization of American government through the creation of a National Council, composed of a small body of men, which would replace the existing legislative and executive branches of government. Members of this National Council would be nominated by political parties and elected in proportion to the popular vote. The National Council would then appoint a chief executive, who would administer government. Such a system, Millspaugh argued, would safeguard the manipulation of government by strong presidents like Franklin Roosevelt, who had gained power "mainly because of his personality, his exploitation of 'emergencies,' of public confusion, and of class feelings, the increasing patronage at his disposal, and the spending and other policies which distributed material benefits to special interests." Of course, Millspaugh added, in 1933 it would have taken "an extraordinary mental grasp, a deeply ingrained intellectual honesty, and an exceptionally strong will to resist the demands of special groups, the disposition to deal with subdivisions of policy, and the temptations offered by demagogic political strategy."[8] Implied, of course, was that Roosevelt lacked such qualities.

The Brookings critique of the New Deal, while focusing on the fiscal restraints of liberalism, assumed that Truman, like his predecessor, was inclined to play politics with the economy, particularly when he promised full employment, a national health system, and the extension of Social Security coverage.

Liberals manifested equal cynicism toward the intentions of the Brookings Institution. Moulton's statements struck most liberals not merely as old-fashioned jeremiads against deficit spending, but as outright reactionary propaganda favoring "big business," the AMA, and other vested interests. The editors of the *Nation* summarized a feeling prevalent in many liberal circles when they charged that the Brookings Institution had become "the outstanding academic servant of reaction in America."[9] They further accused the institution, under the presidency of Harold G. Moulton, of having "energetically prostituted scholarship in the interest of American finance and big business. The planning and the timing of its economic studies have been in the closest correlation with reactionary drives in Congress and with astute public relations campaigns to manipulate public opinion."[10] The editors allowed no room for the possibility that the Brookings Institution expressed legitimate concerns over inflation, increased governmental regulation of industry, and expanding government costs. Nor did liberals doubt, given the unparalleled prosperity that America was experiencing in the immediate postwar period, that the Fair Deal program could be afforded. At the same time, they maintained that the Fair Deal program would serve as a preventive to the postwar depression they foresaw. The logic and the emotion involved in the argument between the Brookings Institution and the liberal New Economists precluded compromise. Thus an irrepressible intellectual war broke out, with each side predicting catastrophe if the other side should win.

The opening shots in this warfare came over wage and price controls, and a full-employment bill introduced in Congress in 1945. Liberals worried equally about inflation and depression. Sometimes they could not make up their minds exactly where the economy was headed. Walter Salant, for instance, a former student of Keynes at Cambridge and later an economist in the Office of Economic Stabilization, warned in the late spring of 1945 of an "inflationary psychology" that would be unleashed at the end of the war by higher wage costs, higher consumer demand, and limited goods.[11] Two months later Salant, writing to the head of the Office of Economic Stabilization, warned of serious "deflationary forces" in the economy.[12] In turn the Office of Economic Stabilization informed Truman, "With the ending of war production and resultant unemployment there is no longer any threat of an inflationary bidding up of wage rates."[13]

This uncertainty over the economy was especially evident in the debate over wage and price controls. The existing controls, which had been enacted during the war in the Emergency Price Control Act and the Stabilization Act, had for the most part successfully restrained inflation during the war years. By the fall of 1945 a major debate took place within the administration and in Congress on the issue of how rapidly the economy should be decontrolled. Many public officials, both liberals and conservatives, feared unemployment and urged rapid decontrol. Others, including Chester Bowles, chairman of the Office of Economic Stabilization, expressed concern with runaway inflation and urged Truman to extend wage and price controls until reconversion from a wartime economy to a peacetime economy was complete.

In the midst of the debate on wage and price controls, liberals in Congress, led by Senator James Murray, a Democrat from Montana, and Senator Robert Wagner, a well-known New Dealer from New York, proposed a Full Employment Act in 1945. Their intention was to legislate Keynesian economics into law by guaranteeing government's commitment to full employment through mandatory spending provisions for public work projects in depressed times. The act expressed a conviction on the part of liberals that depres-

sion inevitably follows a postwar boom.[14] Actually the predicted recession would not occur until 1948, and when it did come, in the
last quarter of that year, it proved to be relatively mild and short-
lived. Instead of recession, during the period from 1946 to 1948 the
economy experienced slight economic expansion with increasing
price inflation. The real GNP increased 3.8 percent during this
period, hardly a miraculous growth rate, but by no means an in-
dication of depression, while the consumer price index rose 18.6
percent.[15] These developments placed Truman in a position of having to worry about both high unemployment and simultaneous
runaway inflation. The two concerns were reflected in his endorsement of the full-employment bill, and his relaxation of wage controls in August of 1945.[16] Price controls were kept as a prophylactic
against further increases in inflation.

Not surprisingly, Moulton refused to accept the liberal dictum
that a depression must follow a postwar boom. Therefore he felt
little ambivalence toward the movements to retain price controls
and enact a bill certifying full employment. He opposed both. He
believed that reconversion to a peacetime status would be relatively
smooth, *if* government withdrew its restrictions on the economy.
The best remedy for inflation and the best promise for high employment was to restore competition in the marketplace. In the fall
of 1945, Moulton contributed a short pamphlet, *Should Price Controls Be Retained?*, to the discussion.[17] The question posed in the title
was obviously rhetorical; Moulton's answer was a blunt no. He argued that the higher prices caused by consumer demand were in-
consequential compared to increasing wage costs. He particularly
assailed Truman's relaxation of wage controls in August of 1945.
Aware that wages were increasing, Moulton nevertheless did not
urge the restoration of controls because, as he observed, "the en-
forcement of wage controls in peacetime" would be an impossible
task for "any political administration" desiring reelection. Similarly, the continuous review of a multitude of prices, which was
being advocated by liberal economists, was so time-consuming that
"the expansion of production and employment would be inevitably
retarded."[18] The best means of controlling inflation, he maintained,
was to gradually end price controls and to allow full production an
opportunity to correct any economic imbalances in the market. Although only twenty thousand copies of Moulton's pamphlet were
printed, it had considerable influence in Congress, particularly because it reinforced what Republicans already thought. Robert Taft,

the conservative senator from Ohio, cited the pamphlet on the floor of Congress to drive home his point that price controls were stunting economic growth.[19]

Moulton also undertook a crusade against the full-employment bill. He relentlessly attacked it in speeches before business groups, charging that the bill was "essentially totalitarian." "In due course," he predicted, "it would mean the end of private enterprise." Harsh words indeed, but they expressed many businessmen's anxieties that the government had gone too far in its attempt to bring prosperity to all. The job would best be left to private enterprise, not some sort of Americanized state socialism. Moulton specifically doubted that any president, even with the best economic advice, could manage a complex capitalist economy. Government, he declared, was drifting into state socialism; the full-employment bill even proposed that the president be vested with "power to formulate production requirements in line with his conceptions as to what is necessary for people's welfare."[20] Just as he had maintained during the Roosevelt years that a capitalist economy could not be planned in every detail, during the immediate postwar years Moulton continued to believe that the Truman administration had undertaken a quixotic search for full employment.

After a fierce fight in the House, a greatly modified version of Murray and Wagner's bill passed under the name of the Employment Act. The most important feature of the act called for the creation of a potentially influential Council of Economic Advisors (CEA). Much to the surprise of many, including those at the Brookings Institution, Truman selected a Brookings economist, Edwin Nourse, to be the first chairman of the CEA.[21] In many ways, Nourse appeared to be a perfect political choice to head a committee whose establishment had created such controversy in Congress. Nourse was a moderate, well liked by management, agriculture, and the economics profession, and he was not opposed by labor or the liberal wing of the Democratic Party. Yet his very strength as an economist proved to be a critical flaw. Nourse carried into his work on the council a firm belief in nonpartisan economics and in the necessity of a balanced budget. He made a subtle distinction between "advising" the President and "advocating" or defending current policies. He therefore refused to testify before the Joint Economic Committee of Congress. Nevertheless, he advocated fiscal restraint as the best means of controlling inflation, a policy considered outdated by liberals on the council. Finally, in 1949, feeling his days on the council were numbered, Nourse openly attacked Truman for fiscal irresponsibility. Truman accepted Nourse's resignation shortly afterwards. Nourse's service on the council revealed the pitfalls that confronted the economist standing for the public interest but practicing his profession in a political milieu.[22]

After the Republicans swept the midterm elections in 1946, they began looking forward to entering the White House for the first time in sixteen years. Their program was simple: they advocated cutting taxes, balancing the budget, and reducing the size of government. They purposely set out to undermine the Fair Deal program.[23] The major problem with the Republican plan, however, was that Truman's own instincts led him to balance the budget.[24] From the first quarter of 1945 through mid-1947 the president masterfully cut budget expenditures from $91 billion, or 41 percent of the GNP, to $24.5 billion, or 10 percent of the GNP.[25] In 1947 the Republicans called for a $6 billion cut in expenditures and a $500,000 reduction in federal employees, but they found upon closer examination that they could cut only a piddling $1.8 million from Truman's proposed budget.[26] Still, the Republicans continued to attack Truman for playing politics with the budget. They sought to distinguish themselves from Truman by pointing out programmatic differences over labor relations, medical care, and Social Security. On these issues, the Republicans perceived that the Brookings Institution provided the intellectual ammunition to waylay the Fair Deal.

With a skyrocketing rate of inflation, the public appeared willing to listen to the Republicans, who continued to advocate tax cuts. Inflation was blamed on organized labor, which had gone out on strike in the coal, steel, auto, and transportation industries. In 1946 alone, 14.5 percent of the work force was on strike. Actually, in 1946 fewer workers were involved in strikes than had been the case following World War I, and an increase in food prices more than offset any gains workers made in 1946, but Republicans and the general public were in no mood to listen to labor's apologies.[27] Now in control of Congress for the first time since 1930, the Republicans, supported by business, turned to amending the Wagner Fair Labor Relations Act of 1935, a major piece of New Deal legislation.

The reform of the Wagner Act had been proposed in a Brookings study written by Harold Metz, *The Labor Policy of the Federal Government* (1945).[28] Metz, who had joined the staff during the war years, undertook this study at the request of the Falk Foundation.

Assisted in the project by Harold Jacobstein, Metz claimed that his work was only descriptive, but an implicit antilabor bias was evident. Metz warned that the rapid growth of unions during the war had upset "the balance of power between labor and capital" by placing labor leaders in a dominant position in the economy. Furthermore, he accused the National Labor Relations Board (NLRB), established under the Wagner Act, of pursuing policies that actually encouraged workers to use unfair labor practices in organizing. "The obligation not to discriminate," Metz wrote, "has been construed by the Board as a positive obligation to protect union employees against nonunion workers." Furthermore the NLRB, as Metz saw it, placed "very few limitations on the workers' use of strikes, pickets, and boycotts." As a result, "workers can utilize concerted action, though in the process they commit illegal acts, and though they seek to accomplish undesirable objectives."[29] Employers therefore have no protection from secondary boycotts, or strikes arising from jurisdictional disputes among rival unions, or from the closed shop. In fact, Metz declared, the NLRB policy worked against the employee's "right to self-determination." Metz recommended that the issues of closed shops, secondary boycotts, and jurisdictional strikes be reexamined. He also proposed that unions that entered into illegal strikes be held legally liable for any damages incurred.[30]

Metz's proposals found their way into Republican labor legislation in the form of the Case bill and the Taft-Hartley Act.[31] The Case bill (1946) went so far as to prohibit, among other things, nationwide bargaining. Truman vetoed the legislation, but the next year the Republicans pushed through Congress the Taft-Hartley bill, a complicated piece of legislation that allowed nationwide bargaining, but outlawed the closed shop, jurisdictional strikes, and secondary boycotts. The bill increased membership on the NLRB from three to five members and, more importantly, permitted states to enact "right-to-work laws," which outlawed union shops. Truman vetoed the Taft-Hartley bill in one of his most strongly worded messages to Congress, asserting that it would reverse the "basic direction of our national labor policy." Three days after receiving this message, Congress overrode the veto, and the Taft-Hartley bill became law. Nevertheless organized labor continued to grow throughout the next decade, increasing its membership from 14 million to 17.5 million workers. Furthermore, the closed-shop provisions of the law proved to be unenforceable in the building trades and on the docks. Nonetheless, a major piece of New Deal labor legislation had been drastically amended by the Republicans with the help of Harold Metz, who later took major credit for proposing the outlines of the bill.[32]

While Truman confronted a hostile Congress on the issue of labor relations, another battle was being fought between his administration and the Republicans over the establishment of national health insurance, as proposed in the Wagner-Murray-Dingell bill. Liberals, who had dreamed of national health insurance since the Progressive Era, had nearly succeeded in having such insurance included in the original Social Security Act of 1935, but the American Medical Association had defeated their plans. They were encouraged to resume their efforts by World War II studies of military draftees, which showed notable inadequacies in the existing system of health care. Furthermore, William Beveridge's *Social Insurance and Allied Services* (1943), calling for extensive social security "from cradle to grave" in England, gave additional impetus to the American movement. Senators Robert Wagner and James Murray revived the issue on a national level when they sponsored a new national health insurance bill in Congress. Although a *Fortune* magazine poll in 1942 showed that an impressive 74.3 percent of the American people favored national health insurance, the Wagner-Murray-Dingell bill quickly became stalled in Congress. Following the war Truman tried to aid the passage of the bill by sending a message to Congress in which he urged the establishment of a comprehensive medical system prepaid through Social Security taxes. The AMA lashed out at the bill, spending over a million dollars to convince the American public of the ills of "socialized medicine."[33]

In the midst of this fight, which was growing increasingly bitter, Senator H. Alexander Smith, Taft's colleague on the Senate Labor and Public Welfare Committee, asked the Brookings Institution to study the issue. The resulting report, *The Issue of Compulsory Health Insurance*, was produced by Lewis Meriam and George W. Bachman, a physician with close ties to the AMA. The study provided a further rebuttal to national health insurance. It concluded that the program would be too political, too expensive, and too detrimental to the nation's economic health. "Compulsory health insurance," Meriam and Bachman declared, "would necessitate a high degree of government regulation and control . . ." and, they emphasized, "the problem of eliminating politics from government administration is extremely difficult."[34] The bureaucracy that would be required to administer a national health program, they said, would open the door "for complete government control of the entire medical profession." Furthermore, they refuted claims by proponents of national health insurance that current medical expenses were exorbitant. For most people, they said, medical expenses amounted to only between 4.0 and 4.5 percent of their budgets. Because medical expenses were so low, it seemed "necessary to conclude that on the average, the lack of medical care among consumers with total incomes of around $2,000 or over . . . is due more to their failure to give medical care a high priority than to a lack of resources."[35] The truth, it appeared, was that "a very substantial proportion of the population is not interested in health as such" and "the will to health cannot be instilled by legislation."

Meriam and Bachman warned, moreover, that the long-term social effects of national medical care held serious ramifications for the entire American society. They agreed that some people needed aid, but they quickly pointed out that "there are certain individuals and families who lack incentive or a sense of responsibility" to provide for themselves. Leisure and freedom from the discipline of a job or of family responsibilities were seemingly more important to these people than "good housing, good nutrition, or good medical care." Yet to take taxes from professional men—"doctors, dentists, for example, and businessmen"—to provide medical insurance for the irresponsible who refused to save would be unfair. Those who advocated high taxes for a national health system should question whether it was beneficial in the long run to impair "the incentives of those whose native abilities, training, experience, and willingness to assume risks [are] . . . so important to the success of any social and economic system."[36] Meriam and Bachman concluded that the existing medical system could best be improved if the national or state governments contributed funds for health research and education; and government should provide systematic care only for those who were willing to pass a means test and were thereby proved to be indigent.

When released, the Meriam report caused an immediate outcry. *Newsweek* magazine described the report as "a blow" to health insurance. Proponents of national health insurance responded immediately.[37] Michael M. Davis, a former Social Security administrator and a longtime advocate of national health insurance, joined forces with liberal economist George Soule to answer the Brookings study in *The Costs of Health Insurance*. Their polemic against the

Meriam report was sent to hundreds of newspapers, particularly black and labor presses. Davis also prepared a special memorandum for Truman showing that families with an income of less than $5,000—80 percent of all Americans—could not possibly meet the costs of a catastrophic illness.[38]

In a hearing before Congress, Davis and Morris Llewellyn Cooke also questioned Meriam's scientific integrity in conducting the study. "We deplore a report," they testified, ". . . that is bias parading as science. . . . We deplore the reactionary position taken by the staff of the Brookings Institution which is far from the progressive outlook of this organization during its early days."[39] Cooke revealed that as soon as he had heard of Meriam's selection to undertake the study, he had written to the chairman of the Brookings board of trustees, Robert P. Bass, demanding that Meriam be removed as project director because of his preconceived hostility to national health insurance. The Brookings Institution countered these charges by releasing all of the correspondence that had been conducted between Cooke, Bass, and Moulton on this matter. These letters, which were published in the *Congressional Record* in 1945, showed that Cooke's reservations about Meriam were based only on hearsay and that Cooke had never read any of Meriam's books.[40]

Cooke might have been able to support his accusations against Meriam if he had known that Meriam and Bachman had corresponded with Morris Fishbein, the reactionary editor of the *AMA Journal*, to seek his advice on a number of key points concerning national health insurance.[41] No doubt Meriam thought of himself as a nonpartisan social scientist serving neither the Republican Party nor the Democratic Party. Nonetheless Meriam, by now a fiscal conservative, seems to have been inclined toward a deep distrust of government's ability to manage a national health program. Shortly before he undertook his study, he expressed a negative view toward government in an article that appeared in the *American Economic Review* in May of 1947. In this revealing article, Meriam frankly said that he had seen too much government in action to have "illusions as to its potentials for perfection. People once wielding the power of government are loath to see it pass into the hands of others. The power they seek so avidly to obtain would be, if exercised by others, a threat to our democratic institutions."[42] Meriam's suspicions of big government precluded any acceptance of a federal national health insurance program.

Meriam's distrust of federal government and his faith in private enterprise was shared by others. His arguments against national health insurance were quickly assimilated by the opponents of the Wagner–Murray–Dingell bill. Robert Taft declared that a tremendous amount of political patronage would be involved if Truman were allowed to establish a medical insurance system, because such a program would require 50,000 to 1,000,000 employees.[43] The AMA distributed free copies of Meriam's pamphlet to doctors throughout the country to put in their waiting rooms. By 1949 national health insurance had fallen by the wayside, another defeat for the Fair Deal.[44]

In 1950 Harold Moulton, who would retire in two years, reported to his trustees that the Brookings Institution had successfully challenged the Truman program of wage and price controls, full employment through mandatory public works, and national health insurance. The institution, he reported, was preparing to fight one last battle with Truman over the extension of the Social Security system. The Brookings Institution was to lose this battle, however. Republicans in Congress were not prepared to turn the clock back to pre-Depression days. Moreover, they feared alienating the voters who had come to expect certain services and benefits from government. In short, Republicans now sought to halt further radical advances in social programming, not to mount a complete counterrevolution. The next decade, therefore, was to be characterized by the politics of incrementalism, the gradual extension of existing programs. And the politics of incrementalism meant increased federal expenditures and, necessarily, a failure to restore a balanced budget. The refusal of the Brookings Institution to accept the political nature of fiscal policy would be evidenced in its principled stand against extending the existing Social Security program further. Nevertheless, the institution's own willingness to support foreign-aid programs and increased defense expenditures undermined its case for fiscal conservatism.

The characteristic Brookings distrust of politics manifested itself in Lewis Meriam's study *The Cost and Financing of Social Security* (1950). The year prior to the publication of Meriam's study, Truman had proposed that Social Security benefits be increased and coverage expanded to include the self-employed and the widows and dependents of war veterans. In Congress, many Republicans had attacked Social Security as, in the words of John W. Byrnes of Wisconsin, "fictitious insurance." Senator Robert A. Taft joined the protest by declaring that Social Security was "not anything in the world but the taxing of people to provide free services to other people."[45] Still, behind this rhetoric most Republicans knew full well that it would be political suicide to oppose the liberalization of Social Security.

Meriam nevertheless worried about the finances of the existing system and suggested that Social Security be put on a pay-as-you-go basis. But his most acute anxiety was that Congress and political appointees would increasingly be able to manipulate the system. "Under the proposed plan [Truman's expanded system], the duty of preventing abuse would have to be entrusted to government employees controlled and directed by politically appointed office." (The ghost of Harry Hopkins, Roosevelt's political appointee in charge of public works during the New Deal, still stalked, it seemed, the halls of the Brookings Institution.) Meriam warned further that political elections "may be won on the promise of making the public assistance program as liberal as possible." Congress, he felt, was particularly sensitive to lobbying interests, above all to "veteran constituents, whose ratio was vitally increased in all districts."[46] Lobbying by such groups would make cuts in aggregate expenditures politically impossible, he wrote, unless Congress acted immediately to turn down Truman's proposal.

Meriam claimed that he was not a partisan-minded conservative. He realized that many people, the elderly and the disabled, needed public assistance. He was nonetheless concerned with runaway costs. His concern led him to make a radical proposal that could have revolutionized social services in this country. He proposed a guaranteed income for the needy. Specifically, Meriam suggested, a "system that guarantees a standard minimum amount of purchasing power" to the needy would permit "a fairly simple solution" to the rising costs, for administration as well as actual benefits, of various public-assistance programs.[47] Meriam did not elaborate on his proposal, expressed in a single sentence, but in any case practical politics in Congress proved to be stronger than any message Meriam might have conveyed about the increasing costs of Social Security. After prolonged deliberation, Congress liberalized eligibility standards and increased benefits by 77 percent. Meriam's proposal for a guaranteed annual income was far too radical to have been enacted during these years of incremental politics.

Throughout all of their studies, the men at the Brookings Institution, Moulton, Meriam, Jacobstein, and Metz, had consistently seen a balanced budget as the means to ameliorate an inflationary economy. Another group of Brookings researchers, however, took a somewhat different tack. This was the International Studies Group (ISG), which had been set up in 1946 under Leo Pasvolsky when he returned to the Brookings Institution after serving seven years as a special assistant to the Secretary of State. ISG studies on issues of foreign aid and defense expenditures were to show an equal concern for efficiency when compared with the work of the Moulton-Meriam group.

Leo Pasvolsky had entered the State Department in 1937 primarily to work on developing a free-trade policy for Cordell Hull. A man easily caricatured by political cartoonists as a short, stocky figure with a disproportionately large, egg-like head and with a bellowing pipe in hand, Pasvolsky became well known in Washington circles as "The Brain." His mastery of detail, his knowledge of economics and geography, and his ability to articulate goals impressed friend and foe alike. Pasvolsky's role in Washington was more than that of mere technician. He proved to be essential during the war, particularly in drafting the plans for the United Nations.[48] Specifically, he deserves much of the credit for designing the U.N. Security Council and for formulating the compromise that led to veto powers for the permanent members of the council. Pasvolsky's achievement in drafting these plans fulfilled Robert Brookings's promise to carry on the Wilsonian dream of international cooperation and free trade. Yet in reaching this goal, Pasvolsky discovered that a coherent ideology, especially one as idealistic as Wilsonian internationalism, was particularly vulnerable to modification in the world of power politics. In the end, the noble vision of internationalism that lay behind the founding of the United Nations would be transformed into an exclusive regionalism found in the North Atlantic Treaty Organization and the Marshall Plan. Nonetheless, Pasvolsky's involvement in the founding of the United Nations enhanced the internationalist reputation of the Brookings Institution.

Pasvolsky left the State Department convinced that the major problem the department had faced during the war was finding properly trained individuals to staff research and policy-making positions. Intent upon bringing expertise to foreign policy, Pasvolsky received a Rockefeller Foundation grant to sponsor the International Studies Group. He staffed the ISG largely with former associates at State, and he brooked little interference from Moulton in the internal affairs of the group. He was able to maintain this independent stance because the ISG attracted the bulk of foundation support received by the Brookings in the immediate postwar years. In fact, the ISG contributed nearly half of the operating revenues of $700,000 in 1949.[49] To many it seemed that there were actually two organizations, one under Moulton, the other under Pasvolsky. Furthermore, the ISG, because of its internationalism, seemed liberal compared to the rest of the institution. This apparently dichotomous situation led the *Chicago Tribune* to describe the Brookings as embodying an "odd mixture of conservatism and globaloney."[50] Yet to emphasize the differences between Moulton and Pasvolsky, as many did at the time, would be misleading. Pasvolsky remained a fiscal conservative on domestic matters, as well as a fervid anti-communist who suspected subversive elements behind the labor upheavals in 1946 and 1947. His fear of Soviet communism clearly manifested itself in his work on the Marshall Plan in 1947.

With the advantage of hindsight, it seems inevitable that differences would arise between the security-conscious United States and the expansionist Soviet Union. By 1947, with Western Europe faltering on the edge of a complete political and economic disaster, the Truman administration was prepared to "get tough" with the Soviet Union. Two successive years of drought in Europe had been followed by a devastating wave of storms, floods, and freezing temperatures. At the same time, American policy makers had become dissatisfied with the United Nations Relief and Recovery Administration, whose aid seemed to bolster Soviet control in Eastern Europe.[51] Under these circumstances, George C. Marshall, speaking at the Harvard commencement ceremony on June 5, 1947, called for a joint U.S.-European program, operating independent of the United Nations, to aid recovery in Europe.

Marshall's proposal evoked little opposition in principle, but immediate questions arose in Congress as to who would administer the program—the State Department, a collection of other agencies, or a new independent agency. For help in resolving this problem, Senator Arthur Vandenberg, chairman of the Senate Foreign Relations Committee, turned to Leo Pasvolsky, whom he had grown to respect while working with him on planning for the United Nations. Vandenberg realized that the 80th Congress, dominated by Republicans, had been pledged to cut expenses and to balance the budget. So Republicans, in order to protect themselves in support of a massive foreign-aid program, proposed that the European Recovery Program (ERP) should be run on a businesslike basis. In

7. Leo Pasvolsky, director of the International Studies Group from 1946 to 1953. (Courtesy of the Brookings Institution Archives)

making his request to the Brookings Institution for its assistance, Vandenberg told Moulton that he shared the opinion of most conservative Republicans that "the actual day-to-day management of the European Recovery Program is a business proposition which should be effectively separated from the State Department.'[52]

Vandenberg's request, made formally on January 5, 1948, gave the ISG only two weeks to submit a plan. The proposal that the ISG drafted, actually completed on January 22, became the "congressional work sheet for the administration of the ERP." The Brookings report assured Congress that it focused "only on those aspects of the problem which bear directly on the administrative arrangement for the European recovery program now under discussion."[53] The plan favored the establishment of an agency separate from the State Department and administered by a single director, who would be appointed by the president. In March Congress passed the Economic Cooperation Act, thus creating a new recovery agency that bypassed the existing United Nations Economic Commission. America now shifted its policy interests to strategic economic recovery and strategic defense alliances.

In participating in the planning for the ERP, the ISG could have presented a policy alternative to the European Recovery Program.[54] And there were many other occasions on which the ISG could have raised questions concerning the direction of American foreign policy. Nevertheless, Pasvolsky and his staff readily accepted the established view that the Soviet Union would have to be confronted militarily. For instance one ISG study, *The Search for Peace Settlements* (1951), concluded that "whichever way we turn, the political malevolence of the Soviet leaders stands out as the great destructive influence" in international affairs. This study castigated American policy makers for not realizing sooner "the extent of Soviet ambitions in Europe or Asia." Now, Americans had no other recourse than the "determined and rapid mobilization by the United States and its allies today" to convince "Soviet leaders that aggression will be resisted and punished."[55] Thus, although the Brookings Institution's studies on domestic affairs advocated balancing the budget, the International Studies Group urged and supported increased defense spending. On this issue, the ISG was in step with the times. In the next decade United States spending on defense would be twice that of any Western European nation. Prosperity would be linked not to fiscal restraint, but to increased appropriations for defense.

The relationship between foreign policy and domestic policy continued, generally, to be unexplored by Brookings economists. The two areas of research remained separate. Furthermore the ISG, even after Pasvolsky's death, continued as a distinct province within the Brookings Institution. Those who came to the ISG deliberately isolated themselves from working with Brookings economists concerned with domestic policy. In large part, this distance between the two groups stemmed from institutional arrangements, but it occurred also because those at the ISG viewed the domestic economists as generally unsophisticated about the larger issues in the world. Moreover, most Brookings economists concerned with domestic policy, assuming that the Cold War was inevitable, failed to apply their cost-benefit analyses to the issue of the arms buildup and whether it made economic sense. As a consequence, Brookings economists used a double standard: they were willing to challenge social programs on the grounds of their being inflationary, but they proved to be unwilling to use the same criterion for evaluating defense policy. Efficiency as a basis of judging policy remained, therefore, a one-edged sword to be used sharply for attacking the Fair Deal domestic program, but a sheathed instrument when it came to defense matters. In fact, Moulton, by 1952, had become so worried that America was not prepared for war that he totally abandoned any concern about the inflationary consequences of defense spending.

His anxiety that the United States was not militarily prepared for another war led to a bizarre turn of events during the presidential election of 1948. In the midst of this campaign, when it appeared that Thomas Dewey would easily defeat Harry Truman, Moulton undertook on his own to write Dewey to recommend General Douglas MacArthur for the post of Secretary of Defense in a Republican administration. Moulton's letter revealed that he was fully aware, and somewhat uncomfortable in knowing, that he was breaking with a Brookings tradition of not becoming involved in what clearly was a political matter. Not only did Moulton's letter arrive in the middle of a heated political campaign; his unsolicited recommendation of the controversial MacArthur for a cabinet post overstepped the bounds of nonpartisan propriety. "For the first time in my career," he wrote, "I am tempted to make a suggestion in the political realm." Nevertheless, he added, "I have been giving much thought in recent years to national defense with particular reference to the unification of the service." The complete overhauling of the military services, he advised, should be "about problem No. 1 for your administration." In order to ensure a complete overhauling of the national defense system, the talents of a military man were called for, particularly a man as dynamic as MacArthur. MacArthur "better than anyone else is capable of formulating a defense program that would be truly unified." Moulton quickly pointed out that "I do not know General MacArthur personally" but "the dictatorial qualities ascribed to him would be assets in this particular situation."[56]

Dewey's secretary politely replied to Moulton thanking him for his suggestion. Dewey, if he had been elected, probably would not have encouraged MacArthur's well-known political ambitions by appointing him to a cabinet post. It seems terribly naive for Moulton to have thought otherwise.

Moulton's letter reveals just how strongly he felt about military preparedness. In supporting MacArthur for the post of Secretary of Defense, Moulton was seeking to bring "efficiency and economy" to the nation's defense establishment. His concern with efficiency and economy was of course in keeping with a Brookings tradition dating back to the founding of the IGR. Yet the institution had also maintained a tradition of advocating realistic and gradual military disarmament. The Japanese attack on Pearl Harbor and the advent of the Cold War in the postwar years shattered the ideal of disarmament. Nevertheless, the dilemma of how to balance a budget while maintaining a strong national defense was to remain problematic for Republicans and Democrats alike. And it was exactly this issue that Moulton avoided. While Moulton harped on the problem of inflation and the need to balance the budget, he equated the public interest with national defense. This equation allowed Moulton to speak for the public interest when he wrote Dewey in 1948. In the end, however, Moulton failed to address the tough questions concerning the effects of huge defense expenditures on inflation, or the meaning of a military-industrial complex in a free-market economy. These questions remained unanswered for the nation in 1948.

Thus when it came to matters of defense, Moulton returned to the older understanding of efficiency: defense was to be judged in terms of administrative or managerial competency. General policy issues, particularly those concerning the inflationary effects of an arms race with the Soviet Union, were outside the domain of the Brookings economists. By narrowing his application of efficiency to administrative matters, Moulton not only harked back to the days of the IGR under Willoughby; he retreated from the ideals he himself had held as a young economist, when he had called for military disarmament as a way of ensuring a balanced budget and economic stability. Moulton's rejection of the Wilsonian vision was, perhaps, inevitable given the complex relations between the United States and the Soviet Union in the immediate postwar years. Nevertheless, Moulton's failure to evaluate defense as a policy issue, not just an administrative problem, and his refusal to weigh the trade-offs between defense spending and inflation, betrayed the responsibilities that he had earlier claimed as an economist.

8·THE CHANGING OF THE GUARD

By 1950 the Brookings Institution appeared to many to be in the doldrums. Milton Lehman, a staff correspondent for the *Nation's Business*, reported in a feature article on the institution: "Before the war, when Brookings granted fellowships to young graduate economists, there was a sharper discussion in the lunchroom. Since then the staff has grown older, and, some alumni believe, a bit stodgier. 'Brookings,' a former fellow declares, 'is now in a cocoon. But it will emerge again and you'll be hearing more of it.'"[1] The *Nation's Business* was not alone in wondering if the Brookings Institution was "keeping up with the times." Even staff members wondered aloud whether the institution had grown too old to be useful.

Many of the most capable members of the staff had left the institution. Edwin Nourse had resigned his position in 1947 to become the first chairman of the Council of Economic Advisors under Truman. Five years later, Lewis Meriam retired to become mayor of Kensington, Maryland, a wealthy suburb of Washington, D.C. (After leaving the institution, Meriam would be persuaded by his son-in-law Charles Thomson, also a Brookings staff member, to change his party registration to Republican.)[2] The loss of Nourse and Meriam was further compounded by the approaching retirement of Harold Moulton. Moulton first submitted his resignation to the board of trustees in 1947, but it was not until 1952 that a successor could be found to replace him. In the intervening years, the institution undertook only short-term projects, a circumstance that further undermined its influence in public policy circles.

The search for Moulton's successor began in 1948. By this time, many members of the board of trustees were aware of the criticisms being voiced in the social science community against the Brookings Institution as it had functioned under Moulton. In fact, as board member Jerome Greene told Joseph H. Willits of the Rockefeller Foundation, "These criticisms are coming not from the ones whose political views make them not like the conclusions of Brookings studies, but from scientists and scholars who do not respect the quality of the work, the quality of the personnel which is being appointed, and the degree of centralization of power in President Moulton's hands."[3] Given the intensity of such criticism, the board decided that Moulton should not be allowed to choose his own successor but that instead an independent search committee should be formed, composed of Harold W. Dodds, president of Princeton University, Karl T. Compton of Massachusetts Institute of Technology, and the chairman of the board of trustees, Robert P. Bass.[4] Within two weeks the committee had compiled a list of fifteen possible candidates for the post.[5] When approached, however, few of these men proved willing to be considered for the job, and those few who did express an interest were dismissed by the search committee for various reasons. Thus the search continued over the next four years.

During this time, the Rockefeller Foundation kept in close touch with the committee. Nonetheless, Joseph H. Willits, speaking for the foundation, told Bass that the foundation "did not have a candidate in mind."[6] Thus there was some surprise in Rockefeller circles when, in late 1948, the search committee approached Robert Calkins, head of the General Education Fund at the foundation, as a possible successor to Moulton. Calkins at that time declined to accept the job, but when the committee again approached him three years later, he finally relented and accepted the post.

Calkins accepted the presidency against the advice of many at the Rockefeller Foundation. Beardsley Ruml, for instance, warned Calkins that the Brookings Institution would not survive the decade.[7] Indeed, the Rockefeller Foundation, as evidenced by the extensive correspondence between the foundation and the search committee, refused to promote Calkins for the job. The search committee found Calkins an attractive candidate largely because of his reputation among economists within academic circles. The final decision to have Calkins succeed Moulton as president of the Brookings Institution remained primarily a professional decision in which economists, not corporate businessmen or foundation officers, played the key role.

Robert Calkins was clearly a man on the rise in economic circles when he was approached in 1948.[8] He offered a sharp contrast to Harold Moulton. He was personable, easygoing, and known for his ability as a mediator. During the 1930s he had become chairman of the politically divided Department of Economics at the University of California, Berkeley; in 1937 he acted as a federal mediator during the San Francisco longshoremen's strike, which violently disrupted the city and shocked the nation. During the war, as cochairman of the Committee for Economic Development, he helped bring together academics and businessmen to lay the foundation for corporate-government cooperation in the postwar period. Calkins's amiability, his ability to compromise, and his down-home charm earned him further promotions. He became the dean of the Columbia School of Business, and in 1947 he was made director of the General Education Fund for the Rockefeller Foundation. He had risen in the "tough" world of academia without having published a single article, popular or otherwise.

Money, men, and reputation confronted Calkins as the major problems of the Brookings Institution. Each was crucially intertwined with the others. Without money and reputation an institution such as the Brookings could not attract top men; without men and reputation, it had difficulty persuading foundations to provide the funds necessary to conduct long-term projects. Calkins quickly discovered these difficulties. In 1952, he was informed by the Rockefeller Foundation that it would not renew the grants that were due to expire that year. Joseph Willits frankly wrote Calkins that it was not the Rockefeller Foundation's "business to lighten the load of Brookings's budget, where there is a considerable amount of weak men on the staff, all of whom need to be weeded out. Our task is not to help carry a budget for weak people, but . . . to leave the financial squeeze on to press out poor people."[9] At this point Calkins must have remembered the last advice Moulton gave him before retiring: "Foundations in changing times and with changing personalities naturally have shifting interests and policies. They like to foster and help new conceptions and new programs."[10] How could Calkins develop new programs and hire new men without money? The new president came to understand that the Brookings Institution would have to live off its remaining funds, whose income amounted to approximately $300,000 a year.

8. Robert D. Calkins and Harold G. Moulton, 1952. (Courtesy of the Brookings Institution Archives)

Financial difficulties were further compounded when Calkins lost the support of the Falk Foundation. The specific occasion for this loss was Calkins's refusal to publish a study by Harold Metz on reducing the costs of government. Shortly before leaving office, Moulton, with the concurrence of Calkins, had undertaken a study on the reduction of federal expenditures, to be supported by a $120,000 grant from the Falk Foundation. Moulton assigned Metz to conduct the study, and Metz began work in February 1952. Problems arose between Calkins and Metz immediately after the completion of the manuscript. Review of Metz's work revealed profound problems; figures were so carelessly used and errors so numerous as to substantially call Metz's conclusions into question. Calkins accused Metz of recommending cuts in federal spending with "no explanation or justification, no consideration of the crite-rion . . . [and] no indication of the effect of a cut upon the government service affected."[11] In defense, Metz took the unusual step of writing directly to the Falk Foundation to charge Calkins with liberal bias.[12] Calkins bluntly denied the charge, adding that the study was being discontinued. As a gesture of goodwill, Calkins offered to return the $120,000 grant, although $70,000 of it had already been spent. Much to Calkins's surprise, the Falk Foundation accepted his offer and requested a refund in full. Although the Brookings Institution was in financial distress at the time, Calkins nevertheless returned the grant. This action placed him in a favorable light with the other major foundations. "Word got around," Calkins recalled later, "that we could not be bought."[13]

Calkins's problems were far from over, however. In the spring of 1953 the Brookings Institution received its greatest loss when Leo Pasvolsky unexpectedly died at the age of fifty-nine. His work at the State Department had greatly enhanced his own reputation and in turn the reputation of the Brookings Institution. Calkins wisely turned to the Rockefeller Foundation for a grant to continue the projects begun by Pasvolsky. In 1953, the Rockefeller Foundation awarded a three-year grant to the International Studies Group to study problems facing the United Nations and other major issues in foreign policy. Then, that same year, the Ford Foundation, through its director Thomas Carrol, a close friend of Calkins, awarded the institution a grant of $1 million to be paid out over a five-year period.[14]

With the financial base of the institution secured, Calkins moved to bring new blood into the staff. Harold Metz, shortly after his dispute with Calkins, left the institution to work for the House Ways and Means Committee as a staff economist. Calkins encouraged other holdovers from Moulton's reign to follow suit. Karl Schlotterbeck resigned; then long-time transportation expert Charles Dearing accepted the position of Deputy Under-Secretary of Commerce for Transportation. Gradually the total staff of the Brookings was reduced from 120 to 60. Of the 20 senior fellows under Moulton in 1951, only 3 from economic studies and 5 from the ISG remained in 1954.[15] Of the economists who remained at the Brookings during this transition period, one of the most important was Wilfred Owen, who had joined the staff shortly after World War II. He had been uncomfortable with the "stuffy and smug" atmosphere at the institution under Moulton.[16] Now, under Calkins's administration, Owen matured as an economist. In 1956 he completed *The Metropolitan Transportation Problem*, one of the first major studies of urban transportation by an economist.

In selecting new men to replace those who were leaving the Brookings Institution, Calkins specifically sought men with liberal credentials and with government experience. As one Rockefeller staff member observed, "Under Moulton contacts in government were limited to the conservative groups in Washington. Calkins, however, is more of a middle of the road economist who is more widely accepted."[17] Walter Salant and Joseph Pechman typified the new Brookings staff members. Both came from prestigious East Coast universities, both had extensive government experience, and both were considered neoclassical economists.

Salant, who became a senior fellow in 1954, cut a striking contrast to the earlier Brookings men. A leading exponent of Keynesian economics in America, he had helped introduce Keynesian economics into government in the late 1930s.[18] After postgraduate study with John Maynard Keynes at Cambridge, Salant had returned to his alma mater, Harvard, to complete his master's degree in economics under Alvin Hansen. Afterwards, in 1939, he had joined the Commerce Department, where he became part of a small group of younger economists in government who helped bring about the Keynesian revolution in federal fiscal policy. Salant had later served as a senior staff economist for the Council of Economic Advisors (1946–52), for NATO (1952–53), and for the Committee on National Trade Policy (1953–54). While on the Brookings staff during the 1960s, Salant continued to move in and out of government, first for the State Department as a deputy leader on an economic survey of Indonesia, and later for the Council of Economic Advisors as director of a report on U.S. balance of payments. A firm proponent of lower tariff rates, he wrote in 1960 the influential *Import Liberalization and Employment*.

Six years after Salant joined the Brookings Institution, Joseph Pechman became a senior fellow. Like Salant he came to the Brookings with extensive government experience, having been a Treasury Department official (1946–53), a member of the Council of Economic Advisors (CEA) (1954–56), and an economist for the Committee for Economic Development (1956–60). He continued to act as a consultant to the CEA during the Kennedy and Johnson administrations. Under Pechman's direction, the institution initiated the important series "Studies of Government Finance." The studies in this series, financed through the Ford Foundation, reestablished the Brookings's reputation among academic economists for scholarly research.

The work of Pechman and Salant reflected the growing ties that the Brookings Institution was establishing with academia and government during this period. In 1955, Calkins decided to strengthen the institution's relations with the academic community by revitalizing the graduate fellowship program, which had been moribund since World War II. The political science and economics departments of the nation's leading universities were encouraged to nominate candidates for one-year fellowships at the institution. During the next ten years over ninety Ph.D. candidates would work in this fellowship program,[19] which coincided with a general resurgence in public policy study.

During the Eisenhower years, Calkins repeatedly sought closer contacts with the federal government, but only with the advent of the Kennedy administration in 1960 were his attempts fully successful. The beginnings of the Brookings's involvement with the Kennedy administration came with a series of memoranda on presidential transition that were prepared at the request of John Kennedy during the 1960 election campaign. In a departure from established institutional policy, the trustees approved Calkins's request to keep the transitional papers from the press and the general public.[20] With Kennedy's election, Brookings men immediately began to enter into government. The Brookings Institution under Robert Calkins and his two successors, Kermit Gordon and Bruce MacLaury, therefore, marked a new era in the history of the Brookings Institution. It seemed that the "New Economics" had indeed triumphed at the institution, once a bulwark against Keynesianism.

Awareness of the early history of the Brookings Institution enhances our understanding of the meaning of nonpartisan research in the early twentieth century, as well as serving as key to the examination of other think tanks and their relationship to public policy. Three general themes have emerged from this study: the multidimensional relationship between corporate capitalism and the origins of nonpartisan research in the United States; the ambiguous and multiple meanings that men have imparted to "efficiency" and to social structures in a democratic capitalist society; and the elitist and antistatist bias of many social scientists since the turn of the century in maintaining the "public interest."

The French sociologist Emile Durkheim once stated that the emergence of "social institutions is due not to reason and calculations but to more obscure causes," to "motives without relation to the effects they produce and which, as a result, they cannot explain."[21] The origin of the Brookings Institution is a case in point. Robert S. Brookings, the capitalist from St. Louis, founded the Institute of Economics and the Graduate School because he held a vague vision that capitalist society could be and should be reformed. As he grew older, his ideas became more practical and more radical (the two are not necessarily contradictory), so that in his later years he spoke of the immorality of corporate interests and the need to redistribute wealth, provide Social Security for the aged and unemployment insurance for workers, and ensure international peace. Nevertheless, the institution that he established, and continued to support, remained more modest in its proposals for changing the world. In fact, the institution that bore Brookings's name became increasingly critical of liberal reform in the years following the death of its founder.

The relationship between Brookings and the institution he established, therefore, takes on a complexity not readily discernible to the ideological-minded. Although in many ways a typical capitalist of his age, Brookings saw the evolution of the corporation as inevitable and for the best; yet he remained highly critical of the system. The social scientists who staffed his institution sought a critical understanding of the capitalist order, but they remained above all else professional economists, elitist in their distrust of partisan politics but confident of the ability of the market economy to ultimately correct, with some help from government, economic and social maladjustments. Perhaps the crucial difference between Robert S. Brookings and the social scientists at the institution remains that Brookings was a builder, whereas they proved, in the end, to be preservers. Background, training, temperament, and perhaps an era divided the founder from the purveyors of his dream. Both sought, it is true, to make the capitalist system more efficient. Yet "efficiency" within a capitalist economy is a concept that proved to be elastic and relative, rather than fixed and absolute.

The purpose of the Brookings Institution, as seen both by its founder and by those who served as staff members, was to offer expert advice in order to provide a needed rationality to the public affairs of the nation. Rationality, however, took at least two forms during the early years of the institute, *rationality of technique* and *rationality of system*. Initially the Institute for Government Research sought to promote bureaucratic efficiency through the rationalization of technique by creating administrative structures, to be managed by specialized professionals, which would provide rational efficiency, continuity of operation, speed, precision, and calculation of results. Headed by a technical expert par excellence, W. F. Willoughby, the IGR envisaged that such efficiency would be in large part accomplished through the passage in 1921 of the Budget and Accounting Act, which promised centralized administration, cost accounting, and the depoliticization of the financial system of the federal government.

With the establishment of the Institute of Economics in 1922, and the subsequent merging of the IGR and IE into the Brookings Institution in 1927, the concept of rationality was broadened to include economic policy, which was defined as including all government action within the economic system. Harold G. Moulton, the first president of the Brookings, was primarily responsible for this extension of the institution's research agenda beyond purely administrative concerns to questions of policy, and thus for the reinterpretation of "efficiency" to mean not only a technical ratio between costs and results within organizations, but rather the overall economic relationship between human costs incurred and benefits produced for the system as a whole. In this sense, Moulton and his colleagues sought to introduce rationality to the entire economic system by evaluating specific economic policies in terms of what produced the greatest good for the greatest number of people.

Neither the IGR nor the Brookings Institution, because of their concern with the immediate, defined public interest in terms of absolute ends. What exactly was meant by the good society remained an ambiguous but an implicitly understood result of the system represented by the institutions, protection of the general welfare by disinterested experts engaged in nonpartisan research and evaluation. Nevertheless, the advent of the New Deal forced the Brookings Institution to address the issue of ultimate ends. With the rapid extension of government into the marketplace, Roosevelt's politicization of the bureaucracy, and the emergence of Keynesian economics, the Brookings Institution gradually came to define the public interest in terms of defense of the marketplace against excessive government intervention. Moulton and his staff viewed the market as a primary mechanism for creating the good society and perceived nonpartisanship as a means for ensuring that partisan forces did not subvert the best interests of the nation. In the course of battling against the New Deal and Keynesian economics, the Brookings

went one step further and translated minimal government interference and a balanced budget into moral imperatives. As a result,
compromise was made impossible.

The role of an elite protecting the public interest, the role in
which the Brookings staff members cast themselves, implied a fear
of partisan interests seen as manipulating and appeasing the base
passions of the masses. The role also required the social scientists at
the Brookings Institution to oppose powerful corporate interests in
America. The public interest provided a symbol that defined the organizational nexus for the institution. Any attempt by Moulton or
others to have rejected this symbol would have undermined the
rationale for the institution's existence. The institution had no
choice, therefore, but to stand its ground against the coal interests
and the isolationists in the 1920s; Roosevelt and the New Dealers in
the 1930s; and the Keynesians and the deficit spenders in the 1940s.
The ideal of the public interest gave the institution its own logic—
indeed, its own history.

The plethora of think tanks operating in the political arena today,
and the increased complexity of the public policy process since
World War II, present a sharp contrast to the situation of the Brookings Institution during the Moulton years. Under Moulton, the institution stood alone in the public policy research field. It is true
that the National Bureau of Economic Research (NBER) made significant contributions during these same years to the general understanding of economics, contributions that had clear policy implications. Nevertheless, the NBER remained primarily concerned with
the collection and analysis of economic data, and less concerned
with the direct evaluation of contemporary economic policy. Although corporate business, for its part, sponsored specific research
groups, this effort primarily served corporate lobbying efforts. And
there were nonpartisan research institutes that operated on municipal and state levels, but their interests in national economic policy
remained of secondary importance. The Brookings Institution in
those years between wars remained, therefore, the single most important research institution in the nation.

Today the Brookings Institution still sees itself as the champion
of the public interest. Yet this ideal seems even more diffuse than
previously because of the rapid growth of other research institutes
in the postwar period, representing a wide spectrum of opinion.
Beginning with the establishment of the Rand Corporation in 1948,
with an annual budget of $3 million largely underwritten by the Air

Force, the postwar period witnessed a mushrooming of private nonpartisan policy institutes. The American Enterprise Institute, initially established in 1943 as a propaganda agency for promoting free enterprise, emerged in the 1960s under its president William Baroody as a clear rival to Brookings. On the left, the Institute for Policy Studies was formed by Marcus Raskin to develop alternative economic policies for the nation.[22]

The emergence of these think tanks has created a powerful influence on governmental policy making. The existence of large, well-financed research institutions influencing government policy decisions was not foreseen by the Founding Fathers when they wrote the Constitution; yet these groups function in effect as a new branch of government by formulating, overseeing, and implementing government policies. They operate outside the electoral process to influence both government administration and the legislative process, but their powers to affect government are not absolute and are moderated by the complexity of government itself, other interest groups, and a diversity of opinion among themselves over policies. The complexity of government today diffuses the power of think tanks but also limits the ability of the electoral process to effect changes in government.

Although these research organizations exert a disproportionate influence on the policy process, they do not represent the dominance, as some social scientists have suggested, of a technological elite which has replaced industrialists and politicians in making decisions that affect the entire society.[23] Experts, as Max Weber observed, are not a creation of modern times. Even preindustrial rulers relied on those with specialized skills to act as political and economic administrators. Such specialists, however, did not displace dominant elites, any more than have experts in the advanced industrial countries. Knowledge does confer power, but in the end, real power stems from the capacity to determine final policy; and in our society this ultimate power lies in "nonspecialists," elected representatives and the political appointees who often head government organizations. At best, research organizations such as the Brookings Institution, the Rand Corporation, and the American Enterprise Institute act as countervailing powers to one another.

The growth of these research organizations remains a peculiarly American phenomenon. The complexity of advanced industrial systems demands expertise, of course, but in Western European countries and in Japan, public policy research and formulation remain primarily within the state. Because economic policy within these other nations remains largely centralized, as evidenced by indicative planning in France, national planning in Norway and Sweden, and the functioning of the Ministry of International Trade and Industry in Japan, private nonpartisan institutes have not flourished in these countries.[24]

Any explanation of this phenomenon must rest in America's history as one of the first democracies in the world, as well as an early industrializer. The democratic tradition in this country caused Americans, during the phase of industrialization in the nineteenth century, to display a strong distrust of the state, which precluded the government from undertaking active planning policies. Further, because the United States underwent industrialization comparatively early, the scale of industry was smaller than in nations that industrialized later and more rapidly, and there was less direct need for government intervention. Thus because individual entrepreneurs could mobilize their own resources, the United States maintained a relatively weak and passive state.[25]

Franklin Roosevelt's attempt to strengthen and to politicize the bureaucratic state in the early 1930s faced inevitable opposition from those who believed the relatively weak traditional state should be protected from partisan intrusion and from what they perceived as a drift toward socialism. By the late 1930s a strong antibureaucratic sentiment had emerged among anti–New Deal conservatives, who genuinely feared the possibilities of a socialist America. The immediate consequence of their anxieties was a direct attack on the leviathan, bureaucracy itself. The conservatives' call for fiscal responsibility through a balanced budget also identified the growth of bureaucracy as detrimental to the nation's well-being. By World War II, conservatives felt confident enough to target specific New Deal agencies for the axe. A particular triumph was the brutal disbanding of the National Resources Planning Board in 1943. After the war, conservatives were able to defeat proposals for national health insurance and for a full-employment bill. As a consequence of such efforts, the United States failed to develop a centralized state-planning apparatus. Rather, Democrats who feared the label of socialist and Republicans who distrusted the political manipulation of the bureaucracy by liberals (those "long-haired men and short-haired women") agreed to a policy of incremental growth of existing New Deal agencies. Instead of developing state-investment policies, adopting long-range economic goals, and undertaking genuine economic reform, both parties accepted limited fiscal and monetary policies instead of state planning in a market economy.

Without centralized state planning, government turned by necessity to private nonpartisan organizations and to universities for much of their research and for policy development and evaluation. The inevitable outcome was the emergence of a huge research establishment operating outside, but heavily dependent on, government. Philanthropic foundations such as Ford and Rockefeller, concerned that scholarly objectivity be maintained, continued to grant research institutions immense sums of money to ensure them some independence from government. The emergence of the postwar research establishment, along with the creation of the government's own internal research agencies—including the Congressional Budget Office, the Library of Congress, and the Council of Economic Advisors, to name only a few—meant that such a plethora of voices would be heard within the public policy arena that any agreement as to a cogent program for economic stability, industrial growth, or social reform would become impossible.

Thus Harold Moulton, who had played so significant a role in articulating the complaints against the National Resources Planning Board, national health insurance, and full-employment proposals, helped create the conditions for the establishment of a myriad of private research institutes in the absence of centralized state planning. Today these new institutes compete with the Brookings Institution for funds, prestige, and influence. The precise meaning of public interest in a democracy, long sought by those associated with the IGR and Brookings, remains as elusive as ever.

Today social history has produced new insights for our understanding of the past. "History from below" has become a watchword for both Marxists and non-Marxists. Yet, as Marxist historian Perry Anderson observes, if our historical understanding is not to be one-sided, historians need to pay equal attention to "history from above."[26] In doing so, historians must develop a more sophisticated view of elites and their relationship to the state. Simplistic descriptions of capitalist hegemony over the public policy process and mechanistic formulas for explaining capitalist-state linkages must be rejected. Historians must assume that individuals and their institutions can play varied, and even exceptional, roles in society, roles that at times may appear neither logical or rational in relation to our understanding of the world. Robert S. Brookings's hopes for a better world were not particularly corporatist; nor were the pur-veyors of his dream, Moulton and his colleagues, simply apologists for the capitalist order.

Moreover, Brookings's dream of a reformed society, an equitable distribution of wealth, a harmony between the social orders, and peace in the world may have been, like El Dorado, an illusion. Nonetheless, it remains a kingdom worth seeking.

NOTES

CHAPTER I

1. Theodore C. Sorenson, *Kennedy* (New York, 1965), 229–30.

2. Quoted in Paul Dickson, *Think Tanks* (New York, 1971).

3. Leonard Silk and Mark Silk, *The American Establishment* (New York, 1980), 157.

4. James Weinstein, *The Corporate Ideal and the Liberal State* (Boston, 1968), 157.

5. R. Jeffrey Lustig, *Corporate Liberalism: The Origins of Modern Political Theory, 1890–1920* (Berkeley, Calif., 1982), xi–xii. Phillips C. Schmitter defines corporation as "a particular model or ideal-type institutional arrangement for linking the associationally organized interests of civil society with dimensional structures of the state" ("Still the Century of Corporatism?" in *The New Corporatism: Social and Political Structures in the Iberian World*, ed. Fredrick B. Pike and Thomas Stritch [Notre Dame, Ind., 1974], 86). For other works on corporate liberalism, as the term is employed by historians, see Gabriel Kolko, *Railroads and Regulation* (Princeton, N.J., 1965); Kolko, *The Triumph of Conservatism* (New York, 1963); Ellis W. Hawley, "The Discovery and Study of a 'Corporate Liberalism,'" *Business History Review* 52 (Autumn 1978): 309–20; Martin J. Sklar, "Woodrow Wilson and the Political Economy of Modern U.S. Liberalism,'" *Studies on the Left*, 1960: 17–47; Joan Hoff Wilson, *Herbert Hoover: The Forgotten Progressive* (Boston, 1975); Hawley, "Herbert Hoover, the Commerce Secretariat, and the Vision of an 'Associative State,' 1921–1928," *Journal of American History* 61 (June 1974): 116–40; Hawley, *The Great War and the Search for Modern Order* (New York, 1972); and Robert Griffith, "Dwight D. Eisenhower and the Corporate Commonwealth," *American Historical Review* 87 (February 1982): 87–112. The relationship of corporate liberalism to think tanks in the twentieth century is developed in David W. Eakins's pioneering study "The Development of Corporate Liberal Policy Research in the United States, 1885–1965" (Ph.D. diss., University of Wisconsin, 1966).

6. G. William Domhoff, *The Higher Circles: The Governing Class in America* (New York, 1970), 157, 182–84.

7. Nicos Poulantzas, *Political Power and Social Classes*, trans. Timothy O'Hagen (London, 1973). Also see David Gold et al., "Recent Developments in Marxist Theories of the Capitalist State," *Monthly Review* 27 (October, November 1975): 29–43, 36–51.

8. Fred Block, "The Ruling Class Does Not Rule: Notes on the Marxist Theory of the State," *Socialist Revolution*, May–June 1977: 6–28; Theda Skocpol, "Political Response to Capitalist Crisis: Neo-Marxist Theories of the State and the Case of the New Deal," *Politics and Society*, 1980: 155–99.

9. Skocpol, "Political Response," 199.

10. Woodrow Wilson, "Democracy and Efficiency" (*Atlantic Monthly*, March 1901), in *Selected Literary and Political Papers and Addresses of Woodrow Wilson* (New York, 1925), 1:112.

11. Jeffrey C. Alexander, *The Antinomies of Classical Thought: Marx and Durkheim*. Vol. 2 of *Theoretical Logic in Sociology* (Berkeley, Calif., 1982), xix–xx, 91.

12. Howard Alrich, *Organizations and Environments* (New York, 1979). For an excellent critique of this perspective, see Mary Zey-Farrell, "Criticisms of the Dominant Perspective on Organizations," *Sociological Quarterly* 12 (Spring 1981): 181–205.

13. James Gilbert, *Designing the Industrial State: The Intellectual Pursuit of Collectivism in America, 1880–1940* (Chicago, 1972), 3.

14. Gilbert, *Designing the Industrial State*, 5.

15. Historians writing of nations other than the United States have been more sensitive to the role individuals can play in large bureaucracies. For instance, see W. Bruce Lincoln, *In the Vanguard of Reform: Russia's Enlightened Bureaucrats, 1825–1861* (DeKalb, Ill., 1982); Richard S. Wortman, *The Development of a Russian Legal Consciousness* (Chicago, 1976); and Chalmers Johnson, *MITI and the Japanese Miracle: The Growth of Industrial Policy, 1925–1975* (Stanford, Calif., 1982), esp. 170–73.

16. David Vogel, "Why Businessmen Distrust Their State: The Political Consciousness of American Corporate Executives," *British Journal of Political Science* 17 (January 1978): 45–78. Also see Stephen Skowronek, *Building a New American State: The Expansion of National Administrative Capacities, 1877–1920* (London, 1982), 3–35. Skowronek astutely argues that "the absence of a sense of the state . . . has been the great hallmark of American political culture," but he also maintains that this country created a strong "centralized state" at the end of the nineteenth century.

CHAPTER 2

1. The political crisis of the nineteenth century in America was quite apparent to foreign observers, especially M. Ostrogorski, *Democracy and the Party System* (New York, 1910), 268–73, 387–90, 398–400; and James Bryce's classic, *American Commonwealth* (London, 1888). Richard T. Ely's shock of returning to American urban life after studying in Germany is revealed in *Ground under Our Feet* (New York, 1938), 65–67; Walter Dean Burnham brilliantly discusses the implications of this political crisis in *Critical Elections and the Mainsprings of American Politics* (New York, 1970),

71–90. Also useful are Alan P. Grimes, *The Puritan Ethic and Woman's Suffrage* (New York, 1967), and *Political Liberalism of the New Nation* (Chapel Hill, N.C., 1953). All recent American historians are indebted to Samuel P. Hays for originally calling attention in a series of monographs to the discussions of depoliticization that were carried on during the Progressive period: "Political Parties and the Community-Society Continuum," in William N. Chambers and Walter Dean Burnham, eds., *The American Party Systems* (New York, 1967), esp. 171–80; "The New Organizational Society," in *Building the Organizational Society: Essays on Associational Activities in Modern America*, ed. Jerry Israel (New York, 1972); and "The Politics of Reform in Municipal Government in the Progressive Era," *Pacific Northwest Quarterly* 55 (October 1964): 157–69. Of the many books on politics in the 1890s, I found J. Rogers Hollingsworth, *The Whirligig of Politics* (Chicago, 1963), the most useful. The preceding period is treated in H. Wayne Morgan, *From Hayes to McKinley: National Party Politics, 1877–1896* (Syracuse, N.Y., 1969). On the discussions among intellectuals concerning this crisis, see Thomas L. Haskell, *The Emergence of Professional Social Science* (Urbana, Ill., 1977), esp. 3–4, 15–47; R. Jackson Wilson, *In Quest of Community: Social Philosophy in the United States, 1860–1920* (New York, 1965); and Jean B. Quandt, *From Small Town to the Great Community: The Social Thought of Progressive Intellectuals* (New Brunswick, N.J., 1970). David W. Noble traces the tensions in reform philosophy in *The Paradox of Progressive Thought* (Minneapolis, Minn., 1958). The relationship among science, technology, and social order is discussed by David F. Noble, *America by Design* (New York, 1977); and James Gilbert, *Designing the Corporate State* (Madison, Wis., 1970).

2. For a summary of the evolution of the idea of an executive budget, see Louis Fisher, *Presidential Spending Power* (Princeton, N.J., 1975), 17–35; and Lewis Kimmel, *Federal Budget and Fiscal Policy, 1789–1958* (Washington, D.C., 1959).

3. Bruere's background is discussed in Augustus Cerillo, Jr., "The Reform of Municipal Government in New York City," *New York Historical Society Quarterly* 57 (January 1973): 51–71; Martin T. Schiesl, *The Politics of Efficiency: Municipal Administration and Reform in America, 1890–1920* (Berkeley, Calif., 1977); and Robert Muccigrosso, "The City Reform Club: A Study in Late Nineteenth Century Reform," *New York Historical Society Quarterly* 52 (July 1968): 235–54.

For a fascinating account of New York politics and society at the turn of the century, see David C. Hammack, *Power and Society: Greater New York at the Turn of the Century* (New York, 1982).

4. William H. Allen, *Efficient Democracy* (New York, 1907), 182.

5. William H. Allen, "Reminiscences," Oral History Project, Columbia University; Jane S. Dahlberg, *The New York Bureau of Municipal Research: Pioneer in Government Administration* (New York, 1966).

6. Mary E. Richmond, "The Retail Method of Reform," in *The Long View: Papers and Addresses* (New York, 1930), quoted in Roy Lubovo, *The Professional Altruist: The Emergence of Social Work as a Career, 1880–1900* (Cambridge, Mass., 1965), 186. See also Allen Davis, *Spearheads for Reform: The Social Settlements and the Progressive Movement, 1890–1914* (New York, 1967).

7. Mary Furner presents a provocative account of the professionalization of the social sciences during this period in *Advocacy and Objectivity: A Crisis in the Professionalization of American Social Science, 1865–1905* (Lexington, Ky., 1975).

8. A typical example of this transition from moral reform to technical expertise is evident in John R. Commons's career. He began his career as a Christian socialist, but eventually became a technical expert in industrial compensation. John H. Commons, *Myself* (Madison, Wis., 1936).

9. Gerald W. McFarland, *Mugwumps, Morals, and Politics, 1884–1920* (Amherst, Mass., 1975), 51. A discussion of professionals and progressivism is found in Wayne K. Hobson, "Professionals, Progressives, and Bureaucratization: A Reassessment," *Historian,* 39 (August 1977): 639–58.

10. John G. Sprout, *"The Best Men": Liberal Reformers in the Gilded Age* (New York, 1968); Ari Hoogenboom, *Outlawing the Spoils: A History of the Civil Service Reform Movement, 1865–1883* (Urbana, Ill., 1961); John Tomsich, *A Genteel Endeavor: American Culture and Politics in the Gilded Age* (Stanford, Calif., 1971); Robert H. Wiebe, *The Search for Order, 1877–1920* (New York, 1967), 170–74. Samuel Haber discusses the relationship between mugwumps and the efficiency and economy issue in *Efficiency and Uplift: Scientific Management in the Progressive Era, 1890–1920* (Chicago, 1964), 101–6. Mugwump attitudes toward democracy and political leadership are quite evident in much of the writing of progressive reformers during this period. See Richard T. Ely, "Progressivism, True and False —An Outline," *Review of Reviews* 51 (February 1915): 209–11; F. W. Blackmar, "Leadership in Reform," *American Journal of Sociology* 16 (March 1911): 626–33; C. H. Grabo, "Education for Democratic Leadership," *American Journal of Sociology* 23 (May 1918): 763–78; Richard T. Ely, *The Coming City* (New York, 1902), 49–59.

11. Edmund Janes James, *Economic Science Discussion* (New York, 1886), 24–28. For other rejections of laissez-faire economics see Francis A. Walker, "The Tide of Economic Thought," *Publications of the American Economic Association* 6 (1891): 20–21; Henry C. Adams, *The Science of Finance* (Boston, 1898); and Adams, *Relation of the State to Industrial Action, Economics and Jurisprudence,* ed. Joseph Dorfman (New York, 1954). The influence of German economics is discussed by Dorfman, "The Role of the German Historical School in American Economic Thought," *American Economic Review* 45, supp. (May 1955): 17–28; and Jurgen Herbst, *The German Historical School in American Scholarship: A Study in the Transfer of Culture* (Ithaca, N.Y., 1965). In political science, natural-rights philosophy had come under attack as well. William F. Willoughby declared in 1891 that the state determined individual and community rights. Furthermore, he continued, "It is required of government today that it shall not be content with the mere exercise of its essential functions, but it shall take full advantage of its optimal powers to better the material conditions of citizens" (*"State Activities and Politics," Papers of the American Historical Association* [New York, 1891], 118). By 1919 Willoughby could declare that only the public believed in natural rights (*An Introduction to the Study of the Government of Modern States* [New York, 1919], 168). Frank Goodnow, *Principles of Constitutional Government* (New York, 1916), maintained that natural-rights philosophy was

static and reactionary. English idealists led by T. H. Green had developed a view of the state as an organic entity, and American political scientists found this concept useful in challenging the natural-rights philosophy. William F. Willoughby's brother, Westel, was America's leading proponent of the organic view of the state. For the best examples of his work see his *Introduction to the Problem of Government* (New York, 1921) and *The Nature of the State—A Study in Political Philosophy* (New York, 1896). For discussions of T. H. Green see James Bryce, "Thomas Hill Green, 1836–1892," in *Studies in Contemporary Biography* (New York, 1903), 85–100; and George H. Sabine, *A History of Political Theory* (New York, 1961), 726–35.

12. E. L. Godkin in the *Nation* (1867), quoted in Grimes, *Puritan Ethic and Woman's Suffrage*, 15–29. See Ely, *Ground under Our Feet*, 125–26.

13. Godkin, *The Gilded Age Letters of E. L. Godkin*, ed. William Armstrong (Albany, N.Y., 1974), 434. Also, see Godkin, *Problems of Modern Democracy* (New York, 1903), esp. 176; Simon Newcomb, "The Two Schools of Political Economy," *Princeton Review* 14 (1884): 291–301; Newcomb, "Review of 'An Introduction to Political Economy,'" *Journal of Political Economy*, 1884–85, 106; and a harsh review of Ely's *Labor Movement in the United States, Nation* 42 (1886): 292–93.

14. Benjamin G. Rader shows Ely's elitism in his fine biography *The Academic Mind and Reform: The Influence of Richard T. Ely in American Life* (Lexington, Ky., 1966), 111–36.

15. Richard T. Ely, *Socialism: An Examination of Its Future, Its Strength, and Its Weakness, with Suggestions for Social Reform* (New York, 1894), v–x. Also, see Ely, *The Labor Movement in the United States* (New York, 1883).

16. Richard T. Ely, *The Past and Present of Political Economy*, Johns Hopkins University Studies in History and Political Science, no. 30 (Baltimore, Md., 1884). A similar point would be made seventy years later by Gunnar Myrdal, in *The Political Element in the Development of Economic Theory* (New York, 1953).

17. This point is developed in Furner, *Advocacy and Objectivity*.

18. The decline in voter participation is discussed in Burnham, *Critical Elections*. There is an extensive literature on the subject, with particular reference to this period.

19. The 1904 election is summarized in Cerillo, "Reform of Municipal Government," 51–71.

20. Quoted in Dahlberg, *New York BMR*, 4. See also Gerald Kurland, *Seth Low: The Reformer in an Urban and Industrial Age* (New York, 1971), 15–50, 178–89.

21. "Brief for the Establishment of an Institute for Municipal Research," City Committee File, Citizen Union Papers, Columbia University. Efficient reform is discussed in Allen, *Efficient Democracy*, 179–301. .

22. For insight into Cutting's ideas on reform, see his *Address Given to the Citizens Union Dinner, January 7, 1902* (New York, 1902) and *The Citizens Union, Its Origins and Purpose: Address Given at the Nineteenth Century Club, April 14, 1903* (New York, 1903).

23. The best discussion of the political and professional attitudes of accountants can be found in John Carey, *The Rise of the Accounting Profession, 1896–1969* (New York, 1969), 1–88. Also, the *Journal of Accounting* provides

a good idea of the flavor of accounting during this period. Other descriptions of accounting are John Bauer, "Accounting," *Encyclopedia of the Social Sciences* (New York, 1948), 404–12; and Ananias C. Littleton, *Accounting Evolution to 1900* (New York, 1966).

24. Sketches of Frederick Cleveland's career are found in *Who's Who* (New York, 1920); "How Taft Is Doing It," *Review of Reviews* 42 (December 1910): 657; "Politics—Sociology—Ethics," *Review of Reviews* 49 (January 1914): 123; Allen, *Efficient Democracy*, 258.

25. Luther Gulick, interview with author, May 21, 1975, New York.

26. Frederick A. Cleveland, ed., Charles Waldo Haskins, *Business Education and Accountancy* (New York, 1904), 22–23.

27. Cleveland, ed., *Business Education and Accountancy*, 22.

28. Bureau of Municipal Research, *How Manhattan Is Governed* (New York, 1906). The work of the BMR is revealed particularly in William H. Allen, "Better Business Methods for Cities," *Review of Reviews* 37 (February 1908): 195–200; Frederick A. Cleveland, "The Basis of Municipal Research," *New Republic* 1 (January 23, 1915): 23–24; Henry Bruere et al., "Efficiency in City Government," *Annals* 41 (May 1912): 3–22. See also Cleveland, "Budget Making and the Increased Cost of Government," *American Economic Review* 6, supp. (March 1916): 50–70; Frank J. Goodnow, *Politics and Administration* (1900; reprint, New York, 1967), 122–30; Cleveland, *Chapters in Municipal Administration and Accounting* (New York, 1907), 102–4, 202–5; Cleveland, "The Need for Coordinating State and National Activities," *Annals* 41 (May 1912): 24, 27; Henry Bruere, "Efficiency in City Government," *Annals* 41 (May 1912): 3–6. A valuable insight into the BMR is gained from a close reading of its official monthly publication, *Municipal Research* (1906–16).

29. For readable accounts of the BMR and New York municipal reform during this period, see Robert A. Caro, *The Power Broker: Robert Moses and the Fall of New York* (New York, 1974), 60–135; Luther Gulick, *The National Institute for Public Service* (New York, 1929); and Raymond Fosdick, *Chronicle of a Generation* (New York, 1958).

30. Dahlberg, *New York BMR*, 152.

31. Raymond Fosdick, "The Mayor's Eye" (1910), in Fosdick Papers, box I, Princeton University.

32. Frederick Cleveland to Charles Norton, October 13, 1910, William Howard Taft Papers, Library of Congress (Microfilm Presidential Series 6, no. 215 [Washington, D.C., 1969]).

33. Edwin R. Lewinson, *John Purroy Mitchel* (New York, 1965), 54–55. On the role of the BMR in the drafting of the New York State Constitution, see Frederick A. Cleveland, "The Short Ballot and the New York Constitution," *Review of Reviews* 52 (August 1915): 195–98; Cleveland, *The Budget and Responsible Government* (New York, 1920), 140–47; George Wickersham, "The New Constitution and the Work of the Bureau of Municipal Research," *Real Estate Magazine*, October 1915, 1–6; Charles A. Beard, "Reconstructing State Government," *New Republic* 4, supp. (August 21, 1915): 1–16; Bureau of Municipal Research, *The Constitution of the State of New York: An Appraisal* (Albany, N.Y., 1915).

34. Caro, *Power Broker*, 63.

35. Quoted in Caro, *Power Broker*, 83.

36. E. A. Fitzpatrick, "Municipal Research—A Criticism," *New Republic* 1 (January 2, 1915): 19–21.

37. Schiesl, *Politics of Efficiency*. See also Frank Mann Stewart, *A Half Century of Municipal Reform: The History of the National Municipal League* (Berkeley, Calif., 1950); and William H. Toman, *The Municipal Reform Movement in the United States* (New York, 1895).

38. Taft is portrayed as a conservative by Donald F. Anderson, *William Howard Taft: A Conservative's Conception of the Presidency* (Ithaca, N.Y., 1968); and Paolo E. Coletta, *The Presidency of William Howard Taft* (Lawrence, Kans., 1973). A more balanced view of Taft's Progressivism is found in Richard Abrams, *Conservatism in a Progressive Era: Massachusetts Politics, 1900–1912* (Cambridge, Mass., 1964), 217–19. Taft's reliance on conservative elements in the party for assistance in gaining the Republican nomination in 1912 may have been shrewd politics once he had broken with the insurgents. See Norman M. Wilensky, "Conservatives in the Progressive Era," *University of Florida Monographs: Social Science* 25 (Winter 1965).

39. Kimmel, *Federal Budget and Fiscal Policy*, 85.

40. Charles Norton, "Memorandum to the President," September 15, 1910; Charles Norton to Charles Hines, August 2, 1910; Cleveland to Charles Norton, "Memorandum," September 17, 1910; "Announcement: The President's Bureau on Efficiency and Economy" (n.d.)—all in Taft Papers.

41. *Dictionary of American Biography*, supp. 2 (New York, 1974): 250–51; *Essays on the Law and Practice of Government Administration*, ed. Charles G. Haines (Baltimore, Md., 1935), v–xv. See also Lurton W. Blassingame, "Frank J. Goodnow: Progressive/Urban Reformer," *North Dakota Quarterly* 40 (Summer 1972): 22–30. In the late 1880's only three schools were offering courses in public administration. Herbert Tuttle taught a course in municipal administration at Cornell, Woodrow Wilson taught one in public administration at Johns Hopkins, and Goodnow began presenting courses in municipal administration and administration law at Columbia in 1884, after study at the École Libre des Sciences Politiques in Paris and further work at the University of Berlin. Goodnow did not publish his great work *Comparative Administrative Law* until 1893. See John C. French, *A History of the University Founded by Johns Hopkins* (Baltimore, Md., 1946), 187–98; and Arthur S. Link, "Woodrow Wilson and the Study of Administration," in *The Higher Realism of Woodrow Wilson* (Nashville, Tenn., 1971), 41.

42. Henry Bruere to Charles Norton, "Memorandum—Suggestions for F. A. Cleveland Regarding a Social Welfare Program for the Nation," November 7, 1910, Taft Papers. Allen stressed that the goal of the IGR was not "penny pinching or economy for its own sake" ("Reminiscences," Oral History Project, Columbia University, 158–59).

43. President's Commission on Economy and Efficiency, *The Need for a National Budget*, 62nd Cong., 2nd sess., 1910, H. Doc. 854, 23, 143, 219; Frederick Cleveland, *Budget and Responsible Government*, 78–79.

44. Joseph Cannon, "The National Budget," *Harpers Weekly* 139 (October 1919): 621; Henry C. Adams, "Problems of Budgetary Reform,"

Journal of Political Economy 27 (October 1919): 621–38; J. P. Chamberlain, "American Budgetary Reform," *Nation* 108 (June 21, 1919): 976–78; W. F. Willoughby, *The Problem of a National Budget* (Washington, D.C., 1912); and Carl Hayden, speech, *Congressional Record*, 67th Cong., 1st sess., May 3, 1921, 987–88.

45. Clearly at the time Taft's concerns with budgeting were seen as Progressive. See four articles by Franklin MacVeagh: "Departmental Economy," *Independent* 69 (December 22, 1910): 1366–69; "President Taft and the Roosevelt Policies," *Outlook* 101 (May 18, 1912): 110–16; "Mr. Taft's Four Years," *Independent* 74 (March 6, 1913): 488–89; "President Taft and the Cost of Government," *Outlook* 102 (October 5, 1912): 235–36. See also W. F. Willoughby, "History of the Budget—Confidential Report" (1921), in Brookings Institution Files, Washington, D.C. (hereafter cited as BIF).

46. Cleveland, *Budget and Responsible Government*, 84–85; and Paolo E. Coletta, *Presidency of Taft*, 130–32.

47. *Congressional Record*, 1912, 48, pt. 1: 1824. See also Henry L. Stimson, "A National Budget System," *World's Work* 38 (September 1919): 528–36; Fritz Marx, "The Bureau of the Budget and Its Present Role," *American Political Science Review* 39 (August, October, 1945): 653–84, 869–98.

48. Frank Goodnow wrote W. B. Monroe that "we ought to put the American Political Science Association behind the movement for a national budget." Subsequently the two men made plans to make the session on economy and efficiency "one of the most important" at the December 1912 session. Frank Goodnow to W. B. Monroe, October 23, November 19, 1912, in Goodnow Papers, Johns Hopkins University.

49. Arthur B. Farquhar to Frank Goodnow, September 10, 1912, in Goodnow Papers.

50. The nine included Charles D. Norton, vice president of the National Bank of New York; Jerome D. Greene, secretary of the Rockefeller Foundation; Raymond Fosdick, adviser to John D. Rockefeller; James F. Curtis, Fosdick's law partner; Anson Phelps Stokes; R. Fulton Cutting; Charles P. Neill, former U.S. commissioner of labor; Frederick Strauss, a banker; and Theodore N. Vail, president of American Telephone and Telegraph. Jerome D. Greene to Robert Calkins, April 29, 1954, BIF. Also, Institute for Government Research, "Confidential Prospectus" (n.d.), BIF.

51. Jerome Greene to Robert Calkins, April 19, 1954, BIF.

52. "Early Interest of the Rockefeller Foundation in Research in Economics and Government" (1952?), BIF; Executive Committee of the Rockefeller Foundation to Brookings Institution, November 30, 1914, BIF. Other early contributors to the IGR included J. P. Morgan, who gave $12,000; Willard Straight, $10,000; R. Fulton Cutting, $10,000. For hostility to the Rockefeller Foundation see "Probe of U.S. Offices," *Washington Post*, July 23, 1916, clipping in BIF.

53. Jerome Greene to Robert Calkins, April 29, 1954, BIF.

• 54. BIF documents: Director in Charge of Research, "Memorandum—Appropriations from the Rockefeller Association," July 28, 1915; Raymond Fosdick to Frederick Cleveland, April 15, 1917; Frederick Cleveland to E. R. Embree (n.d.); W. F. Willoughby to E. R. Embree, November 11, 1918; "A Report on Studies for Rockefeller Foundation, January 1919;

Robert Brookings to W. F. Willoughby, February 17, 1919. The Rockefeller
Foundation awarded $100,000 to the IGR in 1916.

55. The early staff of the IGR included Henry Seidemann, Gustavus A.
Weber, Arthur W. Proctor, H. J. Simons, A. G. Thomas, and Lewis Mer-
iam. All had extensive government service; most had gone to schools in
the East, particularly the Baltimore-Washington area; all had been trained
in either accounting or the social sciences. Director of the Institute for
Governmental Research, *Report to the Trustees* (Washington, D.C., 1916);
Charles Thomson, *The Institute for Government Research* (Washington,
D.C., 1956).

56. Willoughby's own career, compared with those of other staff members, was less indicative of a shift from reform issues to technical concerns.
Nevertheless, it is interesting to note that he began his career working for
the Labor Department, where he was concerned largely with the conditions of working men. Although he would later be president of the American Association for Labor Legislation, a leading Progressive reform association, he would not publish anything on American labor after 1901.

57. *The National Encyclopedia*, vol. 1 (New York, 1930), 212–13. In 1900
Willoughby was commissioned to write a series of pamphlets for the U.S.
Commission to Paris. These pamphlets, which provide an excellent insight
into his views on labor, were reprinted in *Monographs on American Social
Economics*, ed. Herbert B. Adams, vols. 5, 6, 9, 10 (Boston, 1900). See also
Adams, *State Activities in Relation to Labor in the United States*, Johns Hopkins
University Studies, no. 19 (Baltimore, Md., 1901).

58. Edward J. Berbusse, *The United States in Puerto Rico, 1898–1900*
(Chapel Hill, N.C., 1966), 182–83; Truman R. Clark, *Puerto Rico and the
United States, 1917–1933* (Pittsburgh, Pa., 1975), 11–12.

59. William F. Willoughby, "Two Years of Legislation in Porto Rico,"
Atlantic Monthly 90 (July, 1902): 34–42; Willoughby, "The Reorganization of Municipal Government in Porto Rico," *Political Science Quarterly*
24 (September 1909): 409–43.

60. Willoughby's appointment to the Census Bureau is discussed in *Review of Reviews* 40 (September 1909): 266.

61. Willoughby, *Introduction to the Study of the Government of Modern
States*, 81–85, 89–90. Willoughby's twin brother, Westel, a professor of
political science, proposed in 1921 that "the vote of each individual be
given a weight proportionate to the intelligence of the person who casts it."
There is no record that W. F. Willoughby commented directly on his
brother's proposal, although he believed that voting requirements should
be restricted. Westel W. Willoughby and Lindsay Rogers, *An Introduction to
the Problem of Government* (New York, 1921).

62. Willoughby, "State Activities and Politics," 114–18.

63. W. F. Willoughby, "The Problem of Political Education in Puerto
Rico," *Report of the Twenty-sixth Annual Meeting of the Lake Mohonk Conference* (Lake Mohonk, N.Y., 1908), 160–62, 166.

64. Jerome Greene to Robert Calkins, April 19, 1915, BIF.

65. Raymond Fosdick to W. F. Willoughby, January 12, 1917, BIF; W. F.
Willoughby to Raymond Fosdick, January 26, 1917, BIF. In January 1913,
Woodrow Wilson wrote Senator Benjamin Tillman, "Ever since I was a

youngster I have been deeply interested in our methods of financial legislation . . . and one of the objects I shall have most in mind when I get to
Washington will be conferences with my legislative colleagues there with a
view of bringing some budget system into existence. . . ." Quoted in
Henry Jones Ford, *Woodrow Wilson: The Man and His Work* (New York,
1916), 165.

66. Frederick A. Cleveland, "Budgeting Reform Today," *Annals* 41
(May 1921): 258; Kenneth L. Roberts, "Adventures in Budgeting," *Saturday Evening Post*, July 1, 1922, 3-4; Donald Bruce Johnson and Kirk H.
Porter, comps., *National Party Platforms, 1840-1862* (Urbana, Ill., 1966),
166.

67. *Congressional Record*, April 30, 1920, 6349-50.

68. W. F. Willoughby to Robert S. Brookings, July 19, 1919, BIF.

69. *Congressional Record*, April 30, 1920, 6349.

70. A similar question had arisen in 1789 when the Treasury Department was first established. It was decided at that time that the president
could remove an appointee from office in accordance with the general principles of appointment. In 1920, however, Congress did not view the comptroller-general as an administrative office under the jurisdiction of the
president. For the issue involving removal from office see Congressional
Research Service, *The Constitution of the United States* (Washington, D.C.,
1973), 434, 529-35; *Congressional Record*, June 4, 1920.

71. Director of the Institute for Government Research, *Report to the
Trustees* (1919, 1920), BIF.

72. W. F. Willoughby to Robert S. Brookings, November 4, 1920, BIF.

73. Fritz Marx, "The Bureau of the Budget," *American Political Science
Review* 39 (August 1945): 675.

74. Marx, "Bureau of the Budget," 675.

75. Marx, "Bureau of the Budget," 676.

76. Director of the Institute for Government Research, *Report to the
Trustees* (Washington, D.C., 1923); Thomas Sterling to W. F. Willoughby,
March 8, 1923, BIF; Lewis Meriam, *Principles Governing the Retirement of
Public Employees* (Washington, 1918). For Willoughby's involvement in
government reorganization, see W. F. Willoughby, *The Reorganization of the
Administrative Branch of the National Government* (Washington, D.C., 1923);
Willoughby, "Important Features of the Outline of the Reorganization
Plan" (n.d.), BIF; Director of the Institute for Government Research, Re-
port to the Trustees (Washington, D.C., 1923), BIF; and Willoughby et al.,
Proceedings of the American Academy of Political and Social Science (May 1924).

CHAPTER 3

1. See David W. Eakins, "The Development of Corporate Liberal Policy
Research in the United States, 1885-1965" (Ph.D. diss., University of
Wisconsin, 1966); G. William Domhoff, *The Higher Circles: The Governing
Class in America* (New York, 1970), 182-84.

2. Harrison Rhodes, "War Time Washington," *Harper's Magazine* 136
(March 1918): 465-77.

3. Irving Fisher, "Economists in Public Service," *American Economic Re-*

view 9, supp. (March 1919): 5. Also, John M. Clark, ed., "Introduction," *Readings in the Economics of War* (Chicago, 1918); Wesley Clair Mitchell, "The Prospects of Economics," in *The Trend of Economics*, ed. Rexford Guy Tugwell (New York, 1924), 21.

4. Among the biographies of Carnegie, the one that perhaps best captures the man is Joseph Frazier Wall's *Andrew Carnegie* (New York, 1970).

5. The discussion of Brookings's early life relies on two unpublished autobiographies found in the Chancellor files at Washington University. One is dated 1920, the other April 11, 1932. For a complete biography, see Hermann Hagedorn, *Brookings: A Biography* (New York, 1937).

6. "St. Louis," *Harper's Monthly Magazine* 68 (March 1884): 497−517; H. B. Wandell, *The Story of a Great City in a Nutshell* (St. Louis, 1900); Edmund S. Hoch, *St. Louis and Its Exposition* (St. Louis, 1904).

7. "Cupples Station," *Scientific American* 18 (August 29, 1903): 150−51.

8. Hagedorn, *Brookings*, 53−56.

9. Hagedorn, *Brookings*, 58.

10. Alfred D. Chandler, Jr., *The Visible Hand: The Managerial Revolution in American Business* (Cambridge, Mass., 1977), 329−30; Victor S. Clark, *History of Manufacturers in the United States* (New York, 1929), 2:461−62.

11. Gerald T. White, *The United States and the Problem of Recovery after 1893* (University, Ala., 1982), 1−8.

12. "Cupples Station," 151; Hagedorn, *Brookings*, 115−18.

13. Hagedorn, *Brookings*, 127−30; and Alexander Lansday, "The Story of Washington University, 1853−1953" (unpublished), in Washington University Library.

14. See Wandell, *Story of a Great City*, 115.

15. Wall, *Carnegie*, 1005. Wall fails to mention that Brookings traveled with Carnegie on this trip.

16. Wall, *Carnegie*, 1005.

17. Hagedorn, *Brookings*, 184, 191.

18. Hollis Godfrey submitted a list of names to serve on the National Advisory Committee, which later evolved into the WIB. See Hollis Godfrey to Colonel House, June 17, 1916, in House Papers, quoted in Robert D. Cuff, *The War Industries Board: Business-Government Relations during World War I* (New York, 1973), 38. Also, Curtice Hitchcock, "The War Industries Board: Its Development, Organization, and Functions," *Journal of Political Economy* 26 (June 1918): 545−66.

19. Jordan A. Schwarz, *The Speculator: Bernard M. Baruch in Washington, 1917−1965* (Chapel Hill, N.C., 1981), 73−76.

20. William Hard, "Retarding the Allies," *New Republic* 18 (December 29, 1917): 238−40.

21. Also, see Chandler P. Anderson diary, January 22, 1918, Anderson Papers, Library of Congress; and Schwarz, *Speculator*, 73−76.

22. Charles B. Saunders, Jr., *The Brookings Institution: A Fifty Year History* (Washington, D.C., 1966), 21; Melvin T. Urofsky, *Big Steel and the Wilson Administration: A Study in Business-Government Relations* (Columbus, Ohio, 1969), esp. 236−46.

23. For other works on the price-fixing commission, see Frank W. Taussig, "Price-Fixing as Seen by a Price-Fixer," *Quarterly Journal of Eco-*

nomics 33 (February 1919): 205–41; Lewis Haney, "Price Fixing in the United States during the War," *Political Science Quarterly* 34 (September 1919): 434–53; Susan Litman, *Prices and Price Controls in Great Britain and the United States during the War* (New York, 1920).

24. Robert S. Brookings to Harold G. Moulton, December 21, 1928, BIF.

25. For details of Nelson A. Nelson's fascinating experiment in cooperative ownership, see Edward Berkowitz and Kim McQuaid, *Creating the Welfare State: The Political Economy of Twentieth Century Reform* (New York, 1980), 4–10; Robert S. Brookings, *Economic Democracy: America's Answer to Socialism and Communism* (New York, 1929), xxxiii, and *Industrial Ownership: Its Economic and Social Consequences* (New York, 1928).

26. Brookings, *Economic Democracy*, 23. Robert S. Brookings to Harold G. Moulton, March 26, 1932, BIF.

27. Brookings, *Economic Democracy*, 75.

28. This ideal of the evolving nature of capitalism was quite prevalent in business circles in the 1920s. For instance, Raymond Fosdick wrote to John D. Rockefeller, Jr., that "labor in the future is going to have a great deal to say not only about working conditions and wages, but about management, the division of profits, and I am confident that your influence can help shape the introduction of this new age . . . ." Fosdick to Rockefeller, September 5, 1919, Fosdick Papers, Princeton University. Also see Morrell Heald, "Business Thought in the Twenties: Social Responsibility," *American Quarterly* 13 (Summer 1961): 126–39; Paul W. Glad, "Progressives and the Business Culture of the 1920's," *Journal of American History* 53 (June 1966): 75–89; and Joan Hoff Wilson, *American Business and Foreign Policy, 1920–1933* (Lexington, Ky., 1971).

29. Minutes of the executive committee of the IE board of trustees, April 21–22, 1922, BIF.

30. Hagedorn, *Brookings*, 261.

31. "Proposal to the Carnegie Foundation," quoted in full in the minutes of the IE board of trustees, January 5, 1922, BIF. Other research organizations founded during this time were the business-dominated National Industrial Conference Board (1916), the Food Research Institute at Stanford University (1921), and the Committee on Economic Research at Harvard University (1921).

32. For liberal support for the new institutes, see John D. Rockefeller to Jerome D. Greene, November 8, 1920, BIF; D. M. Keezer, "Making the Social Sciences Sociable," *Survey* 55 (October 15, 1925): 80–82. Other discussions of research institutes during this time can be found in the dependable Joseph Dorfman, *The Economic Mind in American Civilization* (New York, 1958), vol. 4; and David Eakins, "Development of Corporate Liberal Policy Research."

33. "Memorandum on the Early History of the Brookings Institution" (n.d.), BIF.

34. Brookings's technique for selling the IGR to corporation and business executives was to point out that they had a direct interest in seeking the introduction of sound procedures in government management. Minutes of the IGR board of trustees, June 17, 1921, BIF.

35. Minutes of the IGR board of trustees, April 18, 1918, April 17, 1919, BIF. See also Harold Moulton, "Memorandum on the Early History of the Brookings Institution," 1956; minutes of the IGR executive committee, March 16, 1920, both in BIF.

36. Robert S. Brookings to Arthur Hadley, January 17, 1924, BIF. Maintaining a nonpartisan stance was vital for raising funds, particularly from the Rockefeller Foundation. A perfect example of this concern was expressed by Harold Moulton in a letter to Brookings in which he recounted: "The Rockefeller reps who were here, as you know, were very much concerned to find out whether or not we were to be controlled by conservative capitalistic opinion. You and I know very well that we are free to pursue the truth, no matter to what conclusions it may lead. In pursuit of the truth, however, we keep our feet on the ground." Moulton to Brookings, January 21, 1921, BIF. Also included in the first board of trustees were Edwin Alderman of the University of Virginia; Charles Eliot, president emeritus of Harvard University; David Kinley, University of Illinois; Charles Walcott, president of the Smithsonian Institution; and Samuel Mather, University of Chicago. Representing business were Whiteford Smith, James J. Storrow, and Charles Hutchinson. During the past fifty-six years, 116 individuals have served as trustees for the Brookings Institution. Two were presidents of the United States, three were Supreme Court justices, three were Secretaries of War or Defense. Five other trustees have served in other cabinet posts, and three as state governors.

37. Minutes of the IE board of trustees, April 21–22, 1922, BIF.

38. Minutes of the IE board of trustees, April 21–22, 1922, BIF.

39. *Industrial Ownership* was published by the Macmillan Company in February 1928.

40. Brookings, *Economic Democracy*, 79–105.

41. *Industrial Ownership*, 56.

42. Quoted in Hagedorn, *Brookings*, 310.

43. Robert S. Brookings to Harold Moulton, March 26, 1932, BIF.

44. Adolf A. Berle and Gardiner C. Means, *The Modern Corporation and Private Property* (New York, 1932), 66–119.

CHAPTER 4

1. Moulton to Brookings, January 11, 1924, BIF.

2. Walton Hamilton, "The Institutional Approach to Economic Theory," *American Economic Review* 9, supp. (March 1919): 9–24. See also Hamilton, "Review of Hoxie's Economics," *Journal of Political Economy* 24 (November 1916): 883.

3. Edwin Nourse, oral biography, Nourse Papers, Cornell Univesity.

4. Wesley Clair Mitchell, "The Prospects of Economics," in *The Trend of Economics*, ed. Rexford Guy Tugwell (New York, 1924), 21.

5. Raymond T. Bye, "Some Developments in Economic Theory," in *Trend of Economics*, 283.

6. Sumner Slichter, "Efficiency," *Encyclopedia of Social Science* (New York, 1937), 5:437–39.

7. W. F. Willoughby to Senator Simmons, May 25, 1917, BIF.

8. Moulton to Brookings, May 8, 1922, January 21, 1924, BIF; Dr. Barbara Moulton, interview with author, Orange Grove, California, October 5, 1974; Jack Moulton, interview with author, Harpers Ferry, West Virginia, May 20, 1975.

9. A good insight into American attitudes toward sports can be gained from the periodical literature at the time. For example; Newton Fuessle, "America's Boss-Ridden Athletics," *Outlook* 130 (April 19, 1922): 642–45; "Portrait," *Colliers*, October 18, 1924, 13; March 14, 1925, 15; October 22, 1927, 10; J. B. Griswold, "You Don't Have to Be Born with It," *American Magazine* 112 (November 1921): 60; "Honor Stagg as Character-Builder," *Christian Century* 48 (October 28, 1931): 1350.

10. Robert Calkins, "Harold Glenn Moulton, 1883–1965," *American Philosophical Yearbook, 1966* (New York, 1966); Joseph Dorfman, *The Economic Mind in American Civilization* (New York, 1949), vol. 3, esp. 413–16; Alfred Borneman, *J. Laurence Laughlin* (Washington, D.C., 1940), 138.

11. J. Laurence Laughlin, *Laughlin Versus Coin: Facts about Money* (Chicago, 1896); Laughlin, *Industrial America* (New York, 1912), 54–55, 65; Dorfman, *Economic Mind*, 3:271–76; A. W. Coats, "The Origins of the 'Chicago School(s),'" *Journal of Political Economy* 71 (October 1963): 487–93.

12. *Cap and Gown, 1907* (Chicago, 1907).

13. Harold Moulton, *Waterways versus Railways* (Chicago, 1912), 1–3.

14. For typical accusations made by reformers against pork barrel politics and appropriations for waterways, see "At the Bung of 'Pork Barrel,'" *World's Work* 20 (May 1910): 12871; Hubert Bruce Fuller, "The Crime of the 'Pork Barrel,'" *World's Work* 20 (August 1910): 13259–73.

15. Moulton, *Waterways versus Railways*, 1–3.

16. Moulton, *Waterways versus Railways*, 446–47. See also Dorfman, *Economic Mind*, 3:413.

17. Moulton's entrance into business economics coincided with the great expansion of this field. The business curriculum in American colleges and universities grew from 9,000 courses in 1915 to 60,000 courses in 1930. Moulton's book *The Financial Organization of Society* (Chicago, 1924) became the standard text in many business courses. For Moulton's orientation in the classroom, see his articles "The Possibilities of a General Survey Course in Finance," *Journal of Political Economy* 29 (May 1921): 368–94; and "Commercial Banking and Capital Formation," *Journal of Political Economy* 26 (May, June, July, October 1918). Discussions of business education in this period can be found in Leverett Lyon, "Business Education," *Encyclopedia of Social Science* (New York, 1937); and Willis J. Winn, "Business Education in the United States: A Historical Perspective," Newcomen Society Address, New York, 1963.

18. Lloyd W. Mints, *A History of Banking Theory in Great Britain and the United States* (Chicago, 1945), 265.

19. As early as 1918 Moulton urged that prices be reduced and wages be maintained in order to ensure further economic growth. H. G. Moulton to Felix Frankfurter, October 30, 1918, quoted in Dorfman, *Economic Mind*, 3:335.

20. Dorfman, *Economic Mind*, 3:416; Harold L. Reed, "The Industrial Outlook," *Journal of Political Economy* 27 (April 1919): 231.

21. Moulton briefly argued for a compensatory spending policy following World War I, but he soon changed his views because he feared the inflationary consequences of a public works program.

22. H. G. Moulton, "The Economic Necessity for Disarmament," *Yale Review* 11 (January 1922): 271, 281; "Memorandum on the Early History of the Brookings Institution" (n.d.), BIF.

23. For an excellent discussion of the founding of the National Bureau of Economic Research, see Guy Alchon, "Technocratic Social Science and the Rise of Managed Capitalism, 1910–1933" (Ph.D. diss., University of Iowa, 1982).

24. H. G. Moulton to Robert S. Brookings, January 11, 1924, BIF.

25. Director of the Institute of Economics, *Annual Report* (1923), BIF.

26. Robert M. Robertson, *History of the American Economy* (New York, 1964), 515.

27. Joseph G. Knapp, "The Path to Public Service," in *In Memoriam: Edwin G. Nourse*, ed. Kermit Gordon et al. (Washington, D.C., 1975). See also two other works by Knapp: *The Advance of the American Cooperative Enterprise, 1920–1945* (Danville, Ill., 1973), 6; and *Edwin G. Nourse: Economist for the People* (Danville, Ill., 1979).

28. Joseph G. Knapp, "Nourse—Dean of American Cooperative Scholars," in *American Cooperation* (New York, 1974), 373.

29. H. G. Moulton to Robert S. Brookings, January 11, 1924.

30. H. G. Moulton to Robert S. Brookings, August 16, 1922.

31. H. G. Moulton, *The Reparation Plan: An Interpretation of the Reports of the Expert Committees Appointed by the Reparations Commission, November 30, 1923* (1924; reprinted New York, 1970).

32. H. G. Moulton to Robert S. Brookings, January 11, 1924, BIF.

33. H. G. Moulton, "War Debts and International Trade Theory," *American Economic Review* 15 (December 1925): 700–716; Moulton, "The American Stake in the War Debts," *Yale Review* 22 (September 1932): 78–96; Moulton, "Will France Get Anything from the Ruhr?" *New Republic* 34 (February 28, 1923): 14–17. Also Moulton, *Germany's Capacity to Pay* (Washington, D.C., 1923); Moulton, *The Reparation Plan* (New York, 1924); Moulton and Leo Pasvolsky, *World War Debt Settlements* (New York, 1924); Moulton and Pasvolsky, *Russian Debts* (Washington, D.C., 1924); Moulton, *America and the Balance Sheet of Europe* (Washington, D.C., 1924); Moulton and Pasvolsky, *The French Debt Problem* (Washington, D.C., 1925); Moulton, *War Debts and World Prosperity* (Washington, D.C., 1932).

34. Director of the Institute of Economics, *Annual Report* (1924), BIF.

35. R. Fulton Cutting and Raymond Fosdick were two associates of the Brookings Institution who were especially active in the reparations issue. Both belonged to the American Association Favoring Reconsideration of War Debts. For other trustees' reactions favorable to lower reparations payments, see Frederic Delano to Oscar Strauss, September 29, 1926, BIF. In 1919 Pasvolsky had reported on the Versailles Conference for the *New York Tribune*. Significantly, he would travel each year to Europe to attend the

annual session of the League of Nations. By the late 1920's Pasvolsky had become a leading expert on the League of Nations.

36. Charles B. Saunders, Jr., *The Brookings Institution: A Fifty Year History* (Washington, D.C., 1966), 31.

37. Virginia Hartley related this incident between Pasvolsky and Leon Trotsky. She said that Pasvolsky told this story to her during his work at the Department of State in World War II. Although no evidence can be found to corroborate the story, it seems plausible given Pasvolsky's involvement in the Russian community in New York. Virginia Hartley, interview with author, Washington, D.C., April 16, 1977.

38. Leo Pasvolsky, "Russian Parliament," *Russian Review*, September 1916: 99–107; Pasvolsky, "Russia's Foreign Trade During the War," *Russian Review*, February 1917: 3, 96–104.

39. Leo Pasvolsky, *The Economics of Communism with Special Reference to Russia's Experiment* (New York, 1921), vii, 64. Later, Pasvolsky would serve as special advisor to Cordell Hull. By this time he had revised his judgment that the Soviet Union and communism would be short-lived. See also his *Economic Nationalism of the Danubian States* (Washington, D.C., 1928), 609; and *Russia in the Far East* (Washington, D.C., 1923).

40. Walton Hamilton and Helen Wright, *The Way of Order in the Bituminous Coal Industry* (Washington, D.C., 1928); Hamilton, "The Plight of Soft Coal," *Nation* 126 (April 4, 1928): 367–69; Hamilton, "The Control of Big Business," *Nation* 134 (May 25, 1932): 591–93.

41. Isador Lubin, *Miners' Wages and the Cost of Coal* (New York, 1924). In 1924 when William K. Bixby, a trustee of Washington University, accused Walton Hamilton's book *The Control of Wages* (New York, 1924) of being socialistic, Robert S. Brookings bluntly replied that "the books we publish would never be received with the academic freedom of expression which they should have if it were understood that they were subject to revision or criticism by the Board of Trustees." Robert S. Brookings to Arthur Hadley, February 15, 1924. For other letters on this subject see Arthur Hadley to William K. Bixby, February 12, 1924; Robert S. Brookings to Harry Wallace, February 18, 1924—all in Chancellor Files, Washington University.

42. Walton Hamilton to Robert S. Brookings, "Curriculum for Economic Division of the School of Economics and Government," March 16, 1923, Chancellor Files, Washington University. Walton Hamilton, "The Institutional Approach to Economic Theory," *American Economic Review* 9, supp. (March 1919): 309–24.

43. Walton Hamilton, "Problems of Economic Instruction," *Journal of Political Economy* 25 (January 1917): 1–13. Also see Claude Fuess, *Amherst: The Story of a New England College* (Boston, 1935), esp. 307–26.

44. On January 23, 1928, Moulton wrote to Brookings that "I have gotten the SSRC a great deal interested in the new institution, and their interest will be of great aid to us in breaking down any prejudices that may be against this kind of institution. . . ," BIF. Also Edwin Nourse, oral history, Nourse Papers, Cornell University; H. G. Moulton to Robert S. Brookings, February 28, 1923, BIF.

45. Saunders, *Brookings Institution*, 39.

46. Walton Hamilton to Robert S. Brookings, memoranda (n.d.), in "Memorandum on the History of the Robert S. Brookings Graduate School," app. 2 (1928?), BIF. See also Robert S. Brookings, *Graduate School General Announcements* (1924–25, 1925–26, 1926–27).

47. Max Lerner File, BIF.

48. W. F. Willoughby to Mr. Brookings, May 24, 1926; "Memorandum on the Early History of the Brookings Institution (n.d.); Director for Government Research, *Annual Report* (1928)—all in BIF.

49. Robert S. Brookings to Walton H. Hamilton, April 12, November 25, 1927, BIF.

50. Leverett Lyon et al., "Report to the Trustees," in Memorandum on the Early History of the Brookings Institution, BIF.

51. Lyon et al., "Report."

52. Director of the Institute of Economics, *Report to Board of Trustees* (1924), BIF.

53. Walton Hamilton, "The Control of Big Business," *Nation* 134 (May 25, 1932): 591–93; Dorfman, *Economic Mind*, 3:425–538.

54. George Wilson Pierson, *Yale: The University College, 1921–1937* (New Haven, Conn., 1955), 259, 577; and William O. Douglas, *Go East Young Man* (New York, 1974), 166.

55. Gustav Peck and George B. Galloway, "On the Dissolution of the Robert Brookings Graduate School," *Survey* 60 (May 15, 1928): 229–31; Harold G. Moulton, "The Other Side," *Survey* 60 (May 15, 1928): 231; "Mr. Moulton's Reply to Questions Asked by Mr. Charles A. Beard," May 26, 1928, BIF.

CHAPTER 5

1. Isador Lubin, *The Absorption of the Unemployed in American Industry* (Washington, D.C., 1929).

2. There is extensive literature on Indian reform during the 1920s and 1930s, but surprisingly, Lewis Meriam and his contribution to Indian reform are usually discussed only in passing. The best treatment remains Randolph C. Downes, "A Crusade for Indian Reform, 1922–34," *Mississippi Valley Historical Review* 32 (December 1945); 331–54. Kenneth R. Phelp has produced a major study of John Collier that devotes a few pages to Lewis Meriam, discussing Meriam's report but failing to discuss his subsequent involvement in the administration of Indian affairs. Phelp, *John Collier's Crusade for Indian Reform, 1920–1954* (Tucson, Ariz., 1977), 90–94, 98–99. Other discussions can be found in Edward Holland Spicer, *Cycles of Conquest: The Impact of Spain, Mexico, and the United States on Indians of the Southwest, 1533–1960* (Tucson, Ariz., 1962); Leo Crane, *Desert Drums: The Pueblo Indians of New Mexico, 1540–1928* (Glorieta, N.M., 1953); S. Lyman Tyler, *A History of Indian Policy* (Washington, D.C., 1973).

3. John Collier, *From Every Zenith* (Denver, Colo., 1963), 68–130.

4. Lewis Meriam to Montrose Moses, February 15, 1919, Rockefeller Foundation Archives (hereafter cited as RFA).

5. Vera Connolly, "The End of the Road," *Good Housekeeping* 88 (May 1929), 164; Phelp, *Collier's Crusade*, 1–24.

6. U.S. Committee on Indian Affairs (House), *Pueblo Indian Land Titles: Hearings, Pursuant to H.R. 13452, H.R. 13674*, 64th Cong., 2nd sess., February 15, 1923, 180; Frank Waters, *Masked Gods: Navaho and Pueblo Ceremonialism*, 2nd ed. (Chicago, 1973), 131–32; "John Collier," *Current Biography*, March 1941, 159–61.

7. Collier remained with the Peoples Institute until 1919. While serving on the staff at the Peoples Institute he helped organize the National Board of Motion Pictures and served as the director of the National Training School for Community Centers from 1915 to 1919. Collier, *Zenith*, esp. 93–95, 115–16.

8. Collier, *Zenith*, 68–103.

9. John Collier, "Our Indian Policy," *Sunset* 50 (March 1923): 13; Collier, "America's Treatment of Her Indians," *Current History Magazine* 18 (August 1923): 771; and Spicer, *Cycles of Conquest*, 172.

10. Quoted in Kenneth Phelp, "Albert B. Fall and the Protest from the Pueblos, 1921–1923," *Arizona and the West*, Autumn 1970: 237–55; Crane, *Desert Drums*; Collier, *Zenith*, 131–32; *Congressional Record*, 1922, 62: 1234–35; *New York Times*, November 19, 1922 (hereafter cited as *NYT*).

11. U.S. Committee on Indian Affairs (House), *Pueblo Indian Land Titles*, 180. Also see U.S. Committee on Indian Affairs (Senate), *Survey of Conditions of Indians in the United States: Hearings before a Sub-Committee of the Committee on Indian Affairs*, 70th Cong., 2nd sess., November 12, 21, 23, 26, 1928.

12. Connolly, "End of the Road," 170. Also see Stella Atwood, "The Case for the Indian," *Survey* 49 (October 1922): 7–11, 57.

13. Walter Woehlke, "Let 'Em Die," *Sunset* 51 (July 1923): 14–15; M. Clyde Kelly, "The Indian and His Master," *Sunset* 50 (June 1922): 17; John Collier, "The Accursed System," *Sunset* 52 (June 1924): 15; Collier, "America's Treatment," 779; and Joseph W. Latimer, "Bureaucracy a la Mode," *Independent* 112 (February 2, 1924): 75.

14. John Collier, *The Indians of the Americas* (New York, 1947), 261.

15. For an enlightening discussion of earlier reform efforts, see Robert Winston Mardock, *The Reformers and the American Indian* (Columbia, Mo., 1971).

16. "Proceedings of the AAA, Central Section, March 23, 1923," *American Anthropologist*, April-June, 1923, 285; *NYT*, January 7, 1923.

17. Woehlke, "Let 'Em Die," 14–15.

18. *NYT*, January 15, 17, 25, February 8, 1923.

19. John Collier, "Are We Making Red Men Slaves?" *Survey* 57 (January 1, 1927): 453.

20. Memorandum, Adeline Otero Warren to Commissioner, "Meeting Federation of Women's Clubs at Los Angeles," June 28, 1924, Papers of Indian Affairs, National Archives (hereafter PIA). Also, for the Bureau of Indian Affairs' attack on Collier, see Charles H. Burke to M. K. Sniffen, August 5, 1924, PIA; John Collier to Officials of the Pueblos, June 25, 1924, PIA.

21. For an insider's look at the bureau's attitude toward the Pueblos, see Crane, *Desert Drums*.

22. Phelp, *Collier's Crusade*, 64. *NYT*, June 19, July 13, February 9, 1924.

23. John Collier to Charles H. Burke, February 2, 1926, 68–3–1925–150, PIA; *American Indian Life*, supp., November 1926; U.S. Committee on Indian Affairs (Senate), *Survey of Conditions*, 4403; U.S. Committee on Indian Affairs (Senate), *Hearings before Senate Sub-Committee . . . pursuant to S.R. 341*, 69th Cong., 2nd sess., 1927, 69.

24. "The Tragedy of the American Indian," *Scientific American* 134 (January 1926): 7.

25. In 1923, three nurses from the American Red Cross were commissioned by Albert Fall to conduct a survey of medical conditions on reservations. The report, dated June 1924, declared that medical conditions on reservations were deplorable. The bureau suppressed the report and dismissed the nurses as being "ultra-professional." "A Study of the Need for Public Health Nursing on Indian Reservations by the American Red Cross," in U.S. Committee on Indian Affairs (Senate), *Survey of Conditions*, pt. 3 (1929), 995–1005. Also see Connolly, "End of the Road," 154; *NYT*, January 29, 1926.

26. Thomas Jesse Jones to Colonel Woods, April 25, 1929, RFA; minutes of the IGR executive committee, May 25, 1928, October 18, 1929, BIF; W. F. Willoughby, "Letter of Transmittal," in *Problem of Indian Administration*, viii–x; Charles Thomson, interview with author, Bethesda, Md., July 25, 1975.

27. Lewis Meriam to Henry Roe Cloud, February 5, 1929, RFA.

28. Obituary, *Washington Star*, October 31, 1972.

29. Charles Thomson, interview with author, Kensington, Md., July 18, 1975; Lewis Meriam, *Public Service and Special Training* (Chicago, 1936), 12.

30. In his youth as well, Meriam had shown a marked tendency toward independence of thought. His father, a dentist in Salem, Massachusetts, was a Republican and an Episcopalian. Meriam became a Democrat, and at Harvard, he flirted with Swedenborgianism, before he joined a Quaker meeting. Later, he would leave the Quakers when the meeting he attended stood for the entrance of Herbert Hoover, then president-elect.

31. Willoughby, "Letter of Transmittal," xiii.

32. Meriam, *Problem*, 59–60, 80–85.

33. Connolly, "End of the Road."

34. Robert Gessner, *Massacre: A Survey of Today's Indian* (New York, 1931), 67; Downes, "Indian Reform," 342–43. See also *NYT*, May 27, 1928.

35. Meriam, *Problem*, 3, 52.

36. Meriam, *Problem*, 439–56.

37. Meriam, *Problem*, 7, 25, 38–42, 44–48, 123–25, 436, 462–64.

38. Lewis Meriam to John Collier, June 8, 1931, John Collier Papers, Yale University (hereafter JCP).

39. Willoughby, "Letter of Transmittal."

40. Lewis Meriam to Guy Moffett, March 21, 1931, RFA; Meriam, *Public Service*, 55.

41. John Collier, "Hammering at the Prison Door," *Survey* 60 (July 1, 1928): 389. Also see Vera Connolly, "Cry of a Broken People," *Good Housekeeping* 88 (February 1929): 30–31.

42. E. B. Meritt to Lewis Meriam, January 18, 1929, RFA; G. Linquist to Charles A. Burke, December 12, 1929, PIA, 26283–1926–101; memorandum, "Review of the Problem of Indian Affairs," Samuel A. Eliot to the Secretary of the Interior, Roy O. West, January 10, 1929, PIA, 26283–1926–100; Meriam to Chorley, January 16, 1929, RFA; memorandum, Meriam to members of the survey staff, January 28, 1929, RFA.

43. Thomas Jesse Jones to Lewis Meriam, quoted in minutes of the Rockefeller Foundation executive committee, May 15, 1929, BIF.

44. Memorandum, "The Reorganization of the Indian Administration and Indian Commissioner," Thomas Jesse Jones to Kenneth Chorley, January 7, 1929, RFA.

45. The Bureau of Indian Affairs would also request grants to fund technical studies on Indian law, education, and land. Memorandum, Guy Moffett, January 4, 1930, RFA; minutes of the IGR executive committee, October 18, 1929, BIF; C. J. Rhoads to Spelman Fund of New York, March 30, 1931, RFA; Lewis Meriam to Roy O. West, January 7, 1929, RFA.

46. *NYT*, March 13, 1928, April 9, 1929.

47. Memorandum, Thomas Jesse Jones to Kenneth Chorley, January 7, 1929, RFA.

48. Lewis Meriam to Francis Fisher Kane, April 24, 1919, RFA; Meriam to W. F. Biglow, April 16, 1929, RFA.

49. Telegram, Kenneth Chorley to Charles James Rhoads, April 11, 1929, PIA; Chorley to Roy L. Wilbur, March 28, 1929, PIA; *NYT*, May 1, 1929.

50. Board of Indian Commissioners, *Annual Report* (1929), 3–4; *NYT*, April 28, 1929, sec. 3, p. 4, col. 5; "Uncle Sam Has a New Indian Policy," *Saturday Evening Post* 201 (June 8, 1929): 5.

51. "Report of the Meeting of the Council of All–New Mexico Pueblo, held at San Domingo, September 12, 1919," in U.S. Committee on Indian Affairs (Senate), *Survey of Conditions*, pt. 2 (January 30–31, February 3, 5, 1931); Collier, *Zenith*, 148–50; Edward Everett Dale, *The Indians of the Southwest* (Norman, Okla., 1929), 155.

52. Meriam to Moffett, January 25, 1932, RFA.

53. John Collier to Haven Emerson, February 4, 1930, JCP.

54. Meriam to Moffett, January 25, 1932, RFA; John Collier, "The Immediate Tasks of the American Indian Defense Association," *American Indian Life*, December 10, 1929.

55. Meriam to Moffett, January 15, 1932, RFA; U.S. Committee on Indian Affairs (Senate), *Survey of Conditions* (1929), pt. 6, esp. 1750.

56. Later appearing before the Senate Committee on Indian Affairs, Rhoads testified, "We were practically new and unless we followed past methods, we could not get by Congress without a mutual understanding." U.S. Committee on Indian Affairs (Senate), *Survey of Conditions*, pt. 1, 2197; R. A. Black, "New Deal for the Red Man," *Nation* 130 (April 2, 1930): 388–90; Mary Ross, "The New Indian Administration," *Survey* 64 (June 15, 1930): 268–69.

57. Quoted in Gessner, *Massacre*, 152.

58. Collier in his memoirs gives a different account of the final break. He says the break came over the commissioners' defense of J. Hagerman, official for the Pueblo Indian reservation, before the Senate investigating committee. This account would set the break as late as spring 1931. *Zenith*, 153. Also Phelp, *Collier's Crusade*, 101; U.S. Committee on Indian Affairs (Senate), *Survey of Conditions*, pt. 20 (1932).

59. Representative Scott Leavitt introduced a bill to establish an Indian claims court (H.R. 7963) in 1929. Congress did not act on this bill, however. *Congressional Record*, 71st Cong., 2nd sess., December 21, 1929, pt. 1: 1051–53.

60. John Collier to Lewis Meriam, February, 1931, JCP.

61. Memorandum, "My Telephone Conversation with Mr. Charles J. Rhoads," Lewis Meriam, June 18, 1929, RFA.

62. Meriam detailed his efforts at reorganization in two lengthy letters to Guy Moffett, dated March 21, 1931, and January 15, 1932, RFA. Also see Lewis Meriam to Kenneth Chorley, September 9, 1929, RFA.

63. Meriam to Moffett, January 15, 1932, RFA.

64. Meriam to Moffett, January 15, 1932, RFA.

65. M. K. Sniffen, "Progress in Indian Affairs," March 10, 1932, BIF.

66. Charles Rhoads to Spelman Fund, March 30, 1931, RFA.

67. *NYT*, August 20, 1930.

68. W. Carson Ryan, Jr., and Rose Brandt, "Indian Education Today," *Progressive Education* 9 (February 1932): 81–86; Lewis Meriam, "Indian Education Moves Ahead," *Survey* 66 (June 1, 1931): esp. 254; Meriam, "Education Appointments in the Indian Service," *School and Society* 34 (November 14, 1931): 658–59.

69. W. Carson Ryan, Jr., "Educational Conferences of Indian Service Superintendents," *School and Society* 34 (December 5, 1931): 764–65.

70. Ryan, "School Facilities for Indians," *School and Society* 37 (June 3, 1933): 706; Commissioner of Indian Affairs, *Annual Report* (June 30, 1931), 6–12.

71. Appropriations for the medical service increased from $3,115,100 in 1930 to $4,352,500 in 1931. Examinations for trachoma increased from 25,000 to 61,426 in the years 1930 to 1933. Commissioner of Indian Affairs, *Annual Report* (June 30, 1931), 12.

72. Department of the Interior, "Memorandum for the Press," March 30, 1931, RFA; Commissioner of Indian Affairs, *Annual Report* (June 30, 1931), 3; *NYT*, March 30, 1931.

73. Lewis Meriam to John Collier, April 4, 1931, JCP.

74. Lewis Meriam to Guy Moffett, March 21, 1931, RFA.

75. *Congressional Record*, 71st Cong., 2nd sess., 1931, 92, 3635, 8505.

76. *Congressional Record*, 71st Cong., 2nd sess., 1931, 92, 8505.

77. Minutes of the Brookings Institution executive committee, October 21, 1929, BIF.

78. John Collier to Lewis Meriam, July 20, 1932, JCP.

79. Lewis Meriam to John Collier, July 14, July 20, 1932, JCP.

80. Lewis Meriam to John Collier, July 14, July 20, 1932, JCP.

CHAPTER 6

1. See Paul Conkin, *The New Deal* (Boston, 1967); James M. Burns, *Roosevelt: The Lion and the Fox* (New York, 1956); Burns, *Roosevelt: The Soldier of Freedom* (New York, 1970), 36–39; Richard Polenberg, *War and Society: The United States, 1941–1945* (Philadelphia, 1972), 6–7.

2. For the most recent expression of this view see Ellis Hawley, "The New Deal and Business," in *The New Deal*, ed. John Braeman (Columbus, Ohio, 1974), esp. 68–74; Kim McQuaid, *Big Business and Presidential Power: From FDR to Reagan* (New York, 1982), 18–62; Robert M. Collins, *The Business Response to Keynes, 1929–1964* (New York, 1981); Ronald Radosh, "The Myth of the New Deal," in *A New History of Leviathan: Essays on the Rise of the Corporate State*, ed. Radosh and M. Rothbard (New York, 1972), 146–87.

3. H. G. Moulton to Frederic Delano, September 28, 1932, BIF; Charles B. Saunders, Jr., *The Brookings Institution: A Fifty Year History* (Washington, D.C., 1966), 31.

4. Speech by H. G. Moulton, "Economic Problems Today," June 1931, BIF. See also Moulton, *The Recovery Problem in the United States* (Washington, D.C, 1937), 174.

5. Barry D. Karl, *Charles E. Merriam and the Study of Politics* (Chicago, 1974), 221–22.

6. Quoted in Saunders, *Brookings Institution*, 55. For similar accusations, see "Statement by Donald R. Richberg, Chairman of the NRA," April 21, 1935, BIF; H. G. Moulton to Frederic Delano, April 21, 1935, BIF.

7. James C. Nelson to author, March 21, 1975; Barbara Moulton, interview with author, Orange Grove, Calif., November 12, 1974.

8. H. G. Moulton, "The Relation of Credit and Prices to Business Recovery," *Annals* 59 (April 1934): 20–26.

9. List of past trustees of the Brookings Institution, BIF.

10. Brookings Institution, *Staff Directory* (Washington, D.C., 1961).

11. H. G. Moulton, "Financial History of the Brookings Institution," 1952(?), BIF.

12. Edwin Nourse, oral biography, Nourse Papers, Cornell University.

13. Peter Avery, *Modern Iran* (New York, 1965), 262–63. Millspaugh's experiences in Iran are recounted in his *American Task in Persia* (New York, 1925).

14. Radio address by H. G. Moulton, "The American Transportation Problem," March 25, 1933, BIF. Also see Moulton, *The American Transportation Problem*, (Washington, D.C., 1933); Jordan Schwarz, *The Speculator: Bernard Baruch in Washington, 1917–1965* (Chapel Hill, N.C., 1981).

15. Moulton, "Financial History"; Moulton, "Prospectus for Falk Foundation Studies," n.d., BIF.

16. J. Ronnie Davis argues that economists before Keynes believed that deficit spending policies offered a way of solving the economic problems of the Depression. In making this argument he relies heavily on the responses of economists to Wagner's survey. Furthermore, he mistakenly seems to think that, because some pre-Keynesian economists approved of emergency government involvement in the market, they were in fact "Keynes-

ians" before Keynes. A closer reading of the economic literature of the 1920s and the 1930s shows that nearly all economists believed in the importance of a balanced budget and feared the inflationary effects of deficit spending. J. Ronnie Davis, *New Economics and Old Economists* (Ames, Iowa, 1967).

17. *Congressional Record*, 72nd Cong., 1st. sess., 1932, 10309–39.

18. Jacob Viner, "Balanced Deflation, Inflation or More Depression," *The Day and Hour Series of the University of Minnesota* (Minneapolis, Minn., 1933).

19. Alvin Hansen, *Economic Stabilization in an Unbalanced World* (New York, 1932).

20. Viner, "Balanced Deflation," 5. Also see Hugh S. Norton, *The Employment Act and the Council of Economic Advisers, 1946–1976* (Columbia, S.C., 1977), 46.

21. James E. Sargent, "FDR and Lewis W. Douglas: Budget Balancing and the Early New Deal," *Prologue*, Spring 1974, 33–43. For a summary of Lewis Douglas's own view see Douglas, "Address," *Consensus*, January 1935, 8–25. Useful insights into Roosevelt's economic thinking can be found in Daniel Roland Fusfeld, *The Economic Thought of Franklin D. Roosevelt and the Origins of the New Deal* (New York, 1956).

22. Quoted in Lewis Kimmel, *The Federal Budget and Fiscal Policy*, 176. See also *Public Papers and Addresses of Franklin D. Roosevelt* (Washington, D.C., 1938), 2:175.

23. Elliott A. Rosen, *Hoover, Roosevelt, and the New Deal* (New York, 1977); Albert V. Romasco, *The Politics of Recovery: Roosevelt's New Deal* (New York, 1983).

24. H. G. Moulton to Frederic Delano, September 25, 1932, March 9, 1933, BIF.

25. Franklin D. Roosevelt to H. G. Moulton, January 26, 1933, quoted in Brookings Institution, *President's Annual Report to the Trustees* (May 19, 1933), BIF.

26. Paul T. David to Robert D. Calkins, May 11, 1951, BIF; C. O. Hardy to Frederick Delano, February 17, 1933, BIF.

27. H. G. Moulton to Frederic Delano, March 9, 1933, BIF.

28. Moulton wrote Robert Brookings in early 1923 to convey his enthusiasm for an "exciting" lecture on Italian fascism he had heard delivered by an Italian economist. H. G. Moulton to Robert S. Brookings, February 28, 1923, BIF.

29. Rosen, *Hoover, Roosevelt, and the New Deal*, 162–72. Also Joseph Dorfman, *The Economic Mind in American Civilization* (New York, 1958), 5:510.

30. Charles Beard, "A Five Year Plan for America," *Forum* 86 (July 1931): 1–11; also Andre Maurois, "Can Capitalism Be Saved?" *Forum* 86 (November 1931), 157. For an overview of planning sentiment see Hawley, "New Deal and Business." Also Helen M. Muller, ed., *Democratic Collectivism* (New York, 1934), 33–36; and "Final Report of the Commission on the Social Studies," *School and Society* 39 (May 26, 1934): 680–83.

31. United States Chamber of Commerce, Committee on Continuity of Business, "Referendum," quoted in Charles A. Beard, *America Faces the Fu-*

ture (New York, 1932), 203. Owen Young is quoted in *The Swope Plan: Details, Criticisms, and Analysis*, ed. J. George Frederick (New York, 1931), 58. Business views are discussed by Kim McQuaid, "Corporate Liberalism in the American Business Community, 1920–1940," *Business History Review* 52 (Autumn 1978): 342–68.

32. Walton Hamilton, "The Affairs Called Industry," in *Price Policies, Big Business and Economic Power in a Free Society*, ed. Hamilton (1934; reprint, New York, 1973), 21.

33. H. G. Moulton, "History and Origins of the NIRA," 1934(?), BIF. For other discussions of the NIRA see John T. Flynn, "Whose Child Is the NRA?" *Harper's Magazine* 169 (September 1934): 385–94; Bernard Bellush, *The Failure of the NRA* (New York, 1975), esp. 1–30; Ellis Hawley, *The New Deal and the Problem of Monopoly* (Princeton, N.J., 1966), 19–52. See also Arthur M. Schlesinger, Jr., *The Coming of the New Deal* (Boston, 1958), chaps. 6–8; and for further insight, Theda Skocpol, "Political Response to Capitalist Crisis: Neo-Marxist Theories of the State and the Case of the New Deal," *Politics and Society* 10 (1980), esp. 156–201.

34. Moulton, "History and Origins of the NIRA"; Moulton to Frederic Delano, September 18, 1932, BIF.

35. Attending this meeting with Wagner were Fred I. Kent of Bankers Trust; James Rand of Remington-Rand; Congressman Clyde Kelly of Pennsylvania; Virgil Jordan, president of the National Industrial Conference Board; and M. C. Rorty.

36. Moulton, "History and Origins of the NIRA."

37. Hawley, *New Deal and Monopoly*, 28, 77; Bellush, *Failure*, 66.

38. See Leverett S. Lyon to Leon Henderson, January 21, 24, 1935; Leon Henderson to W. A. Harriman, "Weekly Report for Week Ending November 17, 1934." Files of Leon Henderson, National Recovery Administration Record Collection, 3797, National Archives; Brookings Institution, *President's Annual Report* (March 31, 1934), BIF.

39. Hawley, *New Deal and Monopoly*, 28.

40. Leverett Lyon, Paul T. Homan, and George Terborgh, *The National Recovery Administration: An Analysis and Appraisal* (Washington, D.C., 1935), 29–82, 138, 387, 290–94. Other works on the NIRA by the Brookings Institution staff include Lyon, *The ABC of the NRA* (Washington, D.C., 1934); Terborgh, *Price-Control Devices in NRA Codes* (Washington, D.C., 1934); Lyon, *The Economics of Free Deals: With Suggestions for Code-Making Under the NRA* (Washington, D.C., 1933).

41. Lyon et al., *National Recovery Administration*, 73–79.

42. Memorandum, "Facts about the Release of the Brookings Institution Study of NRA," n.d., BIF. Chief Justice Hughes had read Lyon's *Economics of Free Deals* in proof. H. G. Moulton, "Memorandum on Special Studies Being Conducted by the Brookings Institution," January 12, 1934, BIF.

43. Edwin Nourse et al., *America's Capacity to Produce* (Washington, D.C., 1933), 2.

44. Harold G. Moulton et al., *The Formation of Capital* (Washington, D.C., 1936), 74.

45. Moulton et al., *Formation of Capital*. Also see Leverett Lyon and Victor Abramson, *Government and Economic Life* (Washington, D.C., 1940), 6, 59–61.

46. H. G. Moulton et al., *Income and Economic Progress* (Washington, D.C., 1935), 24–27.

47. These charges have been substantiated by Gavin Wright, "The Political Economy of New Deal Spending: An Econometric Analysis," *Review of Economics and Statistics* 56 (February 1974): 30–38. Also see L. J. Arrington, "The New Deal in the West: A Preliminary Statistical Inquiry," *Pacific Historical Review* 38 (August 1969): 311–16; Arrington, "Western Agriculture and the New Deal," *Agricultural History* 44 (October 1970): 337–53. For conservative hostility to New Deal relief, see James T. Patterson, *Congressional Conservatism and the New Deal* (Lexington, Ky., 1967).

48. Nourse, oral biography, 171; Edwin A. Nourse et al., *Three Years of the Agricultural Adjustment Administration* (Washington, D.C., 1937), viii. Other Brookings works on the AAA were Joseph S. Davis, *Wheat and the AAA* (Washington, D.C., 1935); Harold B. Rowe, *Tobacco under the AAA* (Washington, D.C., 1939); Nourse, *Marketing Agreements under the AAA* (Washington, D.C., 1935); John D. Black, *The Dairy Industry and the AAA* (Washington, D.C., 1935); D. A. FitzGerald, *Livestock under the AAA* (Washington, D.C., 1935); and Henry I. Richard, *Cotton and the AAA* (Washington, D.C., 1936). Also see Dean Albertson, *Roosevelt's Farmer: Claude R. Wickard in the New Deal* (New York, 1961).

49. Nourse et al., *Three Years*, 448, 461–65.

50. Brookings Institution, *President's Annual Report*, May 22, 1936, BIF.

51. U.S. v. Butler et al., 297 U.S. 61.

52. *Congressional Record*, 74th Cong., 2nd sess., 1936, 561, 7031; John Morton Blum, *From the Morgenthau Diaries: The Years of Crisis, 1928–1938* (New York, 1959), 147–58, 263–65; Martha Swain, *Pat Harrison: The New Deal Years* (Jackson, Miss., 1978), 100–120.

53. Paul Kleppner and Stephen C. Baker, "The Impact of Depression on Mass Political Behavior: The United States in the 1870s, the 1890s, and the 1920s" (Paper delivered at the 1979 Annual Meeting of the American Historical Association, December 1979), 28–33.

54. Blum, *Morgenthau Diaries*, 263–83; Kimmel, *Federal Budget*, 184–90.

55. Kenneth D. Roose, *The Economics of Recession and Revival* (New York, 1969), 24–33. For the political debate over compensatory spending, see Dean L. May, *From New Deal to New Economics: The American Liberal Response to the Recession of 1937* (New York, 1981); and Richard N. Chapman, *Contours of Public Policy, 1939–1945* (New York, 1981), 1–60.

56. Actually this recovery was not unique. Consumption led investment in the upturns that followed the recessions of 1924 and 1927. Roose, *Economics of Recession*, 70–74, 102–18. See also Sumner Slichter, "The Downturn of 1937," *Review of Economic Statistics* 20 (August 1938): 97–110; M. D. Brockie, "Theories of the 1937–38 Crisis and Depression," *Economic Journal* 60 (June 1950): 292–310; Douglas A. Hayes, *Business Confidence and Business Activity*, Michigan Business Studies (Ann Arbor, Mich.,

1951). Concerns with inflation were expressed at the time by E. A. Golden-weiser, "How Can Credit Be Controlled?" *Academy of Political Science Proceedings* (May 1936); Arthur Marget, "Inflation: Inevitable or Avoidable?" *The Day and Hour Series of the University of Minnesota* (Minneapolis, Minn., 1937); and Sumner H. Slichter, "Must We Have Another Boom?" *Atlantic Monthly* 159 (May 1937): 600–607.

57. S. Wells Utley, *The American System: Shall We Destroy It?* (Detroit, Mich., 1936), as quoted in Roose, *Economics of Recession*, 57; Robert L. Lund, *The Truth about the New Deal* (New York, 1936); and the *Atlantic Monthly*'s series of editorials, especially "Blowing the Bubble!" 157 (January 1936): 40–45, and "The Danger of Mounting Deficits," 156 (November 1935): 561–67.

58. Maxwell S. Stewart, "Beware of Inflation," *Nation* 142 (March 11, 1936): 306–9; Alvin Johnson, "Where Inflation Threatens," *Nation* 143 (September 5, 1936): 265–66; "Eccles Warns: Fight Inflation Now," *Business Week* 394 (March 20, 1937): 13–14.

59. Roose, *Economics of Recession*, 24.

60. Robert Aaron Gordon, *Economic Instability and Growth: The American Record* (New York, 1974), 68–69.

61. Franklin D. Roosevelt to V. P., March 20, 1935, Gulick Papers, Institute of Public Administration, New York. See also Richard Polenberg, *Reorganizing Roosevelt's Goverment: The Controversy over Executive Reorganization* (Cambridge, Mass., 1967).

62. H. G. Moulton, *The Recovery Problem of the United States* (Washington, D.C., 1937), 457–60. Although Great Britain did follow an extremely orthodox recovery program, a leading economic historian declared that the British "government had only a marginal influence on Britain's recovery." Sweden, contrary to Moulton, spent heavily during the depression, and in 1933 nearly one-quarter of the unemployed were being given relief work. Derek Aldcroft, *The European Economy, 1914–1970* (New York, 1978), 100–104.

63. Harold G. Moulton, "Economic Essentials Today," speech before the Union League Club, January 31, 1939, BIF; Moulton, "The National Debt—Retrospect and Prospect," speech given to the Citizens Conference on Government Management, Estes Park, Colorado, June 17, 1940, BIF.

64. Leverett Lyon, *Cooperative Research* (Washington, D.C., 1934).

65. "Senator Byrd Talks About 'Presidents I Have Known,'" *U.S. News and World Report* 53 (September 10, 1962): 84–85.

66. H. G. Moulton to Senator Byrd, July 14, 1936, BIF.

67. Stacy May of the Rockefeller Foundation offered to supplement this grant, but Byrd feared that any association with the Rockefeller Foundation would bias public supporters. F. W. Powell to H. G. Moulton, May 8, 1936, BIF; H. G. Moulton to James Buchanan, June 15, 1936, BIF; Charles Thomson, interview with author, Kensington, Maryland, July 18, 1975.

68. President's Committee on Government Administration and Management, *The Reorganization of the Executive Branch of Government* (Washington, D.C., 1937).

69. Memorandum, W. F. Powell to H. G. Moulton, March 11, 1936, BIF. Leverett S. Lyon to Clark C. Wren, November 2, 1936, and C. Wren

to Leverett Lyon, November 3, 1936, quoted in Polenberg, *Reorganizing Roosevelt's Government*, 40.

70. Memorandum, H. G. Moulton to Louis Brownlow, March 24, 1937, President's Reorganization Committee Files, FDR Library, Hyde Park, New York. Daniel Selko, "Financial Administration of the Federal Government," n.d., and "Issues Involved in Government Reorganization," May 7, 1937, BIF. See also Lewis Brownlow, "Memorandum for Moulton," March 11, 1936, President's Reorganization Committee Files, FDR Library.

71. Senator Byrd to W. F. Powell, February 25, 1937, BIF; H. G. Moulton to Senator Byrd, March 2, 1937, BIF; H. G. Moulton to Senator Byrd, March 23, 1937, BIF.

72. Luther Gulick to Herbert Hoover, n.d.; Luther Gulick, "Fundamental Considerations of the Place of Control of Audit in Administration," n.d.; Luther Gulick to Felix Morley, June 11, 1937; J. Harris to Luther Gulick, February 8, 1937. Gulick Papers, Institute of Public Administration. See also Rexford Tugwell, *Enlargement of the Presidency* (New York, 1960), 399.

73. Memorandum, H. G. Moulton to Louis Brownlow, March 24, 1937.

74. Daniel Selko, "Financial Administration" and "Issues Involved."

75. U.S. Congress, *Hearings before the Joint Committee on Government Reorganization* (Washington, D.C., 1937), 276–94, 307–10. For insight into the political strategy of the president's committee, see Joseph P. Harris to Luther Gulick, "List of Witnesses on S2700," n.d.; Luther Gulick to FDR, March 1, 11, 1937; Charles Beard to Luther Gulick, January 25, 1937; Nelson Rockefeller to Luther Gulick, January 22, 1937, Gulick Papers.

76. "State and County Surveys Made by the Institute for Government Research, 1929–1941," n.d., BIF.

77. *New York Times*, April 22, 1937; U.S. Congress, *Hearings before the Joint Committee on Reorganization*, 278.

78. F. Delano to H. Moulton, May 17, 1937, BIF.

79. Harold Moulton, "Memorandum on Mr. D's Opposition," 1937(?), BIF.

80. Moulton, "Memorandum on Mr. D's Opposition." See also Moulton to F. Delano, August 27, 1935, BIF.

81. Brookings Institution, *President's Annual Report*, March 21, 1938, BIF. Collins, *Business Response to Keynes*, presents the best account of the influence of Keynesian economics on American political and business leaders.

82. H. G. Moulton, "Economic Essentials Today," January 29, 1939, BIF.

83. James C. Nelson to author, February 10, 1975. There is a growing literature on this Keynesian revolution. See John K. Galbraith, "Came the Revolution," *New York Times Review of Books* 1 (May 1965): 36; Lawrence R. Klein, *The Keynesian Revolution* (New York, 1966); Robert Lekachman, *The Age of Keynes* (New York, 1966), 79–112; J. Ronnie Davis, *New Economics and Old Economists* (Ames, Iowa, 1971); Herbert Stein, *The Fiscal Revolution in America* (Chicago, 1969); and Alan Sweezy, "The Keynesians

and Government Policy, 1933–1939," *American Economic Review* 62 (May 1972), 116–24. For the business community's response to Keynes, see Collins's important study, *The Business Response to Keynes*.

84. Schwarz, *The Speculator*, 358–63; Eliot Janeway, *The Struggle for Survival* (New York, 1951); "The Conflict in the New Philosophy of the Public Debt," *Finance*, July 10, 1943, clipping in BIF. Also important are Alvin Hansen, "Our National Debt after the War," *Harvard Alumni Bulletin*, May 27, 1944; L. Albert Hahr, *Deficit Spending and Private Enterprise* (Washington, D.C., 1942); Alvin Hansen and Guy Greer, "The Federal Debt and the Future," *Harper's Magazine* 184 (April, 1942): 489–500; and Hansen, "Toward Full Use of Our Resources," *Fortune* 26 (November 1942): 130–33. For Moulton's most representative statements on the subject and insight into his increasing conservatism, see *Controlling Factors in Economic Development* (Washington, D.C., 1949); *Can Inflation Be Controlled?* (Washington, D.C., 1958); "Economic Potentials and Requirements," *Appraisal Journal* 18 (January 1950): 29–34; and "Productivity: The Key to National Security," *Systems*, August 1951, clipping in BIF.

85. "Economics," *Time*, June 10, 1940, 83–84.

86. The official historian of the institution argues that the Brookings staff gradually accommodated itself to the New Deal during World War II. Saunders, *Brookings Institution*, 62.

87. Saunders, *Brookings Institution*, 65.

88. Saunders, *Brookings Institution*, 67–68.

89. Leon Keyserling, "Comment," *American Economic Review* 62 (May 1972): 134–38. See also Byrd L. Jones, "The Role of Keynesians in Wartime Policy and Postwar Planning, 1940–1946," *American Economic Review* 62 (May 1972): 125–33; Louis Fisher, *Presidential Spending Power* (Princeton, N.J., 1975), 44; Herbert Stein, *The Fiscal Revolution in America* (Chicago, 1969), 167–69; Donald Winch, *Economics and Policy: A Historical Study* (New York, 1969), 274–80; Otis Graham, Jr., *Toward a Planned Society: From Roosevelt to Nixon* (New York, 1976), 70–90.

90. See Alvin Hansen, *After The War —Full Employment* (Washington, D.C., 1942).

91. Alvin Hansen to Harold Moulton, June 12, 1943; Harold Moulton to Alvin Hansen, June 22, 1943, BIF. Harold Moulton to Milton Van Slyck, July 31, 1944, BIF.

92. H. G. Moulton to Dexter M. Keezer, December 1946, BIF.

93. Alonzo E. Taylor, General Mills, to H. Moulton, June 3, 1943; Harold Stonier, American Bankers Association, to Harold Moulton, April 8, 1943; Walter H. Wheeler, engineer, to Harold G. Moulton, August 3, 1943; Harold G. Moulton to George B. Roberts, National Bank, December 10, 1943; Melchior Palyi to Harold G. Moulton, July 31, 1943; Senator H. Alexander Smith to Harold G. Moulton, June 3, 1943. BIF.

94. *Congressional Record*, 78th Cong., 1st sess.; 1943, 717.

95. *Congressional Record*, 78th Cong., 1st sess., 1943, 212, A. 108, 1146; Graham, *Toward a Planned Society*, 52–58.

96. Andrew Shonfield, *Modern Capitalism: The Changing Balance of Public and Private Power* (New York, 1965), 302–59. See also Paul A. Baron, "National Economic Planning," in *A Survey of Contemporary Economics*, ed.

Bernard F. Haley (Homewood, Ill., 1952), esp. 358–60. For histories of the NRPB, see Philip A. Warken, *A History of the National Resources Planning Board, 1933–1943* (New York, 1979); and Marion Clawson, *New Deal Planning: The National Resources Planning Board* (Baltimore, Md., 1981).

CHAPTER 7

1. For a critique of the New Economics see Paul A. Baron, "National Economic Planning," in *A Survey of Contemporary Economics*, ed. Bernard F. Haley (Homewood, Ill., 1952), 35. Also see Gerald Colm, "Fiscal Policy and the Federal Budget," *Income Stabilization for a Developing Nation*, ed. Max F. Millikan (New Haven, Conn., 1953); and Leon Keyserling, "Comments," *American Economic Review* 62 (May 1972): 136.

2. Joseph P. Schumpeter, "Capitalism in the Postwar World," in *Postwar Economic Problems*, ed. Seymour E. Harris (New York, 1943).

3. Harold G. Moulton, *Controlling Factors in Economic Development* (Washington, D.C., 1949), 175.

4. Harold G. Moulton, "The World Peace Program" (Speech to the Foreign Policy Association, Philadelphia, December 16, 1944); "Government and Postwar Business Policy" (Speech to American Finance Conference, November 17, 1943); "Government Finance and Economic Development" (Speech to the American Institute of Real Estate Appraisers, November 18, 1949); and "Economic Potentials and Requirements" (Speech to the Ohio Public Expenditures Conference, November 3, 1949). BIF.

5. Moulton, *Controlling Factors*, 186.

6. Moulton, *Controlling Factors*, 268–69.

7. Moulton, *Controlling Factors*, 148; Wilfred Owen, interview with author, Washington, D.C., April 3, 1976.

8. Arthur C. Millspaugh, *Toward Efficient Democracy: The Question of Governmental Organization* (Washington, D.C., 1949), esp. 207–29; also 111–13, 231.

9. "Brookings Popgun," *Nation* 159 (October 21, 1944): 452.

10. "Brookings Popgun," 452.

11. Memorandum by Walter Salant, "Wage and Price Policy," July 30, 1945, Salant Papers, Truman Library, Independence, Missouri.

12. William H. Davis, "Memorandum to the President," August 12, 1945, Official File 407 (1945), Truman Library; Harry S. Truman, "Special Message to Congress Presenting a 21 Point Program for Reconversion," September 6, 1945, in *Public Papers and Addresses* (Washington, D.C., 1961), 264.

13. Craufurd D. Goodwin, ed., *Exhortation and Controls: The Search for a Wage-Price Policy, 1945–1971* (Washington, D.C., 1975), 13–17, 64–66.

14. For example, see Everett E. Hagen, "The Reconversion Period: Reflections of a Forecaster," *Review of Economic Statistics* 29 (May 1947): 95–101. Concern with an approaching depression was evident in a memorandum of the Office of War Mobilization, "Economic Projection Prepared within the Technical Staff of the Office of War Mobilization," September 8, 1945, Official Files of the Office of War Mobilization, Record Group 250, National Archives, Washington, D.C. See also C. A. Blyth, *American Busi-*

ness Cycles (New York, 1969), 88–102; Bert G. Hickman, *Growth and Stability in the Postwar Economy* (Washington, D.C., 1960), 27–70; and Angus Maddison, *Economic Growth in the West* (New York, 1964).

15. Goodwin, *Exhortation and Controls*, 23.

16. Stephen K. Bailey, *Congress Makes a Law* (New York, 1950). See also R. A. Gordon, *The Goal of Full Employment* (New York, 1967), 45–49.

17. Harold G. Moulton and Karl T. Schlotterbeck, *Should Price Controls Be Retained?* (Washington, D.C., 1945).

18. Moulton and Schlotterbeck, *Should Price Controls Be Retained?*, 33.

19. *Congressional Record*, 79th Cong., 1st sess., September 11, 1945, 8111. See also Walter F. George to H. G. Moulton, July 7, 1943, BIF; Moulton's testimony to Congress in *Hearings before the Special Committee on Postwar Economic Policy and Planning*, 75th Cong., 1943, 435–36.

20. Untitled speech by Moulton, March 10, 1945, BIF.

21. Joseph P. Knapp, *Edwin G. Nourse: Economist for the People* (Danville, Ill., 1979); and Edwin Nourse, *Economics in the Public Service* (New York, 1952). The idea for a CEA was first proposed by Lewis Lorwin, a Brookings economist, in 1931. See Lorwin, *Advisory Economic Councils* (Washington, D.C., 1931).

22. For fiscal policy during this period see Donald Winch, *Economics and Policy: A Historical Study* (New York, 1969); Hugh S. Norton, *The Employment Act and the Council of Economic Advisors* (Columbia, S.C., 1977).

23. For Republican strategy, see "The Republicans," *Fortune* 35 (April 1947): 77–85; James T. Patterson, *Mr. Republican: A Biography of Robert A. Taft* (New York, 1972).

24. Harry S. Truman, *Memoirs: Years of Trial and Hope* (New York, 1956), 41. See also Charles Sawyer, *Concerns of a Conservative Democrat* (Carbondale, Ill., 1968).

25. Bert T. Hickman, *Growth and Stability in the Postwar Economy* (Washington, D.C., 1960), 44, 213.

26. A. E. Holmans, *United States Fiscal Policy, 1945–1959* (New York, 1961), 79.

27. Clark Kerr, "Employer Policies in Postwar Industrial Relations," in *Labor in Postwar America*, ed. Coleston E. Warne (New York, 1949), 48–65; R. Alton Lee, *Truman and Taft-Hartley: A Question of Mandate* (Lexington, Ky., 1966), 15–16.

28. Harold W. Metz, *The Labor Policy of the Federal Government* (Washington, D.C., 1945), 39.

29. Metz, *Labor Policy*, 59.

30. Metz, *Labor Policy*, 274–75.

31. Lee, *Truman and Taft-Hartley*, traces the history of the act. Metz discussed his influence on the bill in a memorandum to Robert Calkins, "Influence of Brookings in Government," 1952(?), BIF.

32. Milton Lehman, "The Oracle of Lafayette Square," *Nation's Business* 38 (May 1950): 50–52.

33. See Daniel S. Hirschfield, *The Lost Reform: The Campaign for Compulsory Health Insurance in the United States from 1932 to 1943* (Cambridge, Mass., 1970), 18–19; 45–73; and Monte M. Poen, *Harry S. Truman versus the Medical Lobby* (Columbia, Mo., 1979), esp. 30, 123–34.

34. George W. Bachman and Lewis Meriam, *The Issue of Compulsory Health Insurance* (Washington, D.C., 1944), 41–69.

35. Bachman and Meriam, *Compulsory Health Insurance*, 37.

36. Bachman and Meriam, *Compulsory Health Insurance*, 64–67.

37. "Health Insurance Blow," *Newsweek* 31 (May 24, 1948): 49–50; "Galileo Was Right: Brookings Institution Report on the Issue of Compulsory Health Insurance," *American Journal of Public Health* 38 (September 1948): 1275–76.

38. George S. Soule, *The Costs of Health Insurance* (Washington, D.C., 1949); for Davis's help in writing this book, see memorandum from Frederick Robin to the executive committee of the Committee for the Nation's Health, August 2, 1948, Davis Papers, Truman Library.

39. *Hearings before the Subcommittee of the Committee on Labor and Public Welfare*, 80th Cong., 1948, 2561.

40. *Hearings . . . on Labor and Public Welfare*, 2565–67.

41. Morris Fishbein to George W. Bachman, July 24, 1936, Fishbein Papers, University of Chicago. For later correspondence see Morris Fishbein to George Bachman, February 12, 1953, and George W. Bachman to Morris Fishbein, November 24, 1952, Fishbein Papers. Also see Morris Fishbein, "Medical Insurance Plans," *Vital Speeches* 11 (January 1, 1945).

42. Lewis Meriam, "The Role of Social Security in a Stable Prosperity," *American Economic Review* 37, supp. (May 1947): 335–44.

43. Robert A. Taft, "Should Congress Approve National Compulsory Medical Insurance?" *Congressional Digest* 28 (July 1949): 79–81.

44. C. A. Thomson to Robert Calkins, May 4, 1954, BIF.

45. Quoted in Martha Derthick, *Policymaking for Social Security* (Washington, D.C., 1979), 45–48, 214, 272–79.

46. Lewis Meriam and Karl Schlotterbeck, *The Cost and Finances of Social Security* (Washington, D.C., 1950), 18–19, 36, 115–16.

47. Meriam and Schlotterbeck, *Cost and Finances*, 176–77.

48. Harley Notter, *Postwar Foreign Policy Preparation, 1939–1945* (Washington, D.C., 1949), 181. See also Ruth B. Russell, *The History of the United Nations Charter: The Role of the United States, 1940–1945* (Washington, D.C., 1958). Interviews with former associates of "Passy" provided much of the information for this sketch: Virginia Hartley, interview with author, Washington, D.C., April 16, 1977; Benjamin V. Cohen, interview with author, Washington, D.C., April 19, 1977; Ruth B. Russell, interview with author, Berkeley, California, January 6, 1977; also "Biographical Data," September 24, 1946, BIF. Also see Dean Acheson, *Present at the Creation: My Years in the State Department* (New York, 1969), 9–15; Adolf Berle, *Navigating the Rapids, 1918–1971: From the Papers of Adolf Berle*, ed. Beatrice A. Berle and Travis Beal Jacobs (New York, 1973), 442–43; and Thomas Terry Connally, *My Name Is Tom Connally* (New York, 1954), 279.

49. It should be noted that while Pasvolsky was at the State Department, Cleona Lewis maintained the Brookings's reputation in international economics with the publication of her cross-sectional study of international financial relations, *America's Stake in International Investments* (Washington, D.C., 1938). "The Brookings Seminar on Problems in Foreign Policy: An Account of an Experiment," n.d., BIF; minutes of the board of trustees, Brookings Institution, May 12, 1952, BIF.

50. Quoted in Charles B. Saunders, Jr., *The Brookings Institution: A Fifty Year History* (Washington, D.C., 1966), 76; Virginia Hartley, interview with author.

51. Hadley Arkes, *Bureaucracy, the Marshall Plan and the National Interest* (Princeton, N.J., 1972); Harry Bayard Price, *The Marshall Plan and Its Meaning* (Ithaca, N.Y., 1955), 57–58.

52. Arthur Vandenberg to Harold Moulton, December 30, 1947, BIF.

53. Harold G. Moulton to Arthur Vandenberg, January 22, 1948, BIF.

54. Brookings Institution report, "Administration of the United States Aid for a European Recovery Program Sent January 11, 1948, 80th Congress, 2nd Sess." (Washington, D.C., 1948), in *BIF*.

55. Redvers Opie et al., *The Search for Peace Settlements* (Washington, D.C., 1951), 333–34.

56. Harold G. Moulton to Thomas Dewey, July 21, 1948, BIF.

CHAPTER 8

1. Milton Lehman, "Oracle of Lafayette Square," *Nation's Business* 38 (May 1950).

2. Meriam would be elected for seven two-year terms as mayor of Kensington, beginning in 1952. *Washington Star*, October 31, 1972, clipping in BIF. Also Charles Thomson, interview with author, Kensington, Md., July 18, 1975.

3. Joseph H. Willits, "Memorandum concerning Jerome Greene," May 9, 1947, Brookings file, Rockefeller Foundation Archives, North Tarrytown, New York.

4. Robert P. Bass to Raymond B. Fosdick, September 18, 1947, Brookings file, RFA.

5. JHW [Joseph H. Willits], "Memorandum on Conversation with Robert P. Bass," September 30, 1947, Brookings file, RFA.

6. JHW, "Memorandum."

7. Robert Calkins, interview with James Farrell, November 15, 1976, BIF.

8. This information was gained through a number of informal discussions I had with Robert Calkins when I was a guest scholar at the Brookings Institution during 1976–1977.

9. Joseph H. Willits to Robert Calkins, January 18, 1952, RFA.

10. Harold Moulton, "A History of the Financial Affairs of the Brookings Institution," n.d., BIF.

11. Robert Calkins to Dr. Gow, December 28, 1953, BIF.

12. Harold Metz to Dr. Gow, October 29, 1953, BIF.

13. Calkins, interview with James Farrell.

14. Charles B. Saunders, Jr., *The Brookings Institution: A Fifty Year History* (Washington, D.C., 1966), 98–99.

15. These figures have been calculated from a directory of former staff members compiled by Edna Birkel, n.d., BIF.

16. Wilfred Owen, interview with author, Washington, D.C., April 3, 1977.

17. Kenneth Thompson, memorandum on H. Field Haviland, March 11, 1953, Brookings file, RFA.

18. Walter Salant, interview with author, Washington, D.C., April 2, 1977.

19. Saunders, *Brookings Institution*, 90–91.

20. Calkins, interview with James Farrell.

21. Quoted in Jeffrey C. Alexander, *The Antinomies of Classical Thought: Marx and Durkheim*, vol. 2 of *Theoretical Logic in Sociology* (Berkeley, Calif., 1982), 93.

22. For the best popular overview of these institutions see Paul Dickson, *Think Tanks* (New York, 1971).

23. This discussion of technological elites draws heavily on Anthony Giddens, *The Class Structure of Advanced Societies* (London, 1973), 254–74.

24. For a fascinating history of planning in Japan, see Chalmers Johnson, *MITI and the Japanese Miracle: The Growth of Industrial Policy, 1925–1975* (Stanford, Calif., 1982).

25. William E. Nelson, *The Roots of American Bureaucracy, 1830–1900* (Cambridge, Mass., 1982).

26. Perry Anderson, *Lineages of the Absolutist State* (London, 1974), 11.

Selected Bibliography

Manuscript Collections

Anderson, Chandler P. Papers. Library of Congress, Washington, D.C.

Brookings, Robert S. Chancellor Files. Washington University, St. Louis, Mo.

Brookings Institution. Files. Brookings Institution, Washington, D.C.

———. Rockefeller Foundation Archives, Tarrytown, N.Y.

Bureau of Indian Affairs. Record Collection. National Archives, Washington, D.C.

Citizens Union League. Papers. Columbia University. New York.

Collier, John. Papers. Yale University, New Haven, Conn.

Davis, William H. Papers. Harry S. Truman Library, Independence, Mo.

Fishbein, Morris. Papers. University of Chicago, Chicago.

Fosdick, Raymond. Papers. Princeton University, Princeton, N.J.

Goldenweiser, Emanuel. Papers. Library of Congress, Washington, D.C.

Goodnow, Frank. Papers. Johns Hopkins University, Baltimore, Md.

Gulick, Luther. Papers. Institute of Public Administration, New York.

Meriam Indian Survey. Files. Rockefeller Foundation Archives, Tarrytown, N.Y.

National Recovery Administration. Record Collection. National Archives, Washington, D.C.

New York City. Bureau of Municipal Research. Papers. Institute of Public Administration, New York.

Office of War Mobilization. Record Group. National Archives, Washington, D.C.

Pasvolsky, Leo. Papers. Library of Congress, Washington, D.C.

President's Reorganization Committee. Files. Franklin Delano Roosevelt Library, Hyde Park, N.Y.

Ruml, Beardsley. Papers. University of Chicago, Chicago.

Salant, Walter. Papers. Harry S. Truman Library, Independence, Mo.

Taft, William Howard. Papers. Library of Congress, Washington, D.C.

U.S. Department of State. General Records. National Archives, Washington, D.C.

INTERVIEWS AND ORAL HISTORIES

Allen, William H. Oral History Project. Columbia University, New York.

Calkins, Robert. Interview with author. Washington, D.C., June 4, 1975, March 17, 1977.

Cohen, Benjamin V. Interview with author. Washington, D.C., March 28, 1977.

Gulick, Luther. Interview with author. New York, May 21, 1977.

Hartley, Virginia. Interview with author. Washington, D.C., April 16, 1977.

Knapp, Joseph. Interview with author. Bethesda, Md., July 15, 1975.

MacLaury, Bruce. Interview with author. Washington, D.C., April 5, 1977.

Moulton, Barbara. Interview with author. Orange Grove, Calif., November 12, 1974.

Moulton, Jack. Interview with author. Harpers Ferry, W.Va., May 3, 1975.

Nelson, James. Correspondence with author. February 27, 1975, and March 21, 1975.

Nourse, Edwin. Oral History. Cornell University, Ithaca, N.Y.

Owen, Wilfred. Interview with author. Washington, D.C., April 3, 1977.

Russell, Ruth. Interview with author. Berkeley, Calif., January 6, 1977.

Salant, Walter. Interview with author. Washington, D.C., April 2, 1977.

Thomson, Charles. Interview with author. Kensington, Md., July 18, 1975.

BOOKS AND DISSERTATIONS

Abrams, Richards. *Conservatism in a Progressive Era: Massachusetts Politics, 1900–1912.* Cambridge, Mass., 1964.

Acheson, Dean. *Present at the Creation: My Years in the State Department.* New York, 1969.

Adams, Henry C. *The Science of Finance.* Boston, 1898.

Albertson, Dean. *Roosevelt's Farmer: Claude R. Wickard in the New Deal.* New York, 1961.

Alchon, Guy. "Technocratic Social Science and the Rise of Managed Capitalism, 1910–1933." Ph.D. diss., University of Iowa, 1982.

Aldcroft, Derek. *The European Economy, 1914–1970.* New York, 1978.

Alexander, Jeffrey C. *The Antinomies of Classical Thought: Marx and Durkheim,* vol. 2 of *Theoretical Logic in Sociology.* Berkeley, Calif., 1982.

Allen, William H. *Efficient Democracy.* New York, 1907.

Alrich, Howard. *Organizations and Environments.* New York, 1979.

Anderson, Donald F. *William Howard Taft: A Conservative's Conception of the Presidency.* Ithaca, N.Y., 1968.

Anderson, Perry. *Lineages of the Absolutist States.* London, 1974.

Arkes, Hadley. *Bureaucracy, the Marshall Plan and the National Interest.* Ithaca, N.Y., 1972.

Armstrong, William, ed. *The Gilded Age Letters of E. L. Godkin.* Albany, N.Y., 1974.

Avery, Peter. *Modern Iran.* New York, 1965.

Bachman, George W., and Lewis Meriam. *The Issue of Compulsory Health Insurance.* Washington, D.C., 1947.

Bailey, Stephen K. *Congress Makes a Law.* New York, 1950.

Bellush, Bernard. *The Failure of the NRA.* New York, 1975.

Berbusse, Edward J. *The United States in Puerto Rico, 1898–1900.* Chapel Hill, N.C., 1966.

Berkowitz, Edward, and Kim McQuaid. *Creating the Welfare State: The Political Economy of Twentieth Century Reform.* New York, 1980.

Berle, Adolf. *Navigating the Rapids, 1918–1971: From the Papers of Adolf Berle.* Edited by Beatrice A. Berle and Travis Beal Jacobs. New York, 1973.

Blum, John Morton, ed., *From the Morgenthau Diaries: The Years of Crisis, 1928–1938.* New York, 1959.

Blyth, C. A. *American Business Cycles.* New York, 1969.

Borneman, Alfred. *Laurence Laughlin.* Washington, D.C., 1940.

Brookings, Robert S. *Economic Democracy.* New York, 1929.

———. *Industrial Ownership.* New York, 1928.

Burnham, Walter Dean. *Critical Elections and the Mainsprings of American Politics.* New York, 1970.

Burns, James M. *Roosevelt: The Lion and the Fox.* New York, 1956.

———. *Roosevelt: The Soldier of Freedom.* New York, 1970.

Carey, John. *The Rise of the Accounting Profession, 1896–1969.* New York, 1969.

Caro, Robert A. *The Power Broker: Robert Moses and the Fall of New York.* New York, 1974.

Chapman, Richard N. *Contours of Public Policy, 1939–1945.* New York, 1981.

Clark, Truman R. *Puerto Rico and the United States, 1917–1933.* Pittsburgh, Pa., 1975.

Clawson, Marion. *New Deal Planning: The National Resources Planning Board.* Baltimore, Md., 1981.

Cleveland, Frederick A. *Chapters in Municipal Administration and Accounting.* New York, 1907.

———. *The Budget and Responsible Government.* New York, 1920.

Coletta, Paolo E. *The Presidency of William Howard Taft.* Lawrence, Kans., 1973.

Collier, John. *From Every Zenith.* Denver, Colo., 1963.

———. *The Indians of the Americas.* New York, 1947.

Collins, Robert. *The Business Response to Keynes, 1929–1964.* New York, 1981.

Commons, John H. *Myself.* Madison, Wis., 1936.

Conkin, Paul. *The New Deal.* Boston, 1967.

Connally, Thomas Terry. *My Name Is Tom Connally.* New York, 1954.

Crane, Leo. *Desert Drums: The Pueblo Indians of New Mexico, 1540–1928.* Glorieta, N.M., 1953.

Cuff, Robert D. *The War Industries Board: Business-Government Relations during World War I.* New York, 1973.

Cutting, Robert Fuyon. *The Citizens Union, Its Origins and Purpose:*

Address Given at the Nineteenth Century Club, April 14, 1903. New York, 1903.

Dahlberg, Jane S. *The New York Bureau of Municipal Research: Pioneer in Government Administration.* New York, 1966.

Dale, Edward Everett. *The Indians of the Southwest.* Norman, Okla., 1929.

Davis, Allen. *Spearheads for Reform: The Social Settlements and the Progressive Movement, 1890–1914.* New York, 1967.

Davis, J. Ronnie. *New Economics and Old Economists.* Ames, Iowa, 1967.

Derthick, Martha. *Policymaking for Social Security.* Washington, D.C., 1979.

Dickson, Paul. *Think Tanks.* New York, 1971.

Domhoff, G. William. *The Higher Circles: The Governing Class in America.* New York, 1970.

Dorfman, Joseph. *The Economic Mind in American Civilization.* New York, 1958.

Dorfman, Joseph, ed. *Relation of the State to Industrial Action: Economics and Jurisprudence.* New York, 1954.

Eakins, David W. "The Development of Corporate Liberal Policy Research in the United States, 1885–1965." Ph.D. diss., University of Wisconsin, 1966.

Ely, H. *Ground under Our Feet.* New York, 1938.

Ely, Richard T. *The Coming City.* New York, 1902.

———. *The Labor Movement in the United States.* 1883. Rev. ed. New York, 1915.

———. *Socialism: An Examination of Its Future, Its Strength, and Its Weakness, with Suggestions for Social Reform.* New York, 1894.

Fisher, Louis. *Presidential Spending Power.* Princeton, N.J., 1975.

Ford, Henry Jones. *Woodrow Wilson: The Man and His Work.* New York, 1916.

Fosdick, Raymond. *Chronicle of a Generation.* New York, 1958.

French, John C. *A History of the University Founded by Johns Hopkins.* Baltimore, Md., 1946.

Furner, Mary. *Advocacy and Objectivity: A Crisis in the Professionalization of American Social Science, 1865–1905.* Lexington, Ky., 1975.

Fusfeld, Daniel Roland. *The Economic Thought of Franklin D. Roosevelt and the Origins of the New Deal.* New York, 1956.

Gessner, Robert. *Massacre.* New York, 1931.

Giddens, Anthony. *The Class Structure of Advanced Societies.* London, 1973.

Gilbert, James. *Designing the Industrial State: The Intellectual Pursuit of Collectivism in America, 1880–1940*. Chicago, 1972.

Godkin, Edwin. *Problems of Modern Democracy*. New York, 1903.

Goodnow, Frank J. *Politics and Administration*. 1900. Rev. ed. New York, 1967.

——. *Principles of Constitutional Government*. New York, 1916.

Goodwin, Craufurd D., ed. *Exhortation and Controls: The Search for a Wage-Price Policy, 1945–1971*. Washington, D.C., 1975.

Gordon, Robert A. *Economic Instability and Growth: The American Record*. New York, 1974.

——. *The Goal of Full Employment*. New York, 1967.

Graham, Otis, Jr. *Toward a Planned Society: From Roosevelt to Nixon*. New York, 1976.

Grimes, Alan P. *Political Liberation of the New Nation*. Chapel Hill, N.C., 1953.

——. *The Puritan Ethic and Woman's Suffrage*. New York, 1967.

Gulick, Luther. *The National Institute for Public Service*. New York, 1929.

Haber, Samuel. *Efficiency and Uplift: Scientific Management in the Progressive Era, 1890–1920*. Chicago, 1964.

Hahr, L. Albert. *Deficit Spending and Private Enterprise*. Washington, D.C., 1942.

Hagedorn, Hermann. *Brookings: A Biography*. New York, 1937.

Haines, Charles G. *Essays on the Law and Practice of Government Administration*. Baltimore, Md., 1935.

Hamilton, Nora. *The Limits of State Autonomy*. Princeton, N.J., 1982.

Hammack, David C. *Power and Society: Greater New York at the Turn of the Century*. New York, 1982.

Hansen, Alvin. *Economic Stabilization in an Unbalanced World*. New York, 1932.

Haskell, Thomas L. *The Emergence of Professional Social Science*. Urbana, Ill., 1977.

Hawley, Ellis. *The Great War and the Search for Modern Order*. New York, 1972.

——. *The New Deal and the Problem of Monopoly*. Princeton, N.J., 1966.

Hayes, Douglas A. *Business Confidence and Business Activity*. Ann Arbor, Mich., 1951.

Herbst, Jurgen. *The German Historical School in American Scholarship: A Study in the Transfer of Culture*. Ithaca, N.Y., 1965.

Hickman, Bert G. *Growth and Stability in the Postwar Economy.* Washington, D.C., 1960.

Hirschfield, Daniel S. *The Lost Reform: The Campaign for Compulsory Health Insurance in the United States from 1932 to 1943.* Cambridge, Mass., 1970.

Hollingsworth, J. Rogers. *The Whirligig of Politics.* Chicago, 1963.

Holmans, A. E. *United States Fiscal Policy, 1945–1959.* New York, 1961.

Hoogenboom, Ari. *Outlawing the Spoils: A History of the Civil Service Reform Movement, 1865–1883.* Urbana, Ill., 1969.

James, Edmund Janes. *Economic Science Discussion.* New York, 1886.

Janeway, Eliot. *The Struggle for Survival.* New York, 1951.

Johnson, Chalmers. *MITI and the Japanese Miracle: The Growth of Industrial Policy, 1925–1975.* Stanford, Calif., 1982.

Johnson, Donald B., and Kirk H. Porter. *National Party Platforms, 1840–1862.* Urbana, Ill., 1966.

Karl, Barry D. *Charles E. Merriam and the Study of Politics.* Chicago, 1974.

———. *Executive Reorganization and Reform in the New Deal: The Genesis of Administrative Management, 1900–1939.* Cambridge, Mass., 1963.

———. *The Uneasy State: The United States from 1915 to 1945.* Chicago, 1983.

Klein, Lawrence. *The Keynesian Revolution.* New York, 1966.

Kimmel, Lewis. *Federal Budget and Fiscal Policy, 1789–1958.* Washington, D.C., 1959.

Knapp, Joseph G. *The Advance of the American Cooperative Enterprise, 1920–1945.* Danville, Ill., 1973.

———. *Edwin G. Nourse: Economist for the People.* Danville, Ill., 1979.

Kolko, Gabriel. *Railroads and Regulation.* Princeton, N.J., 1965.

———. *Triumph of Conservatism.* New York, 1963.

Kurland, Gerald. *Seth Low: The Reformer in an Urban and Industrial Age.* New York, 1971.

Lansday, Alexander. *The Story of Washington University, 1853–1953.* 1953. Unpublished.

Laughlin, J. Laurence. *Industrial America.* New York, 1912.

———. *Laughlin versus Coin: Facts about Money.* Chicago, 1896.

Lee, R. Alton. *Truman and Taft-Hartley: A Question of Mandate.* Lexington, Ky., 1966.

Lewinson, Edwin R. *John Purroy Mitchel.* New York, 1965.

Lewis, Cleona. *America's Stake in International Investments*. Washington, D.C., 1938.

Lincoln, W. Bruce. *In the Vanguard of Reform: Russia's Enlightened Bureaucrats, 1825–1869*. DeKalb, Ill., 1982.

Litman, Susan. *Prices and Price Controls in Great Britain and the United States during the War*. New York, 1920.

Littleton, Ananias C. *Accounting Evolution to 1900*. New York, 1966.

Lubin, Isador. *The Absorption of the Unemployed in American Industry*. Washington, D.C., 1929.

Lustig, R. Jeffrey. *Corporate Liberalism: The Origins of Modern Political Theory, 1890–1920*. Berkeley, Calif., 1982.

Lyon, Leverett. *The ABC of the NRA*. Washington, D.C., 1934.
——. *The Economics of Free Deals: With Suggestions for Code-Making under the NRA*. Washington, D.C., 1933.

McFarland, Gerald W. *Mugwumps, Morals and Politics, 1884–1920*. Amherst, Mass., 1975.

McQuaid, Kim. *Big Business and Presidential Power: From FDR to Reagan*. New York, 1982.

Mardock, Robert Winston. *The Reformers and the American Indian*. Columbia, Mo., 1971.

May, Dean L. *From New Deal to New Economics: The American Liberal Response to the Recession of 1937*. New York, 1981.

Meriam, Lewis. *Principles Governing the Retirement of Public Employees*. Washington, D.C., 1918.
——. *Public Service and Special Training*. Chicago, 1936.

Metz, Harold W. *Labor Policy of the Federal Government*. Washington, D.C., 1945.

Millspaugh, Arthur. *The American Task in Persia*. New York, 1925.
——. *Toward Efficient Democracy: The Question of Governmental Organization*. Washington, D.C., 1949.

Mints, Lloyd W. *A History of Banking Theory in Great Britain and the United States*. Chicago, 1945.

Morgan, H. Wayne. *From Hayes to McKinley: National Party Politics, 1877–1896*. Syracuse, N.Y., 1969.

Moulton, Harold G. *America and the Balance Sheet of Europe*. Washington, D.C., 1924.
——. *Can Inflation Be Controlled?* Washington, D.C., 1938.
——. *Controlling Factors in Economic Development*. Washington, D.C., 1949.
——. *The Distribution of Income in Relation to Economic Development*. Washington, D.C., 1936.

———. *The Dynamic Economy (A Play)*. New York, 1950.
———. *Economic Systems*. Washington, D.C., 1948.
———. *The Financial Organization of Society*. Chicago, 1924.
———. *The Formation of Capital*. Washington, D.C., 1936.
———. *Germany's Capacity to Pay*. Washington, D.C., 1923.
———. *Income and Economic Progress*. Washington, D.C., 1935.
———. *Income Distribution under Capitalism*. Washington, D.C., 1936.
———. *Japan: An Economic and Financial Appraisal*. New York, 1931.
———. *The New Philosophy of Public Debt*. Washington, D.C., 1943.
———. *Principles of Money and Banking*. Chicago, 1916.
———. *Productivity, Wages and National Income*. Washington, D.C., 1940.
———. *The Recovery Problem in the United States*. Washington, D.C., 1937.
———. *The Reparation Plan: An Interpretation of Reports of the Expert Committees Appointed by the Reparations Commission, November 30, 1923*. 1924. Repr. New York, 1970.
———. *A Survey of Economic Education*. New York, 1951.
———. *The Thirty Hour Week*. Washington, D.C., 1935.
———. *War Debts and World Prosperity*. Washington, D.C., 1932.
———. *Waterways versus Railways*. Chicago, 1912.
Moulton, Harold G., and Leo Pasvolsky. *The French Debt Problem*. Washington, D.C., 1925.
———. *World War Debt Settlements*. New York, 1924.
Moulton, Harold G., and Karl T. Schlotterbeck. *Should Price Controls Be Retained?* Washington, D.C., 1945.
Moulton, Harold G., Maurice Leven, and Clark Warburton. *America's Capacity to Consume*. Washington, D.C., 1934.
Myrdal, Gunnar. *The Political Element in the Development of Economic Theory*. New York, 1953.
Nelson, William E. *The Roots of American Bureaucracy, 1830–1900*. Cambridge, Mass., 1982.
Noble, David F. *America by Design*. New York, 1977.
Noble, David W. *The Paradox of Progressive Thought*. Minneapolis, Minn., 1958.
Norton, Hugh S. *The Employment Act and the Council of Economic Advisors*. Columbia, S.C., 1977.
Notter, Harley. *Postwar Foreign Policy Preparation, 1939–1945*. Washington, D.C., 1949.

Nourse, Edwin G. *Agricultural Economics*. Chicago, 1916.
———. *American Agriculture and the European Market*. New York, 1924.
———. *Economics in the Public Service*. New York, 1953.
———. *Industrial Price Policies and Economic Progress*. Washington, D.C., 1938.
———. *The Legal Status of Agricultural Cooperation*. New York, 1927.
———. *Marketing Agreements under the AAA*. Washington, D.C., 1935.
———. *The Nineteen Fifties Come First*. New York, 1951.
———. *Price Making in a Democracy*. Washington, D.C., 1944.
Nourse, Edwin G., Joseph S. Davis, and John D. Black. *Three Years of the Agricultural Adjustment Administration*. Washington, D.C., 1937.
Nourse, Edwin G., Harold G. Moulton, Frederick G. Tryon, Horace B. Drury, Maurice Leven, and Cleona Lewis. *America's Capacity to Produce*. Washington, D.C., 1934.
Ostrogorski, M. *Democracy and the Party System*. New York, 1910.
Patterson, James T. *Congressional Conservatism and the New Deal*. Lexington, Ky., 1967.
Phelp, Kenneth R. *John Collier's Crusade for Indian Reform, 1920–1954*. Tucson, Ariz., 1977.
Pike, Frederick B., and Thomas Stritch, eds. *The New Corporatism: Social and Political Structures in the Iberian World*. Notre Dame, Ind., 1974.
Poen, Monte M. *Harry S. Truman Versus the Medical Lobby*. Columbia, Mo., 1979.
Polenberg, Richard. *Reorganizing Roosevelt's Government: The Controversy over Executive Reorganization*. Cambridge, Mass., 1967.
———. *War and Society: The United States, 1941–1945*. Philadelphia, Pa., 1972.
Poulantzas, Nicos. *Political Power and Social Classes*. Translated by Timothy O'Hagen. London, 1973.
Price, Harry Bayard. *The Marshall Plan and Its Meaning*. Ithaca, N.Y., 1955.
Quandt, Jean B. *From Small Town to the Great Community: The Social Thought of Progressive Intellectuals*. New Brunswick, N.J., 1970.
Rader, Benjamin G. *The Academic Mind and Reform: The Influence of Richard T. Ely in American Life*. Lexington, Ky., 1966.

Robertson, Robert M. *History of the American Economy*. New York, 1964.

Romasco, Albert V. *The Politics of Recovery: Roosevelt's New Deal*. New York, 1983.

Roose, Kenneth D. *The Economics of Recession and Revival*. New York, 1969.

Rosen, Elliott A. *Hoover, Roosevelt, and the New Deal*. New York, 1977.

Russell, Ruth B. *The History of the United Nations Charter: The Role of the United States, 1940–1945*. Washington, D.C., 1958.

Sabine, George H. *A History of Political Theory*. New York, 1961.

Saunders, Charles B., Jr. *The Brookings Institution: A Fifty Year History*. Washington, D.C., 1966.

Schiesl, Martin T. *The Politics of Efficiency: Municipal Administration and Reform in America, 1800–1920*. Berkeley, Calif., 1977.

Schlesinger, Arthur M., Jr. *The Coming of the New Deal*. Boston, 1958.

Shonfeld, Andrew. *Modern Capitalism: The Changing Balance of Public and Private Power*. New York, 1965.

Silk, Leonard, and Mark Silk. *The American Establishment*. New York, 1980.

Soule, George S. *The Costs of Health Insurance*. Washington, D.C., 1949.

Spicer, Edward Holland. *Cycles of Conquest: The Impact of Spain, Mexico, and the United States on Indians of the Southwest, 1533–1960*. Tucson, Ariz., 1962.

Stein, Herbert. *The Fiscal Revolution in America*. Chicago, 1969.

Stewart, Frank Mann. *A Half Century of Municipal Reform: The History of the National Municipal League*. Berkeley, Calif., 1950.

Swain, Martha S. *Pat Harrison: The New Deal Years*. Jackson, Miss., 1978.

Thomson, Charles. *The Institute for Government Research*. Washington, D.C., 1956.

Toman, William H. *Municipal Reform Movement in the United States*. New York, 1895.

Tomsich, John. *A Genteel Endeavor: American Culture and Politics in the Gilded Age*. Stanford, Calif., 1971.

Truman, Harry S. *Memoirs: Years of Trial and Hope*. New York, 1956.

Tugwell, Rexford. *Enlargement of the Presidency*. New York, 1960.

Tyler, S. Lyman. *A History of Indian Policy*. Washington, D.C., 1973.

Urofsky, Melvin T. *Big Steel and the Wilson Administration: A Study in Business-Government Relations*. Columbus, Ohio, 1969.

Warken, Philip A. *A History of the National Resources Planning Board, 1933–1943*. New York, 1979.

Waters, Frank. *Masked Gods: Navaho and Pueblo Ceremonialism*. 2nd ed. Chicago, 1973.

Weinstein, James. *The Corporate Ideal in the Liberal State*. Boston, 1968.

Wiebe, Robert H. *The Search for Order, 1877–1920*. New York, 1967.

Willoughby, Westel. *The Nature of the State—A Study in Political Philosophy*. New York, 1896.

Willoughby, Westel W., and Lindsay Rogers. *An Introduction to the Problem of Government*. New York, 1921.

Willoughby, William F. *An Introduction to the Study of the Government of Modern States*. New York, 1919.

———. *The Problem of a National Budget*. Washington, D.C., 1918.

Wilson, Joan Hoff. *American Business and Foreign Policy, 1920–1933*. Lexington, Ky., 1971.

———. *Herbert Hoover: The Forgotten Progressive*. Boston, 1975.

Wilson, R. Jackson. *In Quest of Community: Social Philosophy in the United States, 1860–1920*. New York, 1965.

Winch, Donald. *Economics and Policy: A Historical Study*. New York, 1969.

Wortman, Richard S. *The Development of a Russian Legal Consciousness*. Chicago, 1976.

ARTICLES

Adams, Henry C. "Problems of Budgetary Reform." *Journal of Political Economy* 27 (October 1919): 621–38.

Allen, William H. "Better Business Methods for Cities." *Review of Reviews* 37 (February 1908): 195–200.

Arrington, L. J. "Western Agriculture and the New Deal." *Agricultural History* 44 (October 1970): 337–53.

———. "The New Deal in the West: A Preliminary Statistical Inquiry." *Pacific Historical Review* 38 (August 1969): 311–16.

Atwood, Stella. "The Case for the Indian." *Survey* 46 (October 1922): 7–11.

Baron, Paul A. "National Economic Planning." In *A Survey of Contemporary Economics*, edited by Bernard F. Hawey, 358–60. Homewood, Ill., 1952.

Bauer, John. "Accounting." In *The Encyclopedia of the Social Sciences*, 404–12. New York, 1948.

Beard, Charles. "A Five Year Plan for America." *Forum* 86 (July 1931): 1–11.

———. "Reconstructing State Government." *New Republic* 4 (August 21, 1915): 1–16.

Berkhofer, Robert F., Jr. "The Organizational Interpretation of American History: A New Synthesis." *Prospects* 4 (1979): 611–29.

Black, R. A. "New Deal for the Red Man." *Nation* 130 (April 2, 1930): 388–90.

Blackmar, F. W. "Leadership in Reform." *American Journal of Sociology* 16 (March 1911): 626–33.

Blassingame, Lurton W. "Frank Goodnow: Progressive Urban Reformer." *North Dakota Quarterly* 40 (Summer 1972): 22–30.

Block, Fred. "The Ruling Class Does Not Rule: Notes on the Marxist Theory of the State." *Socialist Revolution*, May–June 1977, 6–28.

Botein, Stephen. "Professional History Reconsidered." *American Journal of Legal History* 21 (January 1977): 60–79.

Brockie, M. D. "Theories of the 1937–1938 Crisis and Depression." *Economic Journal*, June 1950, 292–310.

Bruere, Henry, et al. "Efficiency in City Government." *Annals* 44 (May 1912): 3–22.

Bryce, James. "Thomas Hill Green, 1836–1892." In *Studies in Contemporary Biography*, 85–100. New York, 1903.

Calkins, Robert. "Harold Glenn Moulton, 1883–1965." In *American Philosophical Yearbook, 1966*, 81–82. New York, 1966.

Cannon, Joseph. "The National Budget." *Harpers Weekly* 139 (October 12, 1919): 617–28.

Cerillo, Augustus, Jr. "The Reform of Municipal Government in New York City." *New York Historical Quarterly* 57 (January 1973): 51–71.

Chamberlain, J. P. "American Budgetary Reform." *Nation* 108 (June 21, 1919): 976–78.

Clark, John M. "Introduction." In *Readings in the Economics of War*, ed. Walton Hamilton, 566–88. Chicago, 1918.

Cleveland, Frederick A. "The Basis of Municipal Research." *New Republic* 1 (January 2, 1915): 23–24.

———. "Bonds in Relation to Corporate Finance." *Annals* 30 (September 1907): 412–27.

———. "Budgeting Reform Today." *Annals* 95 (May 1912): 258.

———. "Budget Making and the Increased Cost of Government." *American Economic Review* 6 (March 1916): 50–70.

———. "Carnegie as Economist and Social Reformer." *Annals* 17 (May 1901): 474–80.

———. "Causes of Waste and Inefficiency in National Government." *Review of Reviews* 45 (April 1912): 466–71.

———. "Financial Reports of National Banks as a Means of Public Controls." *Annals* 24 (July 1904): 45–66.

———. "Municipal Ownership as a Form of Governmental Control." *Annals* 28 (November 1906): 359–70.

———. "National Budget." *Survey* 48 (August 15, 1922): 604–5.

———. "The Need for Coordinating State and National Activities." *Annals* 41 (May 1912): 23–29.

———. "Our Present Financial Outlook." *Annals* 21 (March 1903): 280–92.

———. "The Short Ballot and the New York Constitution." *Review of Reviews* 52 (August 1915): 195–98.

Coats, J. W. "The Origins of the Chicago Schools." *Journal of Political Economy* 71 (October 1963): 487–93.

Collier, John. "The Accursed System." *Sunset* 52 (June 1924): 15–16.

———. "America's Treatment of Her Indians." *Current History Magazine* 18 (August 1923): 771–81.

———. "Are We Making Men Slaves?" *Survey* 57 (January 1, 1927): 453–55.

———. "Fate of the Navajos." *Sunset* 52 (January 1924): 11–13.

———. "Hammering at the Prison Door." *Survey* 60 (July 1, 1928): 389.

———. "Our Indian Policy." *Sunset* 50 (March 1923): 13–15.

———. "Persecuting the Pueblos." *Sunset* 53 (July 1924): 50.

———. "Plundering the Pueblos." *Sunset* 50 (January 1923): 21–25.

———. "Pueblos' Land Problem." *Sunset* 50 (November 1923): 15.

———. "Pueblos' Last Stand." *Sunset* 50 (February 1923): 19–22.

———. "Red Atlantis." *Survey* 49 (October 1, 1922): 15–20.

———. "Red Slaves of Oklahoma." *Sunset* 52 (March 1924): 9–11.

Collins, Robert M. "Positive Business Responses to the New Deal: The Roots of the Committee for Economic Development, 1933–1942." *Business History Review* 52 (Autumn 1978): 342–68.

Connolly, Vera. "Cry of a Broken People." *Good Housekeeping* 88 (February 1929): 30–31.

Cuff, Robert D. "American Historians and the 'Organizational Factor.'" *Canadian Review of American Studies* 4 (Spring 1973): 19–31.

———. "An Organizational Perspective on the Military-Industrial Complex." *Business History Review* 52 (Summer 1978): 250–67.

Dorfman, Joseph. "The Role of the German Historical School in American Economic Thought." *American Economic Review* 45, supp. (May 1955): 17–29.

Douglas, Lewis W. "Address." *Consensus*, January 1935, 8–25.

Douglas, Paul. "The Reality of Non-Commercial Incentives in Economic Life." In *The Trend of Economics*, edited by Rexford Guy Tugwell, 182–83. New York, 1924.

Downes, Randolph C. "A Crusade for Indian Reform, 1922–34." *Mississippi Valley Historical Review* 32 (December 1945): 331–54.

Ely, Richard. "Progressivism, True and False—An Outline." *Review of Reviews* 51 (February 1915): 209–11.

Fisher, Irving. "Economists in Public Service." *American Economic Review* 9 (June 1919): 5–21.

Fitzpatrick, E. A. "Municipal Research—A Criticism." *New Republic* 1 (January 2, 1915): 19–21.

Flynn, John T. "Whose Child Is the NRA?" *Harper's Magazine* 169 (September 1934): 385–94.

Fuessle, Newton. "America's Boss-Ridden Athletics." *Outlook* 130 (April 19, 1922): 642–45.

Fuller, Hubert Bruce. "The Crime of the Pork-Barrel." *World's Work* 20 (August 1910): 13259–73.

Galambos, Louis. "The Emerging Organizational Synthesis in Modern American History." *Business History Review* 44 (Autumn 1970): 279–90.

———. "Technology, Political Economy, and Professionalization: Central Themes of the Organizational Synthesis." *Business History Review* 57 (Winter 1983): 471–94.

Glad, Paul W. "Progressives and the Business Culture of the 1920s." *Journal of American History* 53 (June 1966): 75–89.

Gold, David, et al. "Recent Developments in Marxist Theories of the State." *Monthly Review* 27 (October 1975): 29–43; 28 (November 1975): 36–51.

Grabo, W. H. "Education for Democratic Leadership." *American Journal of Sociology* 23 (May 1918): 763–78.

Griffith, Robert. "Dwight D. Eisenhower and the Corporate Commonwealth." *American Historical Review* 87 (June 1982), 87–112.

Hagen, Everett E. "The Reconversion Period: Reflections of a Forecaster." *Review of Economic Statistics* 29 (May 1947).

Hamilton, Walton. "Amherst Program in Economics." *Journal of Political Economy* 25 (January 1917): 1–13.

———. "The Control of Big Business." *Nation* 134 (May 25, 1932): 591–93.

———. "Economic Theory and Social Reform." *Journal of Political Economy* 23 (June 1915): 562–84.

———. "The Institutional Approach to Economic Theory." *American Economic Review* 9, supp. (March 1919): 309–24.

———. "Place of Value Theory in Economics." *Journal of Political Economy* 26 (March–April 1918): 217–45, 375–407.

———. "The Plight of Soft Coal." *Nation* 126 (April 4, 1928): 367–69.

———. "Price System and Social Policy." *Journal of Political Economy* 26 (January 1918): 31–68.

———. "Review of Hoxies' Economics." *Journal of Political Economy* 24 (November 1916): 883.

Haney, Lewis. "Price Fixing in the United States during the War." *Political Science Quarterly* 34 (September 1919): 434–53.

Hansen, Alvin. "The Economics of Unionism." *Journal of Political Economy* 30 (June 1922): 518–30.

———. "Toward Full Use of Our Resources." *Fortune* 26 (November 1942): 130–33.

Hansen, Alvin, and Guy Greer. "The Federal Debt and the Future." *Harper's Magazine* 184 (April 1942): 489–500.

Hard, William. "Retarding the Allies." *New Republic* 18 (December 29, 1917): 238–40.

Hawley, Ellis W. "The Discovery and Study of a Corporate Liberalism." *Business History Review* 52 (Autumn 1978): 309–20.

———. "Herbert Hoover, the Commerce Secretariat, and the Vision of an Associative State, 1921–1928." *Journal of American History* 61 (June 1974): 116–40.

———. "The New Deal and Business." In *The New Deal*, edited by John Braeman, 68–74. Columbus, Ohio, 1974.

Hays, Samuel. "The New Organizational Society." In *Building the Organizational Society: Essays on Associational Activities in Modern America*, edited by Jerry Israel. New York, 1972.

———. "Political Parties and the Community-Society Continuum."

In *The American Party Systems*, edited by William N. Chambers and Walter Dean Burnham, 171–80. New York, 1967.

―――. "The Politics of Reform in Municipal Government in the Progressive Era." *Pacific Northwest Quarterly* 55 (October 1964): 157–69.

Heald, Morrell. "Business Thought in the 1920's: Social Responsibility." *American Quarterly* 13 (Summer 1961): 126–39.

Hitchcock, Curtice. "The War Industries Board: Its Development, Organization, and Function." *Journal of Political Economy* 26 (June 1918): 545–66.

Hobson, Wayne K. "Professionals, Progressives, and Bureaucratization: A Reassessment." *Historian* 39 (August 1977): 639–58.

Johnson, Alvin. "Where Inflation Threatens." *Nation* 142 (September 5, 1936): 265–66.

Jones, Byrd L. "The Role of Keynesians in Wartime Policy and Postwar Planning, 1940–1946." *American Economic Review* 62 (May 1972): 125–33.

Karl, Barry D. "Philanthropy, Policy Planning, and the Bureaucratization of the Democratic Ideal." *Daedalus* (Fall 1976): 129–49.

Keezer, D. M. "Making the Social Sciences Sociable." *Survey* 55 (October 15, 1925): 80–82.

Kelly, M. Clyde. "The Indian and His Master." *Sunset* 49 (December 1922): 17–18.

Kerr, Clark. "Employer Policies in Postwar Industrial Relations." In *Labor in Postwar America*, edited by Coleston E. Warne. New York, 1949.

Keyserling, Leon. "Comment." *American Economic Review* 62 (May 1972): 135–37.

Latimer, Joseph W. "Bureaucracy a la Mode." *Independent* 112 (February 2, 1924): 75.

McQuaid, Kim. "Corporate Liberalism in the American Business Community, 1920–1940." *Business History Review* 52 (Autumn 1978): 342–68.

MacVeagh, Franklin. "Departmental Economy." *Independent* 69 (December 22, 1910): 1366–69.

―――. "Mr. Taft's Four Years." *Independent* 74 (March 6, 1913): 488–89.

―――. "President Taft and the Cost of Government." *Outlook* 102 (October 5, 1912): 235–36.

———. "President Taft and the Roosevelt Politics." *Outlook* 101 (May 18, 1912): 110–16.

Marx, Fritz. "The Bureau of the Budget and Its Present Role." *American Political Science Review* 39 (October 1945): 653–84, 869–98.

Meriam, Lewis. "Education Appointments in the Indian Service." *School and Society*, November 14, 1931, 658–59.

———. "Indian Education Moves Ahead." *Survey* 66 (June 1, 1931): 253–57.

———. "The Role of Social Security in a Stable Prosperity." *American Economic Review* 37, supp. (May 1947): 335–44.

Moulton, Harold G. "America's Stake in the War Debt." *Yale Review* 22 (September 1932): 78–96.

———. "Appraisal of Carver's Economics." *Journal of Political Economy* 28 (April 1920): 322–31.

———. "Banking Policy and the Price Situation." *American Economic Review* 10, supp. (March 1920): 156–75.

———. "Commercial Banking and Capital Formation." *Journal of Political Economy* 27 (July 1919): 590–600, 604–5.

———. "Commercial Credit or Discount Companies." *Journal of Political Economy* 28 (December 1920): 827–39.

———. "The Economic Necessity for Disarmament." *Yale Review* 11 (January 1922): 271.

———. "Economic Potentials and Requirements." *Appraisal Journal* 18 (January 1950): 29–34.

———. "For the Duration of the War." *Century* 97 (January 1919): 391–97.

———. "The Relation of Credit and Prices to Business Recovery." *Annals* 59 (April 1934): 20–26.

———. "Rising Tide of Social Unrest." *Yale Review* 9 (October 1919): 1–16.

———. "War Debts and International Trade Theory." *American Economic Review* 15 (December 1925): 700–716.

———. "Will France Get Anything from the Ruhr?" *New Republic* 34 (February 28, 1923): 14–17.

———. "Will Prices Fall?" *Journal of Political Economy* 27 (November 1919): 782–97.

Muccigrosso, Robert. "The City Reform Club: A Study in Late Nineteenth Century Reform." *New York Historical Society Quarterly* 52 (July 1968): 235–54.

Newcomb, Simon. "Review of *An Introduction to Political Economy.*" *Journal of Political Economy* 1 (1884–85): 106.

―――. "Review of *The Labor Movement in the United States.*" *Nation* 42 (1886): 293–94.

―――. "The Two Schools of Political Economy." *Princeton Review* 14 (1884): 291–301.

Nourse, Edwin. "Defining Our Employment Goal under the 1946 Act." *Review of Economic Statistics* 38 (May 1956): 193–204.

―――. "Early Flowering of the Employment Act." *Virginia Quarterly Review* 43 (Spring 1967): 233–47.

―――. "The Economic Philosophy of Cooperation." *American Economic Review* 12 (December 1922): 577–97.

―――. "Harmonizing the Interests of Farm Producer and Town Consumer." *Journal of Political Economy* 28 (October 1920): 625–27.

―――. "The Hinge between Two Decades." *Virginia Quarterly Review* 37 (Winter 1961): 1–14.

―――. "Nature's Power and the Conscience of Man." *Virginia Quarterly Review* 31 (Summer 1955): 337–52.

―――. "The Place of Agriculture in Modern Industrial Society." *Journal of Political Economy* 27 (June, July 1919): 466–97, 561–77.

―――. "The Promise of American Capitalism." *Virginia Quarterly Review* 38 (Summer 1962): 369–79.

―――. "Proper Sphere of Governmental Regulation in Connection with the Marketing of Farm Products." *American Economic Review* 13 (March 1923): 198–208.

―――. "The Revolution in Farming." *Yale Review* 8 (October 1918): 90–105.

―――. "Some Questions Emerging under the Employment Act." *American Economic Review* 50 (May 1960): 130–44.

―――. "The War and the Back to the Land Movement." *North American Review* 203 (February 1915): 246–55.

―――. "What Is Agricultural Economics?" *Journal of Political Economy* 24 (April 1916): 363–81.

―――. "Will Agricultural Prices Fall?" *Journal of Political Economy* 28 (March 1920): 189–218.

Pasvolsky, Leo. "Russian Parliament." *Russian Review*, September 1916, 99–107.

―――. "Russia's Foreign Trade during the War." *Russian Review*, February 1917, 96–105.

Peck, Gustav, and George B. Galloway. "On the Dissolution of the Robert Brookings Graduate School." *Survey* 60 (May 15, 1928): 229–31.

Phelp, Kenneth. "Albert B. Fall and the Protest from the Pueblos, 1920–1923." *Arizona and the West*, Autumn 1970, 237–55.

Radosh, Ronald. "The Myth of the New Deal." In *A New History of Leviathan: Essays on the Rise of the Corporate State*, edited by R. Radosh and M. Rothbard, 146–87. New York, 1972.

Reed, Harold L. "The Industrial Outlook." *Journal of Political Economy* 27 (April 1919): 225–40.

Roberts, Kenneth C. "Adventures in Budgeting." *Saturday Evening Post* 195 (July 1922): 3–4.

Ross, Mary. "The New Indian Administration." *Survey* 64 (June 15, 1930): 268–309.

Ryan, W. Carson, Jr. "Educational Conferences of Indian Service Superintendents." *School and Society* 34 (December 1930): 764–65.

Ryan, W. Carson, Jr., and Rose Brant. "Indian Education Today." *Progressive Education Magazine* 9 (February 1932): 81–86.

Sargent, James E. "FDR and Lewis W. Douglas: Budget Balancing and the Early New Deal." *Prologue*, Spring 1974, 33–43.

Sklar, Martin. "Woodrow Wilson and the Political Economy of Modern U.S. Liberalism." *Studies on the Left*, 1960, 17–47.

Skocpol, Theda. "Political Responses to Capitalist Crisis: Neo-Marxist Theories of the State and the Case of the New Deal." *Politics and Society*, 10 (1980): 155–99.

Slichter, Sumner. "The Downturn of 1937." *Review of Economic Statistics* 20 (August 1938): 97–110.

———. "Efficiency." In *The Encyclopedia of Social Science*. New York, 1937.

———. "Must We Have Another Boom?" *Atlantic Monthly* 159 (May 1937): 600–607.

Stewart, Maxwell. "Beware of Inflation." *Nation* 142 (March 11, 1936): 306–9.

Stimson, Henry. "A National Budget System." *World's Work* 38 (September 1919): 528–36.

Sweezy, Alan. "The Keynesians and Government Policy, 1933–1939." *American Economic Review* 62 (May 1972): 116–21.

Taussig, Frank W. "Price-Fixing as Seen by a Price Fixer." *Quarterly Journal of Economics* 33 (February 1919): 205–41.

Tugwell, Rexford Guy. "Experimental Economics." In *The Trend of Economics*, edited by Tugwell, 420–21.

Viner, Jacob. "Balanced Deflation, Inflation or More Depression." *The Day and Hour Series of the University of Minnesota* (Minneapolis, 1933).

Vogel, David, "Why Businessmen Distrust Their State: The Political Consciousness of American Corporate Executives." *British Journal of Political Science* 17 (January 1978): 45–78.

Walker, Francis A. "The Tide of Economic Thought." *Publications of the American Economic Association* 6 (1891), 20–21.

Wickersham, George. "The New Constitution and the Work of the Bureau of Municipal Research." *Real Estate Magazine,* October 1915, 1–6.

Wilensky, Norman M. "Conservatives in the Progressive Era." *University of Florida Monographs in Social Science,* 25 (Winter 1965).

Willoughby, William F. "Integration of Industry in the United States." *Quarterly Journal of Economics* 15 (November 1901): 94–115.

———. "Labor Legislation in France." *Quarterly Journal of Economics* 16 (May, August 1901): 390, 413, 551–77.

———. "The Problem of Political Education in Puerto Rico." In *Report of the Twenty-Sixth Annual Meeting of the Lake Mohonk Conference,* 160–62, 166. Lake Mohonk, New York, 1908.

———. "The Reorganization of Municipal Government in Puerto Rico." *Political Science Quarterly* 24 (September 1909): 409–43.

———. "State Activities and Politics." *Papers of the American Historical Association* 5 (New York, 1891), 114–18.

———. "Two Years of Legislation in Puerto Rico." *Atlantic Monthly* 90 (July 1902): 34–42.

Wilson, Woodrow. "Democracy and Efficiency." *Atlantic Monthly,* March, 1901. Reprinted in *Selected Literary and Political Papers and Addresses of Woodrow Wilson,* vol. 1. New York, 1925.

Winn, Willis J. "Business Education in the United States: A Historical Perspective." Newcomen Society Address, New York, 1963.

Woehlke, Walter. "Let 'Em Die." *Sunset* 51 (July 1923): 14–15.

Wright, Gavin. "The Political Economy of the New Deal Spending: An Econometric Analysis." *Review of Economics and Statistics* 56 (February 1974): 30–38.

Zey-Farrell, Mary. "Criticisms of the Dominant Perspective on Organizations." *Sociological Quarterly* 12 (Spring 1981): 188–205.

INDEX

Budget, balanced: and Brookings Institution, 158–59, 176; economists on, 114–15; Arthur Millspaugh on, 147; Harold Moulton on, 69, 164; and Franklin Roosevelt, 115, 126, 127, 173–74; and Harry Truman, 152
Budget, national executive, 18, 28, 37
Budget and Accounting Act: of 1919, 37–38; of 1921, 38, 173
Budget reform: in New York City, 20; and scientific reform, 19; and Taft Commission, 29–32; and World War I, 36–37
Budget system, congressional, 29
Bureaucracy, 146–48
Bureau of City Betterment, 25. See also Bureau of Municipal Research
Bureau of Indian Affairs: and Brookings Institution, 83; and Bursum Bill recall, 90; John Collier as commissioner of, 84; Division of Administration of, 101–2; improvements in, under W. Carson Ryan, 101; and proposal for Division of Planning and Development, 94; technical experts in, 101–2. See also Indian reform; Indian Service
Bureau of Municipal Research, 26–28. See also Bureau of City Betterment
Bureau of the Budget: Brookings Institution study of, 116; establishment of, 38–39; opposition of, to Indian reforms, 95, 99; proposals for, 30, 37; and Franklin Roosevelt, 115, 131–34
Burke, Edward, 96
Bursum, Holm O., 87
Bursum Bill, 87–89
Busch, Adolph, 50
Business, self-regulation of, 118–21
Businessmen: in efficiency and economy movement, 17; and full-employment bill, 151; hos-

tility of, towards labor, 55; on New Deal, 127–28; on planning, 117–18; and Franklin Roosevelt, 105–6; and state, 15. See also State-business relations
Butler, Nicholas Murray, 46
Bye, Raymond, 64
Byrd, Harry F., 130, 132
Byrnes, James, 134
Byrnes, John W., 157

Calkins, Robert: background of, 167; as Brookings Institution president, 166, 169–71
Canals, 67–68
Capacity studies, 122–24
Capital formation, 68–70
Carlisle, John G., 29
Carnegie, Andrew: and Robert Brookings, 43, 50–51; and Bureau of City Betterment, 25
Carnegie Corporation: and Robert Brookings, 50; and Brookings Institution, 12, 41, 111; and Institute of Economics,' 56
Carney, Mabel, 100
Carrol, Thomas, 169
Case Bill, 153–54
Chamber of Commerce, 32, 117
Chase, C. H., 71
Chase, Stuart, 117
Chicago, University of, 66–68
Chorley, Kenneth, 96
Citizens Union, 19, 24, 25
Civilian Conservation Corps, 126, 127
Clark, J. M., 114
Classification Act of 1923, 92
Class interests, 123–24
Cleveland, Frederick: background of, 25; in Bureau of Municipal Research, 26–27; as director of Taft Commission, 29–31; on efficiency and economy, 26; and Institute for Government Research, 32; later life of, 34
Cleveland, Grover, 21
Cloud, Henry Roe, 92
Coal industry, 75–76